Committees and Commissions in India
1977

Concepts in Communication
Informatics & Librarianship-51

***General Editor* : S.P. Agrawal**

Committees and Commissions in India 1977

Volume 15

PART C

A Concept's Project

Compiled by a team of professionals
guided by
VIRENDRA KUMAR

CONCEPT PUBLISHING COMPANY, NEW DELHI 110059

ISBN 81-7022-486-1 (Vol. 15, Part C)

First Published 1993

Published and Printed by
Ashok Kumar Mittal
Concept Publishing Company
A/15-16, Commercial Block, Mohan Garden
NEW DELHI 110059 (India)

Lasertypeset by
Printing Express
H-13, Bali Nagar
NEW DELHI 110015

CONTENTS

PART B

PART C

PART D

26

WORKING GROUP ON AUTONOMY FOR AKASHVANI AND DOORDARSHAN, 1977 – REPORT[1]

Chairman Shri B.G. Verghese

Members Shri U.G. Rajadhyaksha; Dr. Malcolm S. Adiseshiah; Shri Chanchal Sarkar; Shri P.L. Deshpande; Shri Omashankar Joshi; Shri A.G. Noorani; Prof. J.D. Sethi; Shri P.J. Fernandes; Shri C.R. Subramanian; Smt. Nayantara Sehgal

M. Secy. Dr. Ishwar Dass

Appointment

In pursuance of Government's declared policy that All India Radio and Doordarshan should be freed from Government Control to ensuer their functioning in a fair and objective manner, it has been decided to appoint a Working Group to examine the functioning of All India Radio and Doordarshan and make recommendations regarding their future set-up.

And, it is in pursuance of that declared policy that the present Working Group on Autonomy for Akashvani Doordarshan was constituted by the Ministry of Information and Broadcasting by Gazette Notification dated August 17, 1977.

Terms of Reference

(a) To examine the functional, financial and legal aspects of the proposal to give full autonomy to Akashvani and Doordarshan, con-

1. Akash Bharati National Broadcast Trust, New Delhi, Ministry of Information and Broadcasting, 1978, 2 vols.

sistent with accountability to Parliament, keeping in mind the different forms of autonomous organisations existing in other democratic countries in the matters of broadcasting;

(b) To suggest the form and the structure of the autonomous organisation(s) and their relationship with Government;

(c) To consider and make recommendations in respect of the absorption, fitment and replacement of the personnel of the two media in the event of grant of autonomous status;

(d) to formulate a plan of action for expeditious implementation of the proposal, if the recommendations of the working of group are accepted by Governments;

(e) To examine any other allied matters necessary to enable the working groups to make its recommendations on the future set-up of the media.

Contents

Part I: Preface — Akash Bharati; Introduction; Towards Full Autonomy; After Fifty Years; Communication Policy and Broadcasting; Seven Faces of Autonomy; Policy and Organisational Parameters; The Legal Framework; The Board of Trustees; Management and Programme Structure; The Financial Dimension; Commercial Broadcasting; Broadcast Receiver Licences; Franchise Stations; Independent Production Agencies; News and Current Affairs; The external Services; Extension and Distance Learning; Broadcasting as Entertainment; The Training Function; A New Deal for Staff; Engineering and Technology; Future Expansion; Transitional Provisions; Akash Bharati Bill, 1978; Major Recommendations; Organisation Chart; Part II: List of Appendices A1-156.

Recommendations

Preface

1. We envisage an autonomous national trust as the authority under which Akashvani and Doordarshan should grow. This we are naming Akash Bharati—The National Broadcast Trust (NBT).

Communication Policy and Broadcasting (Chapter 2)

2. By their very nature, radio and television are in the public

domain and must serve the public interest. As mass media, radio and television must fit into a wider perception and perspective of a national communications policy or philosophy.

3. An autonomous broadcast organisation, nationally owned and responsible to Parliament and yet under the centre legislatively and for purposes of international relations through external broadcasts and frequency allocations, and P&T and space support appears logical and desirable.

Policy and Organisational Parameters (Chapter 4)

4. Both in terms of its physical presence and programme content, the emphasis of broadcasting will have to shift from its largely urban-elitist moorings to the rural and semi-urban areas and to the urban poor. The quality and proportion of its instructional content will likewise have to increase. The NBT must bridge the urban-rural divide and combine modernity with relevant tradition.

5. The NBT has to be highly sensitive to react swiftly to the needs and sentiments of the different components of its mass audience. At the same time it will have steadfastly to withstand the day-to-day political and other pressures to which its power will expose it.

6. The Working Group are of the view that there should not be autonomous regional corporations or even a federation of State Government Corporations. Instead, a single National Broadcast Trust is proposed under which a highly decentralised structure is envisaged. There will be a larger measure of power delegated to the regional and local levels so that the organisation enjoys the advantage of quick decision-making, sensitivity to local problems, familiarity with local customs and taste, and close linkages with various governments and institutions.

7. The engineers and programme staff have to work as a closely unit team, representing as they do both medium and massage. To, separate the two would be to diminish the efficiency and ever the creativity of the system. Production autonomy would also be undermined by external engineering control.

8. The working group are unable to support the proposal to create two separate corporations for Akashvani and Doordarshan. However, there is need to recognise the distinctive identity of radio and television within the ambit by a new integrated structure.

The Legal Framework (Chapter 5)

9. We are of the opinion that all the national broadcasting services should be vested exclusively in an independent, impartial and autonomous organisation established by law by Parliament to act as a trustee for the national interest.

10. The autonomy of the corporation and its independence from government control should be entrenched in the Constitution itself and the idea of a trust woven into it.

11. It is not necessary that the establishment of the corporation should await a constitutional amendment. The law establishing the corporation can be enacted and the organisation brought into being to be followed subsequently by an amendment of the Constitution.

12. We recommend a draft constitutional amendments in the following terms:

329A (1) All broadcasting shall be organised and conducted exclusively by or under the authority of an autonomous and independent public corporation acting impartially as a Trustee in the public interest, referred to in this constitution as Akash Bharati, the National Broadcast Trust.

(2) The National Broadcast Trust shall consist by a Chairman and Trustees and the appointment of the chairman and the other trustees shall be made by the President from out of a list of names put forward by a nominating panel duly constituted by law.

(3) Subject to the provisions of clauses (1) and (2) and the other provisions of this constitution, the constitution of the National Broadcast Trust shall be such as may be provided by Parliament by law.

13. The statute made in persuance of the constitutional provisions indicated above should expressly declare the corporation to be "a corporate citizen of the country". In the absence by a statutory declaration, the National Broadcast Trust will not be entitled to exercise those fundamental rights like the fundamental right to freedom of speech and expression, Article 19(1)(a), which are available to citizens alone.

14. We recommend that certain specific objectives be laid down in the statute by Parliament which may be regarded as the charter of

the National Broadcast Trust.

The Trust shall:

(a) Uphold the fundamental rights guaranteed under Article 19(1)(a) of the Constitution to freedom of speech and expression.

(b) Safeguards the citizens' rights to be informed freely, truthfully and objectively on all matters of public interest, national or international.

(c) Uphold the impartiality, integrity and autonomy of Broadcasting in the country.

(d) Provide a National Broadcasting service predominantly Indian in content and character.

(e) Promote the interest and concerns of the entire nation, being mindful of the need for harmony and understanding within the country and ensuring that the programmes reflect the varied elements which make up the composite culture of India.

(f) Produce and transmit varied programmes designed to awaken, inform, enlightened, educate entertain and enrich all sections of the people, with due regard to the fact that the National Broadcast audience consists of a whole series of publics.

(g) Serve the rural, illiterate and underprivileged populations, keeping in mind the special needs and interests of the young, social and cultural minorities, the tribal populations, and those residing in border regions and backward or remote areas.

(h) Stimulate and inform the national consciousness in regard to the status and problems of women.

(i) Promote social justice and combat exploitation, inequality, and such evils as untouchability and narrow parochial loyalties.

(j) Uphold the secular ideal and promote a spirit of truth and inquiry in the country among all sections of the people.

(k) Present a fair and balanced flow of information of national, regional, local and international interest including contrasting views, without advocating any opinion or ideology of its own.

(l) Help to raise educational standards by supporting programmes or formal, non-formal and continuing education and open learning systems.

(m) Promote the extension of new knowledge and practices as well as the transfer of technology as an aid to national development and social change.

(n) Provide entertainment and recreation for all sections of the people and encourage all forms of cultural expression — traditional, classical modern and international.

(o) Take special steps to protect the interests of children, the blind, the aged and other vulnerable sections of the population.

(p) Promote comprehension and national integration by broadcasting in a manner that facilitates communication in an among all the languages of India.

(q) Seek to provide comprehensive broadcast coverage through the choice of appropriate technology and the best utilisation of the broadcast frequencies available and to ensure high quality reception.

15. A restricted power can legitimately be given to the Government to require the Trust to refrain from broadcast any matter which has a clear relation to national security, the preservation of public order, and other matters of grave public importance. A power can also be conferred on the Government to require broadcasts in cases of emergency. In broadcasting such announcements the corporation shall announce that such a requirement has been made.

16. The President and the Prime Minister should have access to Akashvani and Doordarshan for national broadcasts. A similar right should extend to the Governors and Chief Ministers of States for State broadcast over regional network.

17. The Central and State Governments should have reasonable access to the broadcast media to explain official policies. Such Ministerial broadcasts should be arranged in consultation with the appropriate authorities in Akashvani and Doordarshan.

18. The leader of the opposition in the Lok Sabha should also be accorded facilities for making national broadcasts. We would recommend a similar procedure with regard to the recognised leader of the opposition, if any, in every State Legislature.

19. Once the National Broadcast Trust comes into being, the Ministry of Information and Broadcasting should shed its direct responsibility for broadcasting and might thereafter appropriately be redesignated as "Ministry of Information".

20. In regard to the relationship between the broadcasting organisations and Parliament, the best compromise between the claims

of autonomy and of accountability is to impose on the Trust a duty to report to Parliament through its budget and an annual report together with its accounts and auditor's comments thereon. The Report should also incorporate the report of the Complaints Board and a review of the operations of the Licensing Board and the franchise stations. Members of Parliament have an interest rights to ask question. But it is expected that they will refrain from so doing on day-to-day issues.

21. The NBT should ascertain the views of the Central and State Governments in the setting of new stations or transmitters.

22. Financial accountability would be ensured through independent commercial audit. In view of the unique characteristics of the broadcast system we recommend that its accounts be commercially audited by approved firm of auditors of standing, and not be subject to the jurisdiction of the Comptroller and Auditor-General of India.

23. The NBT will be the public trustee for radio and television broadcasting services in the country whether now or in the future, including related technologies such as wired broadcasting and cable television.

The Board of Trustee (Chapter 6)

24. At the apex of Akash Bharati or the National Broadcast Trust we recommend a Board of Trustees or Nyasi Mandal consisting of 12 persons, but not to exceed 21 should there be need for inducting members. The Trustees (Nyasis) will be guardians of the charter given to the National Broadcast Trust by statute.

25. The Controller-General of Broadcasting (CGB) heading the Central Executive Board will be ex-officio secretary to the Board of Trustees so as to provide an organic link between these two tiers.

26. We recommend the appointment of a Board of Trustees of 12 members consisting of a chairman and three other full time members who will devote themselves to the fields of current affairs, extension, and culture respectively. They will operate through the CGB.

27. In addition to the chairman and the three other full time trustees we recommend that of the eight other part time trustees at least one other should be highly experienced in the field of finance and management and another should be an eminent scientist or engineer familiar with the technology of broadcasting.

28. We assume and recommend that the Board will invariably consist of both men and women.

29. The Board of Trustees would have the ultimate responsibility for supervision and control, but it should normally and principally fulfil a trusteeship function in upholding and furthering the purposes of the organisation, execution being left to a Central Executive Board and other agencies under the trust.

30. The Director of Audience Research will be required to submit all audience research reports simultaneously to the Board of Trustees as well as to the Central Executive Board.

31. The Trustees shall be appointed for a term of six years, one-third of the members retiring every alternate year. The order of retirement among the initial 12 Trustees should be settled by draw of lots with the proviso that the chairman and the three full time functional Trustees shall be deemed to have a six-year term.

32. One of the most important tasks of the Trustees will be to appoint the Controller-General of Broadcasting, the Directors and other senior personnel up to the level of Controllers, that is, members of the proposed Zonal Executive Boards. They would also name the members of the proposed Licensing Board. Another critical responsibility will be the preparation and submission of the budget and an annual report to Parliament including the working of the proposed franchise stations, together with the audited accounts of Akash Bharati. All major investment and policy decisions bearing on the expansion of the broadcast system, technological choices the quality of service, major programme departures, and issues likely to affect the financial viability of the Trust, including wage and salary revisions, should be subject to approval by the Board of Trustees.

33. The Trustees should be appointed by the President on the recommendation of the Prime Minister from out of a list of names forwarded to him by a nominating panel consisting of the Chief Justice of India, the Lok Pal (an office that with soon come into being) and the Chairman of the Union Public Service Commission. In order to assist them in their arduous responsibility we recommend that the nomination panel should shall co-opt any two other persons of distinction from the world of science, culture and the arts. We would leave it to this panel to determine, its own procedures and having selected the chairman in the first instance to associate him or her in an advisory capacity with the selection of the other Trustees.

34. It would establish a healthy convention were the Prime Min-

ister to consult the Leader of the opposition before submitting the list of names of the Chairman and Trustees to the President.

35. In the case of the Chairman of the Board of Trustees the nominating panel might recommend two or at the most three names out of which one shall be forwarded to the President by the Prime Minister. However, with regard to all other vacancies, the nominating panel should be required to forward 50 per cent more names than there are vacancies to be filled. Should any functional Trustee not be selected, then the nominating panel might have to suggest an alternative name for the particular category.

36. We recommend that the Trustees should enjoy the status of Supreme Court Judges and should be subject to similar disqualifications and procedures for removal. The age bar, however, need not apply.

Management and Programme Structure (Chapter 7)

37. Programming should necessarily be decentralised and producers should enjoy a significant measure of programme autonomy. There will, however, be need for supervision and coordination at higher levels.

38. For purposes of management and coordination of the National Broadcast Organisation there need to be four operational tiers: National, zonal, regional, and the stations.

39. We recommend the constitution of five zones, namely, Southern, Western, Central, Eastern and Northern.

40. The regions are seen as a tier that would need to be added as the Akashvani network grows.

41. The Central Executive Board will be a policy planning and directing agency with its operating responsibility limited to the Central News Room, the Monitoring unit, the External Service Division, and the Transcription Service for programme exchange. Operational management will largely vest with the Zonal Executive Boards, the programming function being principally that of the stations.

42. Radio and television will operate as separate streams below the zonal apex although even at the national level there will be two separate functional heads who will provide the specialised skills required for the proper development of these two different media.

43. A Central Executive Board consisting of the Controller-General of Broadcasting (CGB) and 12 other Directors will be

responsible for implementing the policies and directives of the Board of Trustees. The Directors will each be responsible for Akashvani, Doordarshan, Current Affairs, Engineering, Finance, Personnel, and Audience Research respectively. In addition, there will be five Zonal Directors who would each head a Zonal Executive Board.

44. The Directors of Akashvani and Doordarshan will be the principal media heads. For other inputs such as engineering, finance, personnel, and audience research they will have to depend on the Directors incharge of each of these departments. Extension policy will not be made by the National Broadcast Organisation. But editorial control will rest with it.

45. The Director, News and Current Affairs will guide the Central News Room headed by a General Manager coordinating the works of the Editor Akashvani, the Editor, Doordarshan, the Foreign Editor, and the Editor Monitoring Unit.

46. Technical personnel in Akashvani and Doordarshan should be interchangeable. For the same reason, even on the programme side, where the degree of media specialisation admittedly has to be higher, people should be able to move between television and radio so that the careers of versatile and talented broadcast are not unduly inhibited.

47. We recommend the inclusion in various selection boards of one eminent outsider from out of a standing panel as an independent external expert who shall take the chair and whose concurrence should be necessary.

48. Auditioning boards should be set up at the Zonal level under the Zonal Director who should be assisted by producers and eminent artists and art critics in making selections and gradings.

49. Internal audit should be constituted as an autonomous deptartment under a Chief Internal Auditors reporting to the CGB.

50. The office of the Director of Audience Research will service both Akashvani and Doordarshan, as well as the proposed franchise stations. All audience research reports should be submitted to the Board of Trustees for information.

51. We recommend the appointment of three Managers each in charge of Legal Services, Planning and Information Services.

52. At each zone we recommend the establishment of a Zonal Executive Board (ZEB) headed by the Zonal Director.

53. The Regional Controller's office should be kept small and perform a supportive and coordinating role, especially with regard to

local stations.

54. The local stations should be headed by a station manager who should have no more than essential staff assisted by local and community participation.

55. The station manager should be responsible for organising listening as viewing groups within the range of his transmitters.

56. There should be functional Advisory Committee at various levels, each serviced by a small secretariate.

57. We recommend the establishment of a Complaints Board or Nyaya Mandal, a quasi-judicial body of four persons selected by the Chief Justice of India.

58. It will deal with complaints from the public relating to charges of unjust or unfair treatment including unwarranted invasion of privacy and misrepresentation provided the right of recourse to the courts is waived. The findings should be published by the NBT in its programme journals and broadcast in special programmes.

59. The NBT should evolve a suitable broadcast code in place of the AIR Code 1970 which is too restrictive.

60. There should be a Broadcast Review Commission in every seven years.

The Financial Dimension (Chapter 8)

61. It would be best to transfer the existing assets of Akashvani and Doordarshan valued at about Rs. 75 crores as an outright grant to the National Broadcast Trust by an Act of Parliament.

62. The National Broadcast Trust will not be liable to corporate taxation. Its profits, if any, will be ploughed back for programme improvement and system expansion along lines approved by Parliament which will scrutinise its annual report and accounts.

63. The Government should initially bridge the NBT's revenue deficit for a period of five years after which it should be expected to stand an its over feet or raise additional resources by charging for broadcast time made available by it to various users including the Central and State Governments.

64. We recommend that the Trust be authorised to borrow from the market or even from the Government at low rates of interest against its capital assets.

65. For its capital budget the NBT should receive as an outright grant the amount outstanding in the Non-Lapsable Fund as well as

annual grants until 1982 of all the amounts already agreed to under the heading of replacement and Renewal for Akashvani and Doordarshan. The NBT should prepare a long-term capital budget, the first five year segment of which should be discussed with the Planning Commission and Government on the basis of which the Government should be committed to a block grant made available in annually budgeted amounts in accordance with a phased programmes.

Commercial Broadcasting (Chapter 9)

66. We recommend that the National Broadcast Trust should undertake a comprehensive review of commercial broadcasting rates and procedures so as to place the marketing of broadcast time on a footing.

67. Commercial broadcasting has been able to tap only a little more than six per cent of the national advertising outlay, an unduly small figure. There is no reason, why this proportion should not rise to between 15 and 20 per cent.

68. The NBT could examine the opening up to commercial broadcasting of other channels which are already available to a limited extent for sponsored programmes. The advertising content must be closely monitored and the drive for commercials must not be allowed to intrude on or distort programmes values.

69. We recommend against any advertising over the proposed franchise stations which universities and other educational institutions may be licensed to operate.

71. We suggest that the NBT call a meeting of the concerned associations and interest to review the advertising codes and standards. Representatives of consumer associations with such a review and they should also be included in the commercial broadcast advisory panels that we recommend be set up.

Broadcasting Receiver Licences (Chapter 10)

72. The NBT should discuss the possible issue of broadcast receiver licence stamps with the appropriate authorities as an alternative to the present system. Broadcast Receiver Liecencing should neither inhibited the sale of sets nor deter the annual renewal of licences where required or encourage evasion.

73. Broadcast receiver licence fees should be revised upwards to

Rs. 25 for radio sets and Rs. 75 for television sets. The present concessional fee of Rs. 7.50 for radios costing less than Rs. 150, as well as for community listening sets and for educational establishments. hostels and welfare institutions should be continued at the present rates. However, a one-time licence fee for single-band sets may be fixed at Rs. 100 or Rs. 12 and collected at the point of sale with special concessions for the blind. The Licence fee for additional sets in the non-concessional category should be one-third of the basic licence fee.

Franchise Stations (Chapter 11)

74. The National Broadcast Trust should be authorised to grant broadcast franchise whether for radio or television to approved educational institutions. Such a franchise recommendation by the National Broadcast Trust should automatically be converted into a broadcast licence by the Ministry of Communications, the specific frequencies being allocated and coordinated by the Ministry's wireless Adviser.

75. The franchise should be granted an NBT Licencing Board manned by part time Commissioners. The licences should be granted for three-year period at a time and should be renewed on satisfaction of performance. The franchise stations should not broadcast news bulletins but should relay these from the Akashvani/Doordarshan network. They should be placed under the general supervision of the NBT and should be answerable to the Complaints Board as well as to the Trustees. Who would be empowered to issue written directives.

76. We would disallow commercial advertising over these educational stations but we envisage great possibilities in programme exchange both among franchise stations and between them and Akashvani and Doordarshan.

Independent Production Agencies (Chapter 12)

77. We recommend that independent radio and television programme production agencies and assisted to acquire a gain access to the necessary production facilities. This will draw in a wide pool of talent and promote variety, programme innovation. Specialisation and excellence. It will also provide an element of competition to Akashvani and Doordarshan.

78. The principle of 20 per cent "reservation" for independent

programme access has been evident in the working of the Government owned Films Division for some years and establishes a precedent which should be extended to the NBT. In addition, the Franchise Stations, universities and others could produce independent programmes which should have to the Akashvani and Doordarshan networks on their own merits.

79. Sponsored programmes by industrial houses or other private institutions should be outside the "reserved" quota even though these are produced for Akashvani or Doordarshan by private agencies.

80. The availability of 16 mm laboratory facilities would provide an incentive to young producers and film makers to set-up independent units to make films and features which they could sell to Doordarshan and to the Franchise stations.

81. It should be possible for Akashvani and Doordarshan to rent out their studios and facilities to recognised independent production groups on certain terms during idle hours if any. The National Broadcast Trust might also consider establishing both sound and television facilities in selected centres outside of Akashvani and Doordarshan which should be available on hire.

82. The existence of independent programme production companies operating in sound, film and video alongside the Franchise stations and advertising companies would provide and alternative source of employment for all categories of broadcast personnel. We see great advantage in this, not least in the mobility it will provide in what has so far been a largely monopolistic situation and in the possibility of expanding programme exports and international programme exchange.

News and Current Affairs (Chapter 13)

83. Akashvani and Doordarshan must be committed to certain national values but ought not to have editorial opinions of their own. They must avoid any partisan or ideological slant out, instead, offer a balanced and objective presentation of all news of relevance to the Indian or external audiences they serve. They must take care to present contrasting of viewpoints and analyses in a constant endeavour to examine events from every angle and perspective.

84. The principles of "fairness", "accuracy" and well-rounded "objectivity" apply not only to the news but to all current affairs programmes. Balance however does not imply a mechanical balanc-

ing of views in each programme, but rather an overall balance achieved over a series of programmes.

85. The Central News Room must be strengthened if the quality of service is to improve. It is clearly inadequate to have the various Indian Language bulletins and to some extent even the Hindi news bulletins serviced by mere translations of the predominantely English pool copy.

86. The cadre link between the CIS and the News Services Division must be severed on the lines we have suggested and Akashvani must train newsmen who can voice their despatches instead of writing them.

87. The slow (dictation) speed news bulletins is service that could be expanded and enriched to assist the growth of community papers in remote areas.

88. The news rooms at the State Capitals and other regional news centres of Akashvani should be strengthened.

89. Intensive coverage of tribal; hill, and hitherto remote or neglected and backward areas must be a special responsibility of Akashvani and Doordarshan if they are to serve the needs of the reward masses and articulate the aspirations of the underprivileged and forgotten.

90. Special news bulletins in simple formats should be fashioned to reach distinctive pockets, especially in the border regions.

91. Akashvani and Doordarshan must make a special effort to encourage development news reportage and the coverage of special areas like sport, science, health, education, the arts, labour, farming and so on.

92. A foreign desk should immediately be set up under a senior Foreign Editor in the proposed Central News Room.

93. It should be Akashvani's policy to strengthen its Asian and Indian ocean coverage so that this region, to being with, becomes one in which it should be able to boast of prompt, complete and informed coverage, spreading outwards to other and more distant regions as and when possible.

94. The Monitoring units should be strengthen, expanded and placed on a sounder footing.

95. We recommend interchange of personnel among the foreign language cadres of the News Services Division, the Monitoring unit and the External Services of Akashvani.

96. The trend reports and weekly analysis as well as other spe-

cial publications of the Monitoring Unit could be made available as priced publications.

97. Akashvani and Doordarshan should not sky away from controversy. They should project issues of social justice.

98. Current affairs speakers and panelists need to be drawn from a wider area than Delhi or the other metropolitan cities and from disciplines other than journalism, politics or the academic world.

99. Anniversary features need to be selective, carefully planned, imaginatively presented and evaluative rather than adulatory.

100. The lack of reference and library facilities, news clippings and research assistance should be made good as a matter of priority.

101. Each Doordarshan Kendra must have a news room with a news editor and professional editing and reporting staff.

102. Doordarshan should have its own network of correspondents and stringers, some of these cameramen doubling as radio correspondents, handling portable video tape recorders for speedy and convenient electronic news gathering.

103. Any step towards the development of a television news agency would be welcome and should be encouraged.

104. Doordarshan should be equipped with dubbing and subtitling equipment to facilitate programme exchange within the country as well as abroad.

The External Service (Chapter 14)

105. Given its limited resources Akashvani should concentrate on the country's neighbours loosely defined as the Indian Ocean Community and North Asia.

106. We recommend that both the capital and revenue budget for the External Services Division of Akashvani and proportionate part of the capital and revenue budget of the Monitoring Unit should be borne by the Government of India.

107. A common news service cannot be half-controlled and half-free since the same news organisation serves both the domestic as well as the foreign listener (and viewer). Autonomy must therefore cover external broadcasts as much as internal broadcasting and there can be "no half-way house".

108. We suggest the need for an external broadcasting cadre. Which can develop area and subject-matter specialisation in regard

to foreign affairs, foreign economic relations and cultural exchange.

109. The salary scales offered to language specialists in the Monitoring Unit, News Service Division, and External Services Division will have to be improved in order to attract these particular talents. As in the case of knowledge of Indian Languages other than one's own mother-tongue. Hindi and English we would recommend the payment of a language bounty for knowledge of an continuing proficiency in additional foreign languages.

110. Audience Research is an important for external broadcasts as for internal broadcasting.

111. The quality and format of the Indian calling could be improved and it should be possible with better editing and content to carry some limited Indian advertising.

Extension and Distance Learning (Chapter 15)

112. Indian school and extension broadcasting should pay more attention to delivery of the message relevant feedback and follow up. They must be coordinated with other communication personnel and implementing agencies or systems in the field.

113. The multi-media approach needs constant emphasis. Radio instruction and educational television must be appropriately backed up with print and other support.

114. The proposed new local radio stations with their closeness to the people should powers new kinds of community programming for open learning. This will call for training and resources and a strong interface with other institutions and authorities.

115. The broadcast media should cater to the non-formal sector because learning can be programmed for different age groups and needs and taken to homes, fields, factories and informal classrooms.

116. Akashvani should draw an its archives to create a valuable cassette tape library on which schools and universities could draw as and when required.

117. We would lay special emphasis on the need to promote popular science over radio and television.

118. A strong interface between the education and extension authorities at all levels and the broadcasting system should be developed.

119. Since health precedes medicine, and good health longevity and low infant mortality rates are powerful and natural factors in-

hibiting family size, the broadcast media should play a more important role in health education.

120. School television programming must be integrated into the classroom with full teachers support. The subject supervisor, producer and presenter of school programmes should work as a single team.

121. The entire approach to women's programming needs change. There should be no talking down to women or any tendency to limit programmes literally to matters of household interest including nutrition and childcare. The very title "Home" tends to suggest restricted horizons. The message of equality, including sexual equality, and social change should permeate all programmes rather than just "women's programmes" and should certainly be addressed as much to men as to women.

122. Tribal programming calls not merely for genuine sympathy, knowledge and sensitivity but for the provision of minimum facilities such as jeeps special allowances for isolation and hardship, portable equipment and considerable delegation. Special staff need to be recruited for tribal stations and the proposed new generation of local stations should have a specially selected cadre of young local people who know the language and have a deep feeling and respect for the tribal populations and their culture.

123. In the hill regions of North East India as in some other areas broadcasting faces a special problem—the many languages that the people speak. A possible answer might be the development of a mobile cassette library. Each village in a language area would get a community cassette tape recorder and a whole series of tapes recorded in Akashvani Studios. The cassettes would be circulated by jeep and replaced after a suitable time.

124. The NBT may after some years consider selling time to Departments of the Government that have educational programmes or extension messages to communicate. This would result in more realistic cost-benefit analyses and ensure the establishment of adequate organisational links, feedback loops, and support services with matching inputs.

125. The NBT should review with the Central and State Government the kind of interface that exists or need to be developed between the broadcast organisation and concerned Departments or extension institutions.

126. We recommend a fresh look at the need for community lis-

tening despite the ubiquitous radio transistor, especially among the weaker sections and in backward areas where there is a clear and present need for a densification of broadcast diffusion. Special schemes should be worked out for making available receiving sets at concessional prices to selected groups or approved individuals who take on the responsibility of organising group listening.

127. Radio and television or extension must be supported by other media, including print. The task of print support should however, be a responsibility that Government and other institutions must share with the NBT.

128. Radio and television must form part of multi-media systems and it should be the endeavour of the NBT to encourage and ensure the development of a systems approach that includes the use of radio-vision, cassette tape recorders, and film, tape, and video libraries.

129. We recommend that teachers and agricultural and health extension workers should be trained in the use of the media so that they come to regard radio and television as allies rather than rivals and are able better to use these media to enhance their own effectiveness.

Broadcasting as Entertainment (Chapter 16)

130. Radio and television have individuals as their target audience, a factor that makes the listener or viewer more critical in accepting programmes, with the option to switch off or twin the knob to another channel or station.

131. The terms of royalty and copyright need to be reviewed. The system of "close bookings" and ceilings on the number of appearances or fees collected in a month or a year must also be removed if talent has to be encouraged and Akashvani and Doordarshan are to build their own radio and television personalities.

132. With newer stations being established in smaller towns and in the districts, programme makers will immediately be faced with the problem of talent. Groups of stations might therefore do well to farm clusters or "cultural Janapadas". Individual stations should however be able to boast of a particular programme—specialisation which they should be on a position to "export" through a well organised systems of programme exchange between stations, regions and zones.

133. With the development of Akashvani all listeners will have

access to three channels—national, regional and local. Programming in each channel will need to be suitably mixed and varied.

134. A great deal of programme initiative must be left to producers and individual production teams and not merely to Station Managers. There should be scope for experimentation with regard to ideas, techniques, and formats.

135. There must be a concurrent devaluation of financial and budgetary powers alongside a decentralisation of programming and administration.

136. Actual production at Akashvani and Doordarshan Kendras should appropriately be classified under three main headings namely planning, production and presentation.

137. It should be possible to develop, a team mode of production in which a producer, technician, script-writer and social scientist function as a single team, pretesting programmes in the field before producing prototype programmes which become precursors to a regular series.

138. We recommend independent programming facilities for the SITE-continuity Kendras at Jaipur, Raipur, Gulbarga and elsewhere if their programmes are to be at all relevant and evoke interest.

139. Akashvani and Doordarshan must have adequate facilities to maintain their archives which are of great cultural and historical value.

140. Akashvani needs to train its musicians in orchestration and harmony and expose them to western and other music from which these concepts derive so that they are then better able to develop Indian orchestration and choral singing which could have a great future and open up whole new vistas for Indian Music.

141. The new generation of Akashvani Stations should each be equipped with a reasonably sized auditorium where live shows and concerts can be held and broadcast with audience participation.

142. Akashvani should review the format and content of Vividh Bharati so as to develop a genuine radio-originated light entertainment programme inclusive of film music, which could become a vehicle for which experimentation and innovation in terms of styles, formats and artists.

143. We recommend the idea of encouraging talented and eminent individuals to write, produce and present radio and television programmes with the help of production and other facilities extended to their by Akashvani and Doordarshan.

144. The present system of auditioning music artists needs change. A central audition board is unnecessary. Zonal boards should instead be established and given a set of norms. Music producers at stations should be involved in the matter of selection of artists as standards and tastes differ from region to region.

145. Children's programmes merit the greatest attention and the very best production talent. This is where cultural tastes can be influenced and interests awakened in the world around. Some school learning could also be imported through song and music to which children quickly and joyously respond.

146. The tendency for Yuva Vani programmes to cater predominantly to urban and student youth should be corrected.

147. With the development of regional and local stations it should be possible to devote more time to regional sporting events and traditional or novel sports and pastimes. Radio and television could do much to promote physical fitness.

148. Akashvani and Doordarshan could do with more and better programme journals. Given the right to print advertisements like any other journal they could earn some modest revenue.

149. Akashvani could produce discs and tapes of Great Masters, national concerts, and folk music on a commercial basis.

150. Party political and election broadcasts must be subject to an approved code.

151. We recommend the establishment of a strong audience research division.

152. Akashvani and Doordarshan should involve its listening and viewing public at all levels through functional programme advisory committees.

153. The NBT should strengthen existing links with the Asian Broadcasting union and establish links with the European Broadcasting union and similar bodies for purposes of programme exchange and professional contact.

154. The internal and international transcription service of Akashvani and Doordarshan must be suitably strengthened and equipped to foster and stimulate programme exchange.

The Training Function (Chapter 17)

155. All broadcasters should know something about communication processes and policies relevant to Indian needs and cir-

cumstances besides an understanding of communications system as a whole.

156. A training reserve is required in all cadres of Akashvani and Doordarshan.

157. Besides the three existing training schools at Delhi, Hyderabad and Shillong, at least two others are needed so that there is one in each zone.

158. There should be a whole system of refresher courses in training academics to which all staff are brought at regular intervals in their career.

159. The news and current affairs staff should receive training in broadcast journalism.

160. There should be facilities for language learning and orientation courses for engineering and programming personnel who are posted to unfamiliar and sensitive areas such as North East India.

161. There should be a broadcast staff college where selected personnel who show promise and are likely to move up into senior decision-making programme or technical levels should be able to spend some time.

162. Graduation from the staff college should equip both engineering and programmes personnel to move to higher responsibilities in "staff" appointments if they show the necessary interest and aptitude.

163. A basic foundation course for both programmes and technical cadres could help establish a new tradition and wider competence than is evident or accepted at present.

164. We recommend that the FTTI be converted into a national institute for film and television training awarding diplomas in both disciplines, with a technical component as well. Doordarshan should be suitably compensated and assisted to establish a separate staff training school elsewhere.

165. For radio too the foundation courses should be taken over by universities and other specialised institutions and the NBT should over a period of time only need to provide induction training and refresher courses at higher levels.

166. The technical training facilities of both Akashvani and Doordarshan require considerable strengthening and expansion. The resources of the present Staff Training Institute (Technical) are fully stretched and it must be suitably expanded or replicated. As in the case of programme training, the best engineers should be assigned to

the training schools and a posting here should be considered a distinction.

167. The NBT should offer apprenticeship and short duration in-service facilities for university or diploma trainees to work under operational conditions.

168. The NBT's requirements of trained administrators and managers can be met by simple in-house facilities supplemental by the existing management institutes.

A New Deal for Staff (Chapter 18)

169. We recommend that there should be parity between all categories of staff in the NBT and that all programme staff including staff artists should be brought under a single unified cadre. It should be possible for a recruit to any one of three broad service categories, namely technical, programme (including news) and "administration" to rise to senior staff positions at the top.

170. Salary scales and fees should be reviewed so as to ensure that Akashvani and Doordarshan attract and retain the requisite talent which they are not always able to do today. Promotional avenues should also be enlarged for all services on an equitable basis in order to prevent stagnation and frustration.

171. The NBT should have machinery to foster cordiality and understanding with and among all sections of its staff by periodic discussions in staff councils between the management and staff representatives who should be encouraged to put forward ideas and suggestions.

172. Consistent with the ethos of the NBT as a non-profit trust and an essential service, we recommend the establishment of a grievance machinery at various levels which should be automatically activated in the case of any difference or dispute.

173. Staff welfare services and amenities should get due attention.

174. Staff should be entitled to study leave in accordance with stipulated procedures if they wish to undertake approved study, research or training.

175. Over-categorisation should be avoided and seniority and rank should be determined by time scales with efficiency-bars rather than by a whole hierarchy of designations.

176. All those who are retained in service after the normal age of

retirement should be re-employed subject to medical fitness on short-term renewal contracts.

177. We recommend that the present staff artists become regular employees of the NBT. Integration of programme staff should be left to special programme staff integration panels working to certain accepted norms. Experience, length of service and assessment of talent should be taken into consideration in fitting personnel of all programme services into a unified programme cadre.

178. We recommend that all Grade I posts of and above the rank of News Editor in the News Services Division, Regional News Units. Monitoring Units, etc., be filled by open competition. All members of the CIS cadre, wherever employed, as well as staff artists and outsiders who fulfil the requisite qualification will be eligible. For the rest, we recommend that all members of the CIS cadre, and not just those currently with Akashvani—be given the option to join the NBT.

179. CIS personnel who opt for service in the NBT should be served by a special selection panel and the existing "CIS quota" of 219 in Akashvani and Doordarshan should be filled from among those selected. The should thereafter be regarded as permanent employees of their NBT and should sever their connections with the CIS.

180. Similar selection and fitment procedures are recommended in respect of Akashvani and Doordarshan posts encadred in the Central Secretariat Service, the Central Secretariat Stenographer's Service, and the Central Secretariat Clerical Service, all belonging to the Information and Broadcasting Ministry's cadres. Similar fitment and selection procedures should be followed for filling in the posts in the Pay and Accounts Sections of the NBT. Deputations should also be given the option as others and be subjected to identical procedures.

181. Non-gazetted engineering staff should be eligible for promotion to gazetted positions of higher responsibility provided they pass an appropriate departmental examination which should include certain basic theoretical papers pertaining to broadest engineering, due account being given to the experience and performance of the person concerned.

182. We recommend direct recruitment of the lower ranks with provision for suitable promotion quotas between different tiers which should be filled on the basis of departmental selections and examinations. However, merit critical should not be relaxed in the process of departmental promotion though we see no reason to impose any age

bar at any stage within the organisation.

183. Those persons who prefer to specialise should be enabled to stay on in specialised jobs rather than graduate to staff or managerial appointments. They should however be offered promotions *in situ* through suitable time scales. We do not think it necessary for the NBT to insist on graduate or any other degree, diploma or certificate for non-technical staff. We would, however, recommend the provision of self-learning and training facilities within the NBT so that there are possibilities for career advancement.

184. It should be a necessary requirement that a person should have gained a certain variety of experience in different appointments before he or she qualifies for a staff job. Similarly, junior staff jobs should regarded as training grounds for senior staff appointments and the latter for selection to top management posts.

185. We recommend lateral entry at higher levels so as to provide necessary infusion of fresh blood and ideas to ensure the best possible talent for sensitive senior posts.

186. The posts of Controller-General of Broadcasting Directors, and General Managers should be tenure posts of not more than five years. This should not preclude reappointment.

187. Confidential reports of members of the staff should be written by their immediate administrative superiors as well as by their professional heads of department. This will ensure a certain balance and reflect more accurately the record of the persons concerned. In the case of very senior personnel, it may be desirable that evaluation is made by a group rather than by individuals who are in the hierarchy.

188. All employees of the NBT irrespective of the discipline to which they belong should be given an appointment letter which should be in the nature of a contract terminable with one, three, or six months notice on either side depending upon the level of the appointment or post held. Entirely new recruits should be initially taken on one or two years probation.

189. The NBT should encourage the formation of a single staff association with distinctive wings to represent the service interests of all employees so as to promote an effective dialogue with the management.

190. Existing employees as are taken over by the NBT should be offered protection in respect of their present benefits such as emoluments housing, medical facilities, pension and gratuity, leave travel

and educational benefits. Existing employees (including staff artists) should continue to be entitled to the allotment of pool accommodation from the Government for a transitional period.

Engineering and Technological Aspects (Chapter 19)

191. We recommend that the technological options relating to Akashvani's "ITU Plan" the VHF alternative, and the possibilities of introducing low-frequency transmissions should be carefully considered by a High level team of experts that the NBT should constitute as early as possible. These technological choices involve not merely questions of investment cost and quality of reception but also patterns of programming. Therefore a realistic and objective cost-benefit study should be made before any irrevocable decisions are taken with all their long-term implications.

192. The emphasis on Research in the NBT should be on those areas of work which cannot be carried out effectively elsewhere. The development of hardware should have lower priority than other specialised problems.

193. The Research Department should be headed by a very senior engineer who can assist in long term planning and assurance of a quality service by reporting to the top management. Its strength will have to be increased considerably, necessary facilities added, and activities expanded and rearranged in specialist groups.

194. It may be desirable to set apart for R&D a definite percentage of say three per cent of the gross annual revenue expenditure on technical operations.

195. The volume of plant and equipment required for NBT's expansion justify the setting up of a separate manufacturing units for broadcast equipment. BEL could be asked to set up a separate unit or, in the alternative, the Government could establish a broadcast Electronics Corporation on in the public sector.

196. A number of technological developments such as slow-scan television, bandwidth reduction, etc., suggest the need for R&D in these areas and, it necessary, their funding by the NBT.

Future Expansion (Chapter 20)

197. While we acknowledge that television is a powerful and effective, medium, India should give first priority to the development

and densification of radio for atleast the next 10 to 15 years.

198. Whatever the choice or mix of technology we would strongly recommend that Akashvani must develop a determined rural extension thrust which is best done through the rapid development of low-power local stations.

199. In the sitting of the proposed new local stations, preference should be given to backward districts including drought prone, tribal and hill areas, subject to the availability of the minimum infrastructure, accessibility and a dependable power supply. The State Governments should be consulted.

200. The NBT should undertake to organise special maintenance services in tribal and backward areas and in approved radio densification clusters. It should combine this wherever possible with the purchase and sale of approved quality sets. Manufacturers should also be encouraged to set up joint after-sales service and maintenance units for rural clients. The Central and State Governments should suitably assist these efforts.

201. The State Governments should considered bearing the cost of licence fees in certain areas and in approved radio densification clusters.

202. Radio listening clusters linked to a "mother station" could develop special educational, extension and other programmes on the SITE model. Hire purchase of sets with concessional bank loans should be encouraged.

203. In certain areas, wired broadcasting may be feasible as in Arunachal where "town broadcasting" systems have been installed in each of the district headquarters.

204. The existing Doordarshan network and on-going schemes will provide television coverage to an area with a potential audience of 100 million. The densification of television viewing within this area would seem to be an obvious priority.

205. Low-cost television technology as experimentally tried out by the Space Applications Centre would seem particularly appropriate for rural areas. If the cost effectiveness of such facilities is demonstrated by some pilot projects which the NBT itself can undertake then the case for a relativity more rapid expansion of this mode of television would be established.

206. The Commissioning of INSAT in 1981 will facilitate National Network of Doordarshan programmes. Otherwise we recommend the use of INSAT in the first instance primarily for establishing

direct reception in North-East Islands and Lakshadweep because the undulating terrain and dispersed habitations there under terrestrial television a highly expensive proposition.

207. Urban programming must show due concern for the needs of the large class of urban unprivileged who, like rural listeners and viewers, need to be provided with community and group listening and viewing facilities.

208. The NBT should undertake research and experimentation in multi-media operations and in the cognitive use of radio and television. There is promise in radiovision, cassette tape recorders used with educational radio, and slow-sean television.

209. There is need for reducing the cost of television and radio sets, including FM radio transistors, if radio and television densification are to move ahead rapidly small assembles of radio and television receivers should be encouraged to form marketing cooperatives of consortia and sell standardised equipment under common brand names.

Transition Provisions (Chapter 21)

210. We hope that the Akashvani Bharati Bill will be approved by the cabinet in time to be formally introduced during the current session of Parliament so that it can be taken up for consideration during the monsoon session and enacted by September or October.

211. As an earnest or its decision to confer full autonomy on Akashvani and Doordarshan we recommend that the Government may direct them to follow the charter spelt out in chapter 5, the Legal Framework. This will immediately introduce a change in the character and outlook of these two broadcast organisations and inform them with the spirit of our recommendations. A Central News Room on the lines we have recommended should be established as early as possible as it is in the area of news and current affairs that an immediate impact can be made.

212. The Ministry of Information and Broadcasting should immediately set up a Broadcast Autonomy Cell to process this report and prepare working papers for preparatory action and cabinet decision.

213. Rationalisation of the staff structure and unification of leaders in accordance with our recommendations will call for detailed work. This task should be entrusted to an expert body of

consultants such as an Indian Institute of Management so that its report is available to the NBT as soon as it comes into being.

214. As soon as the Akash Bharati Bill receives the President's assent, Akashvani and Doordarshan should be accorded a special Transitional Status and serviced by the Broadcast Autonomy Cell.

215. The Akash Bharati Act should come into force with effect from January 1, 1979 and certain transitional sections even earlier, if necessary. From, say, October 15, 1978 onwards Akashvani and Doordarshan should be placed under an Officer-on-Special Duty heading a Transitional Board of Management to undertake the staff work relating to transfer of assets and liabilities to the NBT and to work out procedures whereby the CIS cadre and other staff on eputation will be enabled to exercise an option regarding whether to go over to the proposed NBT or return to their parent services.

216. The Transitional Management Board should prepare an independent budget for the NBT for 1979-80 which the Trustees should formally approve and forward to Government.

AGRICULTURAL CREDIT SCHEMES OF COMMERCIAL BANKS, 1977 – REPORT[1]

Report of the Expert Group

Chairman Dr. Gunvant M. Desai, Professor, Indian Institute of Management, Ahmedabad

Members Shri V.N. Bahadur; Shri R.L. Wadhwa; Shri R. Balasubramanian; Shri S.P. Nair; Dr. N.D. Rege; Shri S. Narayanaswamy; Dr. S. Bose; Shri R. Vijayaraghavan

M. Secy. Shri A. Seshan

Appointment

The Reserve Bank of India, (RBI) set-up an Expert Group [comprising representatives of Government of India, commercial banks, Agricultural Refinance and Development Corporation (ARDC), Agricultural Finance Corporation Ltd., (AFC), RBI and experts in certain disciplines in agriculture and allied activities] in consultation with the Government of India in August 1977.

Terms of Reference

The Expert Group was given the following terms of reference:

(i) To review the different types of schemes formulated by the commercial banks for extending short, medium and long-term financial assistance to various agricultural and allied activities, and

(ii) To suggest, in the light of its findings and taking into consideration the technological and other changes, the general

----

1. Report, Reserve Bank of India, 1978

pattern of new schemes which banks could frame and implement so as to meet the credit requirements of farmers and agriculturists.

Contents

Introduction; Commercial Banks' Finance for Agricultural Sector: An Overview; Formulation of Credit Schemes; Implementation of Credit Schemes; Related Issues; Summary of Conclusions and Recommendations, Annexures and Appendices.

Recommendations

Modalities of Scheme Formulation

6.3.1 We endorse the "area approach" in the formulation of agricultural credit schemes. Concerted efforts should be made to prepare location-specific credit schemes for all purposes. The term "area approach" should mean that the credit schemes are based on location-specific realities with respect to (i) the range of activities for which they are prepared keeping in view the forward and backward linkages between purposes for which credit schemes are formulated and other activities which have a bearing on these purposes, and (ii) factors which affect the scope of lending and viability of loans for the different categories of borrowers. (Paras 3.6.2, 5.5.1 and 5.5.6)

6.3.2 The commercial banks should give due importance to the tasks of formulating and appraising agricultural credit schemes at all levels. This implies strengthening of Agricultural Finance Department at the head office, establishment/strengthening of Agricultural Finance Cell at the zonal offices with adequate and technically competent staff, appointment of Farm Representatives at the regional/divisional/area level and providing increasing number of rural and semi-urban branches with Agriculture/Technical Field Officers. At all these levels, there should be grater involvement of relevant officers in the scheme formulation task than has been the case so far. (Paras 3.3, 3.5, 3.6.3)

6.3.3 There should be a close rapport between the office of the Director of Institutional Finance in each State and the commercial banks operating in that State. On the basis of the agricultural development programmes of the State Governments and the feed-back received from the DCCs, the Director of Institutional Finance should indicate priority areas (functional and geographical) to the commercial banks for formulation of credit schemes. Those State/Union Territory Governments, which have not yet established the office of the Director of Institutional Finance, should do so without delay. A senior officer of the rank of a Secretary/Commissioner should be appointed as Director of Institutional Finance and his office should be strengthened. (Paras 3.6. 4 and 4.12.25)

6.3.4 The Commercial Banks should develop close contacts with the Regional Offices of the ARDC to identify opportunities for developing credit schemes, and increasingly use the guidelines developed by the ARDC to formulate their credit schemes, irrespective of whether refinance is required. (Para 3.6.5)

6.3.5 The AFC may consider establishing offices in each State in a phased manner to play an active role in the formulation of major credit schemes for the State Governments and the commercial banks. In the State Level Coordination Committees and DCCs, the AFC should be associated. It should also be given substantial role in carrying out evaluation of major credit schemes. The findings of these studies should be utilised in the formulation of agricultural credit schemes. (Paras 3.6.6 and 4.12.29)

6.3.6 The Lead Banks and the DCCs should not only monitor the progress of credit schemes but critically examine the problems experienced in the implementation of the existing credit schemes to identify new credit schemes in the areas of functionally inter-related activities (e.g., supplies of inputs, further development of marketing and processing facilities, rural electrification, etc.). For this purpose, among other things, the feedback from the Task Force to Facilitate Implementation of Credit Schemes should be utilised. (Paras 3.3.6, 3.6.7, 4.8.7, 4.12.21, 4.12.24, 4.12.25 and 5.5.2)

6.3.7 District Credit Plans, prepared by the Lead Banks, should contain some discussion on (i) the nature and source of data used and various assumptions made in working out the economics of credit schemes included in them, (ii) balancing of the agricultural credit schemes for direct finance with those for indirect finance; and (iii) forward and backward linkages of the bankable credit schemes proposed in them. (Paras 3.6.8, 5.2.7 and 5.5.6)

6.3.8 To identify opportunities for developing credit schemes for specific villages and blocks, Branch Managers should be invited to the meetings of the block development committees. Similarly, there should be regular interaction between branch staff, on the one hand, and development staff, input dealers and organisations and individuals involved in the marketing of agricultural output, on the other hand. Schemes, however, should be based on purposive groundwork/surveys after the opportunities are identified in this manner. The main objective of the groundwork should be to examine critically the viability of these opportunities to develop sound schemes and to assess the scope for lending under such schemes to different categories of borrowers. (Paras 3.3.2, 3.3.3, 3.3.6 and 3.6.9)

6.3.9 The task of compiling district-wise data on the loan operations of credit institutions and making them available to agencies involved in the formulation of agricultural credit schemes should be entrusted to the Regional Offices of the RBI (Para 3.6.12)

6.3.10 The State/Union Territory Governments should issue instructions to district administration, Groundwater Departments, Directorates of Agriculture and other relevant departments to provide data to the agencies formulating agriculture credit schemes. (Para 3.6.12)

Improvements/Modifications in Credit Schemes

6.3.11 For the same purpose, the terms and conditions of loans to the same category of borrowers should be uniform in the credit schemes of all banks operating in a district/groups of districts. The RBI should evolve such uniformity in consultation with the commercial banks. (Paras 3.4.13, 3.4.20, 3.4.28, 3.4.33, 3.4.38 and 3.6.14)

6.3.12 Each credit scheme should explicitly spell out the assumptions made in working out the economic viability and repayment schedules of loans. Similarly, functional linkages between activity financed by a credit scheme and infrastructural support and other complementary activities which have a bearing on the viability of the scheme should be pointed out. (Paras 3.4.4 to 3.4.6, 3.4.9 to 3.4.11, 3.4.16, 3.4.17, 3.4.29, 3.4.36, 3.4.40, 3.6.15, 3.6.17, 4.8.5 and 4.8.6)

6.3.13 Arrangements for the supply of inputs and other materials as well as for marketing and storage of output should be worked out at the stage of formulating credit schemes. Such functional linkages should be strengthened by formulating credit schemes for indirect finance on location-specific basis (Paras 3.6.19, 3.6.21 and 5.5.1)

Crop Loans

6.3.14 Crop loans should be given both for irrigated and unirrigated conditions. (Para 3.4.14)

6.3.15 The recommendation made by the All India Rural Credit Review Committee on the adjustments to be made in the method of arriving at the actual amount of loans for individual cultivators, and incorporated by the RBI in its manual on *Production-Oriented System of Lending for Agriculture*, should be strictly adhered to. (Para 3.4.15)

6.3.16 Schemes for marketing finance against pledge/hypothecation of produce should be developed and implemented in a coordinated manner with the crop loan schemes. The present ceiling of advances against foodgrains for exemption from selective credit control stipulations should be raised from Rs. 2,500 to Rs. 5,000. (Para 3.4.18)

Credit Schemes for Minor Irrigation

6.3.17 The eligibility criterion for a loan to construct a well should be fixed on the basis of minimum owned land as well such considerations as productivity of land, possible changes in cropping pattern and crop varieties, availability of ready markets for output and cost of a well. (Para 3.4.21)

6.3.18 Besides conventional aspects such as construction of wells/tubewells pumpsheds, and installation of pumpsets, credit schemes for minor irrigation should cover such aspects as sprinklers, lining of canals, water courses and channels, which will improve the performance of minor irrigation facilities (Para 3.4.24)

6.3.19 State Governments should identify the opportunities and develop credit schemes for repairs and desilting of tanks as well as to bring water harvesting technologies from research stations to cultivators' fields in due consultation with the ARDC, the AFC and commercial banks. (Paras 3.4.24 and 2.4.26)

Credit Schemes for Farm Mechanisation

6.3.20 The scope of credit schemes for farm mechanisation should increasingly include such things as small tools and implements, bullock carts with pneumatic tyres, mould board ploughs, dusters, sprayers, threshers and power-tillers. (Para 3.4.27)

6.3.21 In the credit schemes for tractors, economic viability of loans should be rigorously worked out and precautions to ensure proper maintenance of machines should be built. (Paras 3.4.29, 3.4.31)

Credit Schemes for Dairying and Poultry

6.3.22 Whenever these schemes are taken to widen the asset base of low-income groups, security-oriented eligibility criteria, (e.g., mortgage of land and requirements of guarantors acceptable to banks) should be dropped (Paras 3.4.34, 3.4.38)

6.3.23 These schemes should be based on sound location-specific groundwork. They could be for financing of several inter-related activities in regions where major development efforts are being made by the State Governments. They could also be for financing of the purchase of a minimum of a couple of milch animals of local variety/small poultry units to broaden the asset base of the weaker sections. While formulating these credit schemes careful attention should be paid to veterinary support, marketing arrangements for production, supplies of fodder and feed and managerial capabilities of borrowers for the enterprise. Repayment schedules of loans should be worked out after making reasonable allowance for domestic consumption of the product. (Paras 3.4.35 to 3.4.37, 3.4.39 and 3.4.40)

Range of Activities and New Purposes to be Covered by Credit Schemes

6.3.24 Commercial banks should diversify the purposes for which they formulate agricultural credit schemes by (i) developing credit schemes for activities which are inter-related with the existing credit schemes (Para 3.6.19), (ii) developing credit schemes for unconventional purposes (Para 3.6.20) and (iii) formulating credit schemes exclusively for different segments of the low-income groups. (Paras 3.4.25, 3.4.30, 3.6.22 and 3.6.23)

Appraisal of Credit Schemes at the Sanctioning Stage

6.3.25 Credit schemes should be critically appraised at the stage of sanctioning them. The following aspects need particular attention: (i) economic viability of loans, (ii) repayment schedules of loans, (iii) infrastructure support to and functional linkages of, the purpose of loans with other activities and development programmes, (iv) scope of giving loans to the weaker sections under the scheme, and (v) staff required to implement the scheme. (Para 4.2.2, 4.2.3, 4.12.2 and 4.12.3)

6.3.26 The task of pre-sanction appraisal of schemes up to specified amounts should be decentralised up to zonal/regional levels in a phased manner in those commercial banks where this function is still carried out at the head offices. The bank offices at these levels should be provided with adequate and competent staff for this purpose. (Paras 4.2.4 and 4.12.4)

Canvassing Loan Applications

6.3.27 The efforts to enlarge the coverage of borrowers from low-income groups should be more vigorous. "Group Guarantee" approach should be followed not only to get guarantees for individual crop loans but also for joint ownership of assets. The Commercial Banks should play a catalytic role in forming groups for joint ownership of assets and also for group actions in arranging for input supplies and marketing of output. (Paras 4.3.4 and 4.3.5)

Sanctioning of Loans to Individual Borrowers

6.3.28 Concerted efforts should be made in the following directions to minimise the difficulties in sanctioning loans to individual borrowers (Paras 6.3.29 to 6.3.33)

Legislation on the Lines Recommended by the Talwar Committee

6.3.29 All State/Union Territory Governments should pass legislation incorporating all provisions of the Model Bill recommended by the Talwar Committee and effectively implement it without further delay. (Paras 4.8.4, 4.9.9 and 4.12.6)

Land Records and Revenue Pass Books

6.3.30 All State/Union Territory Governments should expeditiously take up a time-bound programme to bring the records of rights up to date. They should also take up issuing Pass Books containing details of land held and rights therein, sources of irrigation, *taccavi* loans issued and encumbrances, and evolve mechanisms to up-date these Pass Books so that they can be given legal status. Wherever such Pass Books have been (or are being) issued, the commercial banks should take them as *prima facie* evidence of rights in land, and use them as the starting point to process the loan applications. (Paras 4.4.3, 4.4.9, 4.4.10, 4.5.1, 4.5.2, 4.8.2, 4.12.7 and 4.12.8)

Powers to Branch Managers

6.3.31 Once a credit scheme is sanctioned for implementation by a particular branch, the Branch Manager should be given powers to sanction individual loan applications under it. Also, Branch Managers should have minimum sanctioning powers up to Rs. 5,000 in respect of loans not covered by area-specific schemes. As far as possible, Managers of rural branches should not be transferred for a period of 3 years as sanctioning loans for the agricultural credit schemes requires a good feel of environment. (Paras 4.4.7, 4.4.10 and 4.12.9)

Simplification of Forms and Procedures

6.3.32 The Commercial Banks should simplify and standardise their loan application forms and documentation formalities for giving loans with a view to reduce the number of required documents and to make the life of the documents longer. The simplified application norms and documents evolved by the Datey Group and the Khanna Group for Regional Rural Banks may be adopted by other commercial banks with suitable modifications (Paras 4.4.1 to 4.4.6, 4.4.9, 4.4.10, 4.5.1, 4.5.2 and 4.12.10)

6.3.33 Non-encumbrance certificate should not be required for crop loans up to Rs. 5,000. In the case of crop loans for Rs. 5,000 or more, it should not be insisted upon, as far as possible, with each fresh application. (Para 4.12.11)

6.3.34 The requirement of sureties often causes great hardships to the weaker sections. It should be dispensed with except in the case of Group Guarantees. Once mortgage on land is taken, there should be no further requirement of a guarantee. (Paras 4.12.12 and 4.12.13)

6.3.35 Wherever extracts of Land Records and/or Non-encumbrance Certificates are required, the Commercial Banks should themselves get these documents on behalf of the borrowers. The State Governments should issue the necessary instructions, allowing the revenue officials to take specified reasonable remuneration for giving the extracts/certificates to banks. Commercial banks may charge this amount to the loan accounts of the borrowers. (Para 4.12.14)

Disbursement of Loans

6.3.36 The disbursement of loans in kind is a desirable practice but it should not become an end in itself. The basic objective should be to avoid the possible misutilisation of loans. To ensure this, the emphasis should be on working out arrangements with input distribution agencies well in advance, if necessary by taking up schemes of indirect finance for them. (Paras 4.5.1 to 4.5.3 and 4.12.15)

6.3.37 In the case of loans for the purchase of animals and birds, the discretion to disburse loans in cash or kind should be left to the Branch Managers as everywhere it may not be possible to make payment to the suppliers. (Para 4.12.16)

6.3.38 For land development and construction of wells, disbursement should be by instalments according to the progress of the work. (Para 4.12.17)

Supervision of Credit Schemes

6.3.39 Supervision of credit schemes should imply not only ensuring that the loans are utilised for the purpose for which they are given but also paying attention to the proper functioning of the several activities on which the viability of the credit schemes depends. Branches of commercial banks should be provided with adequate and trained field staff for this purpose. Also, there should be regular interactions between branch staff and relevant officials of development administration, other functionaries and individuals. The purpose of these interactions should be to seek solutions to the problems because of which the loans may not generate intended increase in the net incremental incomes of the borrowers. (Paras 4.7.1 to 4.7.5 and 4.12.18)

Task Force to Facilitate Implementation of Credit Schemes

6.3.40 A Task Force to Facilitate Implementation of Credit Schemes (TFCS) should be created at the district level. It should seek solutions to the specific difficulties brought to it by branches of the commercial banks operating in the district. It should also act as an effective feedback mechanism for the development administration and the DCC particularly with respect to location-specific difficulties experienced by borrowers and branches of Commercial Banks in implementing agricultural credit schemes. Two objectives of the feedback should be (i) to ensure proper dovetailing of development efforts and credit schemes, and (ii) to facilitate the deliberations in the DCC to serve the objectives for which this machinery has been established. (Paras 4.4.3, 4.4.9, 4.4.10, 4.5.3, 4.7.4, 4.7.5, 4.8.2, 4.8.3, 4.8.5 to 4.8.7, 4.9.4, 4.12.19 to 4.12.22, 4.12.24 and 4.12.25)

6.3.41 The TFCS should meet once a month. The Task Force should consist of District Collector (Chairman), a representative of the Lead Bank and a senior officer of the collectorate as the Convener. Also, in each meeting, representatives of the concerned branches should be co-opted as members. Functionaries of the district administration and non-officials (e.g., input dealers, local leaders and others) who could help in solving the problems should be invited to the meeting of the TFCS. (Para 4.12.23)

6.3.42 One of the items of agenda in the meetings of the DCC should be discussion on the resume of the working of the TFCS in the period intervening between the meetings of the DCC, and the issues raised by the TFCS for the consideration of the DCC. The agenda notes and minutes of the meetings of the DCC should be sent to the Director of Institutional Finance and the Chairman of the State Level Coordination Committee. (Para 4.12.25)

6.3.43 The RBI and State Governments should take steps to establish the TFCS. The Lead Banks should organise workshops in their districts to familiarise the branch staff of different commercial banks operating in the district with the objectives and *modus operandi* of the TFCS. The commercial banks should take necessary steps in this direction. (Para 4.12.23).

Recovery of Loan

6.3.44 The commercial banks should evolve a machinery to get up-to-date information on the recovery of loans for different purposes, identify causes behind poor recoveries of loans and take timely corrective actions. The task of gathering the above information, analysing it and suggesting appropriate corrective actions should become an integral function of the Monitoring and Evaluation Cells which are being set up by the commercial banks. (Paras 4.9.3 to 4.9.7 and 4.12.26)

6.3.45 The State/Union Territory Governments should share the responsibility of recovering the loans in the case of agricultural credit schemes sponsored by them. (Paras 4.9.8, 4.9.9 and 4.12.27)

Monitoring and Evaluation of Credit Schemes

6.3.46 All commercial banks should establish Monitoring and Evaluation Cells. These cells should not only watch the progress in lending but also gather information on the difficulties experienced in implementing the agricultural credit schemes. Such information should be utilised both for follow-up actions at various levels as well as to draw lessons in modifying the existing schemes and in formulating the new credit schemes. (Paras 4.10.1, 4.10.3, 4.10.4 and 4.12.28)

6.3.47 The commercial banks, the ARDC and the AFC should take up on a regular basis the task of evaluating the agricultural credit schemes. The purpose of these studies should be an objective assessment of (i) borrowers' difficulties in getting and utilising the loans, (ii) difficulties experienced by the branches of commercial banks in implementing the schemes and, (iii) impact of credit schemes in raising the incomes of different categories of borrowers. While evaluating a credit scheme, a comparison should be made between actual and intended impact of the scheme and reasons for the divergence between the two should be identified. The commercial banks should sponsor some of the evaluation studies with the AFC and academic institutions. Findings of the evaluation studies should be utilised in the formulation and implementation of the agricultural credit schemes. (Paras 4.10.5 and 4.10.6)

6.3.48 At the national level, data collected by the RBI through half-yearly Special Return on Agricultural Loans-I on the commercial banks' lendings through cooperatives should be on the same lines as commercial banks' direct lendings to the agriculturists. In the annual Special Return on Agricultural Loans-II, the data on overdues should be collected according to different purposes of loans and holdings size. The RBI should also keep a close watch on the balance between direct and indirect finance to the agricultural sector by compiling and analysing the data in as disaggregative a manner as possible. The RBI may consider utilising these data/findings to inform Directors of Institutional Finance in different States and also the consultative/coordination committees established at the State and district levels about the various aspects of credit provided by the commercial banks for agricultural development in their respective regions. (Paras 4.10.2, 4.12.30 and 5.5.4)

Commercial Banks' Loans to Farmers through Intermediaries

6.3.49 This line of lending should not be viewed as an easy alternative to formulating and implementing credit schemes of direct finance to the agricultural sector by the commercial banks. The commercial banks should assist the intermediaries in formulating and critically appraising their credit schemes. (Paras 5.2.4, 5.2.8 and 5.5.5)

Village Adoption Scheme

6.3.50 The Village Adoption Scheme should aim at an integrated development of the village economy in all its aspects. It should also aim at meeting the credit needs of all members of the weaker sections in the adopted villages within 3 to 5 years, particularly by developing credit schemes exclusively meant for different categories of low-income groups such as small and marginal farmers, landless labourers, tenant cultivators, share-croppers and others. These schemes should have two features: (i) terms and conditions should be suited to the circumstances of the low-income groups (e.g., simple documentation formalities, flexible and easy requirements of margin money and sureties, longer repayment periods, lower interest rates, provisions for rescheduling of repayment and moratorium on the payment of interest and principal, and if necessary, additional loan to overcome genuine difficulties), and (ii) there should be possibilities in these schemes for joint ownership of assets. Commercial banks should make concerted efforts to implement these schemes by seeking active and meaningful collaboration of official and non-official agencies of the area. (Paras 5.4.1 to 5.4.8 and 5.4.10)

6.3.51 The progress and experiences of the Village Adoption Scheme with above objectives should be reviewed on a regular basis both by the commercial banks and the RBI. Lessons emerging from these experiences should be utilised to improve the working of the

Village Adoption Scheme as well as to develop strategies for enlarged coverage of the weaker sections in the non-adopted villages by appropriately modifying the recommendations we have made in different parts of this report. (Paras 3.6.16, 3.6.22, 3.6.23, 4.3.5, 4.12.2 and 4.12.3)

6.3.52 The RBI may consider issuing guidelines on the demarcation of areas for different credit institutions for this purpose in the light of the recommendations of the Working Group to Study Problems Arising out of the Adoption of Multi-agency Approach in Agricultural Financing. (Paras 5.4.5 and 5.4.9)

Staff Requirements for Agricultural Credit Schemes and their Training

6.3.53 To formulate and implement agricultural credit schemes on the lines recommended in this report, the commercial banks should critically examine their manpower planning and training of staff for this line of lending. Some of our recommendations will considerably reduce the workload on the branch staff in routine but time-consuming operations. On the other hand, adequate and technically competent staff will have to be provided at different levels for substantive tasks, particularly to formulate sound location-specific credit schemes, to appraise these schemes critically at the sanctioning stage, to establish meaningful rapport with other agencies at the implementation stage, and to monitor and evaluate their performance. (Paras 3.3.5, 3.3.6, 3.6.3 to 3.6.5, 3.6.8, 3.6.9, 4.2.2 to 4.2.4, 4.3.1, 4.3.4, 4.3.5, 4.4.9, 4.4.10, 4.4.11, 4.5.2, 4.7.2, 4.8.8, 4.9.4, 4.10.4, 4.10.5, 4.12.2, 4.12.4, 4.12.29 and 5.4.10)

6.3.54 In the training of staff concerned with agricultural credit schemes, various aspects of formulating and implementing these schemes (discussed in this report) should get more emphasis than has been the case so far. In this type of training, experience-based teaching materials and case studies should be widely used. In the training of field officers, general aspects of banking should also be covered. (Paras 3.6.10 and 3.6.11)

6.3.55 The practice of appointing experienced Agricultural/ Technical Field Officers as Managers of rural branches should be adopted by all commercial banks. Incentives in the form of weightage for future promotion and/or increment for consistently outstanding performance in formulating and implementing agricultural credit schemes should be given to the staff concerned with agricultural credit schemes. (Para 3.6.11)

SECOND REVIEW COMMITTEE TO REVIEW THE WORK OF ICSSR DURING THE LAST 10 YEARS AND SPECIALLY DURING THE FIFTH FIVE YEAR PLAN, 1977 – REPORT[1]

Chairman Prof. V.M. Dandekar
Members Dr. Ramkrishna Mukherjee; Dr. Samuel Paul; Dr. G. Ram Reddy
M. Secy. Dr. V.A. Pai Panandiker

Appointment

The Indian Council of Social Science Research constituted in August 1977 the Second Review Committee.

Terms of Reference

(i) To review the work of the ICSSR during the last 10 years and especially during the Fifth Five-Year Plan; and

(ii) To make proposals for the development of the work and programmes of the ICSSR over the next 10 years and especially during the Sixth Five-Year Plan.

Contents

Introductory; Establishment of the Indian Council of Social Science Research, its Policies and Programmes; Research Grants; Fellowships; Research Institutes; Training in Research Methodology; Area Studies, International Collaboration and Foreign Assistance; Regional and State Centres; Publication, Documentation and Data Archives; Structure, Organisations and Finances; Antonomy; Over-

1. Indian Council of Social Science Research, New Delhi, 1978, 113 p.

view and Recommendations; Annexures.

Recommendations

12.1 The establishment of the Indian Council of Social Science Research (ICSSR) is, clearly one of the important landmarks in the development of social sciences in India. Its work in the past nine years has fully justified its establishment. Its functioning during this period has been on the whole satisfactory and in our opinion it has made a significant contribution to the development of social science research in the country. Above all, it has created a forum for the scientists in the country to meet, communicate, and address themselves to their social responsibilities. In the course of our review, we have examined various aspects of its working naturally focusing attention on where, in our opinion, review, revision, and reorganisation are needed. We shall now bring such points together and present our suggestions and comments in the form of specific recommendations.

Need to Broaden the Base of Social Science Research

12.2 As we have noted, before independence the development of social science research in India occurred along with the growth of the Indian universities and the establishment of a number of research institutes, most of which were privately founded. The government did not play much active role. Since independence, there has occurred a large expansion in the number of universities, number of colleges affiliated to them and number of social science teachers working in them. But there did not occur a corresponding expansion either in centres for social science research or number of social science research workers engaged in research. By and large, social science research in the country has remained concentrated in a few established university departments, a few established research centres, and relatively small number of research workers. Social science research did not percolate below these levels, in particular to affiliated colleges and to social science teachers working in them. In consequence, it failed to broaden its base.

12.3 With the establishment of the Research Programmes Committee of the Planning Commission in 1953, substantial funds for social science research became available but the base remained narrow as before. In the period of 16 years since its establishment in

1953 and the establishment of the ICSSR in 1969, the Research Programmes Committee financed about 400 research projects in social sciences. We do not have a distribution of these projects as between different centres or persons. But we suppose, it remained very narrowly based.

12.4 The establishment of the ICSSR in 1969 and its functioning in the past 9 years have not made much change in this respect. As we have already noted, out of the 708 research projects financed by the ICSSR between 1969 and 1977, almost 600 have gone to the established university departments and research institutes and barely 56 to teachers in affiliated colleges. Nearly a quarter of the research projects are located in Delhi. It is true that the university training of a large majority of social science teachers in affiliated colleges, and of many in a number of university departments and even of research institutes, is not adequate for them to undertake research. It will be unrealistic and unfair to the ICSSR not to recognise this fact. But, at the same time, to let this majority remain outside the mainstream of social science research is undesirable and will undoubtedly prove detrimental to the development of social sciences in the country. The ICSSR must wake up to this danger.

12.5 In our opinion, this constitutes a major gap in the research promotional policies of the ICSSR. In fairness, we should say that the failure is not solely of the ICSSR; in a sense, it is a failure of the total social science community in the country. For instance, this aspect of its responsibility does not receive even a mention in the functions of the ICSSR as laid down in its Memorandum of Association, nor much serious attention since then. Consequently it has remained neglected. The ICSSR must now take urgent notice of this aspect of its responsibility and take active steps to broaden the base of social science research in the country by promoting participation and involvement of the large social science community outside the established university departments and research institutes.

12.6 A major difficulty, it seems, is the absence of channels of communication between the ICSSR and this vast majority of the social science community. We should mention that until now the ICSSR assistance did not reach the social science teachers in affiliated colleges not because their research proposals were found inadequate or unsatisfactory – this might have happened in a few cases – but because a large majority of them did not know even the existence of the ICSSR or the assistance to social science research it offers. Hence, the firs step necessary is to establish lines or a network of communication which will reach these persons effectively.

12.7 The Newsletter of the ICSSR is one such instrument. We understand that the ICSSR distributes it very widely. In our discussion with the Chairman, University Grants Commission, the Chairman offered to give space for ICSSR information in the UGC Newsletter. This should be pursued. But, evidently, the culture of seeking information through Newsletters or other written communications is not yet developed. Until it develops, spoken word appears necessary. The Regional Centres of the ICSSR are providing useful services but they are too few for this purpose. To multiply their number at the present level of financing is not feasible. Hence, after careful deliberation, we have come to the conclusion that, for a minimum effective communication between the ICSSR and the social science teachers in the affiliated colleges, it is necessary to establish an ICSSR Information Centre in each university. Many teachers from the affiliated colleges visit their respective university headquarters frequently for various purposes and an Information Centre located there will, in our judgement, greatly help to establish communication between them and the ICSSR.

12.8 We recommend that the ICSSR should take immediate steps to establish ICSSR Information Centres in all the universities. Such a centre has to be run necessarily in collaboration with the university. We suggest the following minimum collaboration. The university should agree to spare a room, preferably in its Administration Building or in the Social Science Building, appropriately furnished and serviced. The university should also agree to depute one of the social science teachers, if necessary in rotation, who will be available at the Information Centre at least one hour every working day. The ICSSR should agree to pay such a teacher an honorarium of Rs. 100 p.m. and give the Centre one typist-cum-clerk equipped with one typewriter (in the employ of the ICSSR either directly recruited or taken on deputation from the university). The minimum service to be provided by the Centre is to maintain a library of all publications of the ICSSR and a ready reference to all programmes and schemes of assistance of the ICSSR. The ICSSR's each direct expenditure should be limited to Rs. 10,000 per annum. The university may be persuaded to make an equal cash contribution. Depending upon the availability of funds and the enthusiasm of the social science teacher deputed to supervise the Centre, the Centre may offer many other services to the social science teachers visiting the Centre to seek information. The ICSSR should agree to open its Information Centres at all the universities which may agree to provide even the minimum facilities mentioned above without insisting on matching financial contribution.

12.9 The ICSSR Information Centres in the universities will serve a useful but limited purpose. More active steps will be necessary to develop research competence in a recognisable number of social science teachers in the affiliated colleges and help them establish a tradition of social science research in their respective colleges. The ICSSR has tried to organise training in Social Science Research Methodology. These have not proved greatly useful. With formal courses, it seems Research Methodology tends to develop into a science in itself rather than a tool of research. Moreover, an M. Phil. degree is soon likely to be a necessary qualification for all university/college teachers and the M.Phil. degree courses will in almost all universities, include a course in Research Methodology. When this materialises, the ICSSR should turn to somewhat non-formal or loosely structured method of developing and improving the research competence among social science teachers.

12.10 In this, the ICSSR will have to enlist active collaboration of research institutes and university departments. There are a number of well-established research institutes and departments in the country. Some of the institutes, lying outside the university system, are directly funded by the ICSSR. The ICSSR proposes to establish few such institutes in regions where research base is weak. We welcome this. We also welcome the ICSSR concept of developing them into 'centres of excellence' provided it does not preclude them from recognising their social obligation towards the less fortunately places colleagues in affiliated colleges. Let the ICSSR call upon all research institutes, whether within the university system or the ICSSR system, and university departments, to join in the task of broad-basing the social science research in the country by extending it to the social science teachers in affiliated colleges.

12.11 Specifically, we recommend the following:

(a) In the case of institutes financed by the ICSSR, it should be a requirement built into the ICSSR grant that these institutes conduct every year a given number of seminars or workshops for teachers in affiliated colleges in their neighbourhood in which the faculty of the research institutes will present the research methods adopted in their on-going research and the results of the recently completed research.

(b) ICSSR should request all other research institutes (not financed by the ICSSR) to organise similar seminars/ workshops and provide necessary funds for the purpose.

(c) Whenever the ICSSR approves and finances a research project from any established university department or research institute, there should be provision for organising similar seminars/workshops around the research project built into the research grant.

(d) ICSSR should welcome and support all proposals from university departments and research institutes whereby they may extend their research facilities, consultation and guidance to social science teachers in the affiliated colleges and young research workers in the neighbourhood. In particular, ICSSR should encourage and welcome research proposals which offer opportunity to the college teachers and young research workers to actively participate.

These are illustrative of the lines along with the facilities of the university departments and research institutes may be utilised. Several other propositions may be conceived and tried.

12.12 Social science teachers, located in isolated colleges lacking adequate library facilities, and uninitiated in research, need guidance as to what is research, what are the areas to be researched and what are the appropriate research methods. The Surveys of research in different disciplines completed by the ICSSR, which are now being updated, and the listing of gaps in research in various areas have been a useful activity of the ICSSR. If possible, the ICSSR may periodically appoint committees to review the research proposals being currently submitted, not only to the ICSSR but also to the UGC and other funding agencies, and point out gaps and imbalances in the current research. They may indicate, what in their opinion, should be the priorities. More importantly, they may outline the scope of, and appropriate research methods for, each theme so identified. This is a service badly needed by the vast majority of social science teachers who must be drawn into the research activity.

12.13 Research proposals coming from the new entrants should be supported even if they do not fall in the priority areas identified as mentioned above. But proposals coming from established university departments and institutes should be checked for priority. But, beyond this, we do not think that the ICSSR should actively sponsor research in one priority area or another. In particular, we do not think it advisable for the ICSSR to have Standing Advisory Committees to promote and sponsor particular themes of research or to have Programme Divisions to nurse such research through the instrument of establishment scholars, university departments and institutes. The experience of the Sponsored Research of the ICSSR has not been altogether satisfactory. In spite of liberal funding, it has not been always possible to promote the sponsored programmes. Leading scholars, departments and institutes are either too busy with several other commitments or they do not see the priorities where the ICSSR sees them. Hence, they have often to be persuaded to participate in the sponsored programmes of the ICSSR. This has strengthened the already existing tendency of the ICSSR research funds flowing into a few well-established channels of university departments, institutes and individuals. We are also afraid that such high pressure promotion of sponsored programme may result in disproportionate allocation of funds depending upon the promotional abilities of one group of research workers or another. Because of these several considerations, we recommend that the Sponsored Research Programmes of the ICSSR, in its present form, should be discontinued or withdrawn. The present commitments should, of course, be fulfilled.

Role of Established University Departments and Research Institutes

12.14 It is not our intention to suggest that the ICSSR funding of the established university departments and research institutes should be drastically curtailed. Far from it, we recognise that these departments and institutes have an important role to play in broadening the base of, as well as, deepening the content of social science research in the country. Hence, to avoid misunderstanding, we wish to clarify our position more specifically. Firstly, we suggest that proposals of research on familiar lines should be preferred if they come from new entrants. Indeed we would suggest that such proposals coming from established university departments and institutes should be considered only if they involve active participation of social science teachers from affiliated colleges and young research workers. For instance, a large majority of the research proposals involve empirical, fact-finding survey research. Such research provides useful training for young research workers or new entrants. We suggest that the ICSSR should prefer such proposals if they come from or at least actively involve new entrants. In our opinion, there is no justification in supporting such proposals if they are exclusively located in established university departments or institutes. Secondly, we suggest that the ICSSR should expect the established university departments and institutes, with large research facilities and personnel, to submit proposals of research which either have a light priority or which require considerable library and other facilities and a team of research workers who can devote, if not full time, at least a substantial part of their working time to research. When such proposals are submitted, the ICSSR should examine them and, though considerable academic latitude must be left to the established departments and institutes, the ICSSR should insist on a time-bound programme of its execution which may spread over two or three or even more years. In all such cases, the ICSSR should carefully examine the estimates of cost but should relax normal financial ceilings on single proposals.

12.15 Besides research in the priority areas which the ICSSR may identify through its committees, we have in mind two types of research which, in our view, the ICSSR should particularly support in the established university departments and institutes. As already mentioned, a large part of current social science research is empirical, fact-finding survey research. This is a welcome development. However, because of the mechanics of such research, the amount of time it takes to complete the field work and to process the data, such research has tended to be self-contained. As a consequence, the kind of research which uses secondary data, serial, massive, or fragmentary, and collates such data within a framework of social science analysis of broad dimensions, has neglected. Such research requires mature and patient scholarship and its results may not always have immediate policy implications and hence may not often be judged of high priority. We do not want to call such research 'fundamental' and juxtapose it with the other to be called 'applied' because such labelling can be misleading. But we wish to emphasise that only a substantial body of research of this kind can deepen the content of social science research and inspire and attract younger talent. Indeed, it is research of this kind which constitutes a genuine and lasting advance of social sciences. In our opinion, this is the responsibility of the established university departments and institutes. Some of the research projects which the ICSSR has approved and are called 'Major Projects' probably belong to this category. It will not be fair for us to comment on the merits of the particular projects. Hence, without implying a blanket approval of the particular projects, their budgeted costs or the procedures by which they were approved, we wish to record that we approve the concept of Major Projects if they will cover the type of research projects we have referred to above. Such projects will require large costs and longer periods to complete. Hence, the ICSSR should examine them carefully before they are approved and arrange for a periodic review of their progress after they are sanctioned. But if they are the proposals coming from mature scholars of proven ability and with institutional support necessary for their timely and orderly execution, they deserve to be considered generously. Narrow considerations and overcaution are not always justified.

12.16 There is yet another type of research which has remained neglected and which in our opinion is essential for the development of social science in the country. It is also eminently suitable for locating in established university departments and institutes. We have in mind the social science literature presently available to the students and research workers in this country. The bulk of this literature is of western origin and for our purposes is available in English language. The major part of all worthwhile writing in social sciences by Indian scholars is also in English. All this literature is not accessible to a large majority of the growing body of students, teachers and research workers. There are two reasons. Firstly, the library facilities have not expanded in proportion to the expansion in the number of students and the number of colleges. Secondly, because of the shift to regional languages in undergraduate classes, and sometimes even in postgraduate classes, the students' preparation in English is often inadequate for them to be able to read the literature in the original. This is a serious situation and in our opinion deserves urgent attention from the ICSSR. We recommend that a programme of selection of relevant social literature, its editing, translation into major regional languages and publication in cheap editions should receive a high priority in the ICSSR programme. This has often been neglected on grounds that this does not constitute proper research. Without wanting to enter into the semantics, we emphasise that, whether or not it is research, the activity is not easy and can only be undertaken by senior mature scholarship in the country and that this needs active promotion and support. Established university departments and institutes should play their part. We understand that the UGC has a similar programme in operation. We suggest that the ICSSR should explore the possibility of developing a joint programme with the UGC.

12.17 Thus, it will be clear that it is not our intention to exclude established university departments and research institutes from the ICSSR assistance. On the contrary, we envisage for them a very important role in the development of social sciences in the country. To the extent they accept the corresponding social responsibility and offer to play their part, we recommend that the ICSSR should give them full and liberal financial support. Established departments and institutes have remained far too self-contained and senior scholars far too self-centred in the past. The development of social sciences and promotion of social science research have often been identified with the development of a few what are called 'centres of excellence'. This is a dangerous illusion and must be given up before it is too late.

Research Grants

12.18 We have a few minor suggestions to make pertaining to the administration of research grants. They are as under:

(i) The ceiling of Rs. 50,000 for any single project should be raised to Rs. 75,000 and in exceptional cases up to Rs. 100,000.
(ii) The procedure for appointment of consultants should be streamlined. We recommend two lines of action. One, the ICSSR should prepare a panel of eminent social scientists to act as consultants for projects in each discipline. In addition, the Project Director of each proposal should be asked to recommend, if he so desires, a list of six possible consultants who may evaluate his proposal. This should receive due consideration. The final selection of the consultants should be made by a Committee consisting of the Chairman, the Member-Secretary, the Executive Director of the Department of Research Grants and Fellowships, and the Director of the relevant Division of Research Grants. We also suggest that the names of consultants who after accepting the assignment

do not make their report on time on more than two or three occasions should be brought before a meeting of the ICSSR and, if considered fair and appropriate, their names dropped from the panel.

(iii) In order to ensure timeliness of completion of a project, the consultants should be asked to comment in detail about the time budget.

(iv) For the same reason, a Project Director should be asked about his existing research and other commitments to ensure that he does not overstretch himself.

Fellowships

12.19 Next to research grants, fellowships remain the most important activity of the ICSSR. Our main recommendations are the following:

National Fellowships

12.20 The National Fellowships should be continued as at present except that the ceiling on the amount of fellowship may be raised to Rs. 3,000 per month. Besides, the national fellows should be given a higher contingency grant of Rs. 10,000 per annum and research assistance wherever necessary. We support the recent decision of the ICSSR that each proposal for such a fellowship should be accompanied by a detailed bio-data of the social scientist and of the grounds on which the national fellowship is recommended. However, we do not approve the present concept of the National Fellowship being purely an honour or a recognition bestowed on the scholar. If it is only matter of bestowing an honour, there are more appropriate ways of doing it. For instance, the ICSSR may offer to bring together and publish the collected works of the scholar. Or, the ICSSR may arrange to bring out a volume of essays in his honour contributed by senior social scientists. We believe that the fellowship must have a *quid pro quo* and, therefore, while offering the National Fellowship, the ICSSR should make it clear that a substantial work is expected and evolve a *modus operandi* whereby the progress is periodically reported.

Senior Fellowships

12.21 The ICSSR offers four types of Senior Fellowships: (a) For Indians working abroad to work in India; (b) For non-Indians to work in India; (c) For Indian social scientists to work in India; and (d) For Indians to work abroad. In relation to (a), though the experience is not entirely satisfactory, we suggest that no major changes need be made since the experience is limited. In relation to (b) the scheme has to be made more liberal if it is to attract Asian, African, and perhaps Latin American social scientists. Specifically, we suggest: (i) The visiting scholar should be given maximum Indian salary of his academic status; (ii) he should be given free, furnished accommodation appropriate to his academic status; (iii) in special cases, a conveyance allowance not exceeding Rs. 500 p.m. may be given; and (iv) he may be permitted to receive additional emoluments, at home or in India, from his employer or home government, but from no other source.

12.22 In relation to (c), namely, senior fellowships for Indian social scientists to work in India, we recommend that the financial liberalisation we have suggested in the case of National Fellowship should also apply here. Evidently, there are also certain practical and procedural problems concerning these fellowships. We recommend that the ICSSR should discuss them with the University Grants Commission and the universities. In relation to (d), namely, senior fellowships for Indians to work abroad, we have noted that the scheme is too expensive to continue on any scale. However, whenever such facilities can be provided through other means such as the Cultural Exchange Agreements, we emphasise that the ICSSR should try to secure terms and conditions for Indian scholars similar to those we have recommended for foreign scholars under scheme (b). In particular, in addition to the fellowship the Indian scholar may have secured abroad, he should be permitted to draw part or whole of his normal emoluments, at home, from his employer. Indeed, we recommend that, in case his employer is unable to pay even part of his normal emoluments, the ICSSR should give him a fellowship equal to his basic salary as family allowance at home.

Fellowship for Young Social Scientists

12.23 Since this is a new scheme and there is no adequate experience, we do not wish to make any changes therein and suggest that the experience should be evaluated after some time. We, do, however, feel that this scheme has considerable potential.

Post-Doctoral Fellowship

12.24 The Post-Doctoral Fellowships could be redesignated simply as fellowships to differentiate them from the senior fellowships. The selection to these fellowships should be made more rigorous and the ICSSR should ensure that the fellowships is not used as a mere stop gap arrangement by the social scientist concerned.

Assistance to Doctoral Students

12.25 With regard to the scheme relating to salary protection, short-term fellowships, contingency grants and study grants, we do not recommend any changes. We, however, feel that the scheme of doctoral fellowships is too big a charge on the budget of the ICSSR and that, in any case, the number is too large for the ICSSR to do anything meaningful. Besides, this is properly a responsibility of the UGC and the UGC is expanding the number of such fellowships. Hence, we recommend that the ICSSR should discontinue this scheme except the existing commitment. This would free more than Rs. 10 lakhs per year to work out other activities which we consider important.

Research Institutes

12.26 In relation to the Research Institutes maintained or supported by the ICSSR, our principal recommendations are as follows:

(i) On the question of ceiling for grants-in-aid to the research institutes by the ICSSR, we recommend that the present ceilings of Rs. 7.5 lakhs for recurring and Rs. 25 lakhs for non-recurring should remain in the Sixth Plan period;

(ii) The ICSSR at present insists on a matching provision of 50 per cent to be raised by the research institutes. While this principle is sound, we would like to suggest that project funds raised by a research institute should be treated as a contribution of the research institute towards its share. For purposes of annual allocations, previous year's performance of the research institute in raising project money should be considered;

(iii) We do not, however, share the view that the ICSSR grants should be given on a 100 per cent basis. Two exceptions have so far been made in this respect. We suggest that, in the two cases, any additional grants from the ICSSR over and above the present commitments, should be subject to matching contribution by the institutes;

(iv) The practice of block grants to the research institutes is basically sound and we do not think it would be appropriate for the ICSSR to tie the grant to specific items;

(v) The most important question, however, is regarding the relationship of the ICSSR with the research institutes supported by itself. We are of the opinion that, just as the autonomy of the ICSSR itself should be treated with utmost respect, the same principle should extend to the research institutes. The ICSSR's direct control over these should therefore be minimal. However, the ICSSR should ensure that each Research Institute's Governing Board exercises proper planning, direction and control over the research institute concerned. Such a relationship alone, in our view, would be appropriate for building the nature of future linkages between the ICSSR and the research institutes supported by it;

(vi) We understand that there is a proposal to reserve 1/3 or 1/4 of senior posts in institutes supported by the ICSSR for visiting fellows coming from other institutes or universities. We think this will be useful. However, this should be kept as an objective and not made a rigid formula. We feel that, in the short run, because of housing and other problems, it would not be easy to create the facilities necessary for visiting fellows to come from other institutes and universities;

(vii) We consider the matter of relationship between the research institutes and university system to be of considerable importance. It would be in the interest both of the universities as well as research institutes to provide for a better interface between them. The ICSSR should take initiative to bring together the research institutes and the local universities and discuss the manner in which this relationship should be developed. In particular, possibilities of the faculty of the research institutes participating in the university post-graduate teaching and research guidance should be explored and encouraged. Similarly, the ICSSR supported research institutes should actively offer facilities to university teachers to visit and use their facilities;

(viii) The question of proliferation of research institutes is an important one. While the country as vast as India can legitimately claim the need for large number of research institutes, we are of the view that multiplication of institutes without building a critical minimum faculty size is not in the interest either of the country, the ICSSR or social science research. We, therefore, recommend that the existing research institutes should first be enabled to develop properly before new ones are promoted or established, except in regions which do not have sufficient social science research base, such as Madhya Pradesh, Orissa and Assam. We would recommend establishment of new research institutes or strengthening of existing selected institutes in these areas; and

(ix) We strongly feel that the role of research institutes in developing younger social science research talents in the country should be explicitly recognised and, if necessary, made mandatory as a condition for receiving grants from the ICSSR. We have already made our detailed recommendation on this point in the above. These recommendations, if implemented, will help a great deal in the development of the social science research institutes under the auspices of the ICSSR and the overall objective of developing social science research in India.

Training in Research Methodology

12.27 In view of the fact that formal courses in research methodology for social science research are likely to be incorporated in the M. Phil. courses now being instituted in all the universities, we suggest that the ICSSR should provide for less formal and less structured courses in research methodology linked to the research projects in operation. We believe that the established university departments and research institutes, supported by the ICSSR as well as others, have a major responsibility in the matter. We have already made our detailed recommendations.

Area Studies

12.28 In consonance with our general recommendation that the ICSSR should not have special Programme Divisions, to promote researches in particular subjects or areas, we recommend that the present Programme Division for Area Studies and International Collaboration should be abolished and the Statutory Committee for Area Studies may be designated Committee for International Collaboration. This does not mean that Area Studies should be discontinued. Research proposals in Area Studies, particularly in neighbouring countries, should be examined like other research proposals and if found suitable, should be approved for necessary financial support. In certain cases the normal financial ceiling on single projects may have to be relaxed.

International Collaboration

12.29 The international collaboration programme of the ICSSR has been mostly skewed in favour of the western world, despite the intentions of the ICSSR. We suggest that the ICSSR should take immediate corrective action to shift the focus to Asia, particularly South and South-East Asia, Africa, and the Arab countries.

12.30 The development of relationship between the ICSSR and the various international bodies in social science research is desirable and we recommend that the ICSSR should continue to play an active role.

12.31 There is considerable concern amongst the social scientists about the direct approach by institutes to foreign funding agencies. It is sometimes suggested that all foreign funds should be channeled through the ICSSR which should then allocate them to applicant institutes according to appropriate policies in this regard. While we appreciate the underlying concern, we are not sure that the concentration of such large funds and accompanying patronage in the hands of the ICSSR will be desirable for its own healthy functioning. We suggest that, if necessary, the Government may examine the question in its totality.

Regional and State Centres

12.32 The Regional Centres are playing a useful role. But, it seems to us, they have as yet not fully developed the regional concept. This, together with the fact that a number of activities of the ICSSR will in due course have to be extended into regional languages, makes it necessary that the ICSSR develops the State Centres to supplement the Regional Centres. The ICSSR has already a plan to establish the state Centres. We recommend that the ICSSR should take up the matter with the respective State Governments and establish such centres wherever the cooperation of the State Governments is forthcoming.

12.33 We suggest that the ICSSR should decentralise some of its functions to the Regional/State Centres. In particular, approval and sanction of smaller research proposals costing up to Rs. 7,500 as also preliminary scrutiny of research proposals received in regional languages may be delegated to the Regional/State Centres.

12.34 We attach great importance to the production of social science literature in the regional languages. We recommend that for this purpose the ICSSR should develop a programme jointly with the UGC and operate it through its Regional/State Centres.

Publications

12.35 It seems that the Publication Division of the ICSSR is suffering from many problems of distribution and sales. We recommend that early steps should be taken to distribute as fast as possible, if necessary, at subsidised prices, the publications of the ICSSR.

12.36 We recommend that the ICSSR should not give any direct publication grants for the publication of theses, books, etc. Instead, in deserving cases, the ICSSR should agree to buy, at cost, a certain number of copies of a publication and distribute them, at cost, to universities, colleges, institutes and other libraries which are willing to enter into agreement with the ICSSR for purchase of such books. We recommend that the ICSSR should work out an appropriate scheme for this purpose, give it the widest publicity and a trial for a period of five years.

12.37 We do not appreciate the ICSSR itself undertaking publication of specialised journals such as the *Journal of Asian Studies*. We recommend that the possibility of locating the *Journal of Asian Studies* at a suitable institution should be explored, failing which the journal may be discontinued.

Documentation

12.38 We recognise that documentation is an essential function of the ICSSR. However, it seems to us that much documentation effort of the ICSSR has not been sufficiently used except by the Ph.D. students. We recommend that the ICSSR be more selective in further documentation in the next few years with wider publicity given to these services.

Data Archives

12.39 With respect to the Data Archives, we find that the services are ahead of their demand. We suggest that, in the next few years, the ICSSR should confine its efforts in this field to bringing together tabulated data which remain unpublished for want of printing space.

Administrative Structure

12.40 We are sorry to note that the administration of the ICSSR has tended to be bureaucratic both in its structure and procedures. We recommend that early steps should be taken to reorganise it so that it rests with competent senior level academicians with a small supporting staff.

12.41 We think that, considering the numerous activities of the ICSSR and the large number of Divisions into which they have to be organised, the Member-Secretary needs the support and assistance of two senior executives above the Directors of the Divisions. We recommend that the several Divisions should be organised into two Departments in charge of the two Executive Directors.

12.42 Earlier, we have disapproved the administration of the ICSSR being organised into Programme Divisions. We have suggested a certain reorganised structure. We suggest that the ICSSR should examine its convenience and adopt an appropriate reorganisation of the Divisions.

12.43 We recommend that the senior staff of the ICSSR Secretariat should, as far as possible, be brought on deputation for a period of three to five years from academic institutes and universities. In order to facilitate this, the ICSSR must give high priority to provision of accommodation to such senior staff coming on deputation.

Campus

12.44 It is high time that the ICSSR develops a campus of its own which will accommodate its offices, housing for at least the senior staff on deputation, and a hostel for visiting social scientists. We understand that the ICSSR has negotiates a 15-acre plot presently housing the Russian Centre of the Jawaharlal Nehru University in South Delhi. We emphasise that it is of the utmost importance for the future development of the ICSSR that it proceeds urgently to complete this agreement.

Discrimination between Natural and Social Sciences

12.45 We have noted a number of instances in which the Social Sciences, as compared to National Sciences, are discriminated against. We recommend that the ICSSR should take up these matters with the Government of India and ensure that the Social Sciences are treated on par with the Natural Sciences.

Autonomy

12.46 We record our appreciation of the manner in which the Government of India has exercised its control over the ICSSR. However, we feel that the time has now come to relax this control and grant the ICSSR a degree of autonomy.

12.47 We recommend that the ICSSR should request the Government of India that the Government, as a token of its acceptance of the above proposition, should agree to amend the Memorandum of Association of the ICSSR and remove Article 8(a) which states: "The Government of India may give directives to the Council in respect of its policies and programmes." We emphasise that at the very minimum, the ICSSR must be considered fully autonomous at least in respect of its policies and programmes.

Chairman of the ICSSR

12.48 We recommend that the Chairman of the ICSSR should be appointed by the Government of India from among a panel of three prepared by a Selection Committee consisting of a nominee of the ICSSR, a nominee of the UGC and a nominee of the Government.

Social Scientist Members of the ICSSR

12.49 We recommend that every year the six retiring social scientist members should be replaced by the Government from a panel prepared by the sitting Social Scientist members and the Chairman. We have described the procedure in the relevant chapter.

Other Members

12.50 We recommend that the remaining six members should be nominated by name and that they should not be permitted to send their nominees/representatives to the meetings of the ICSSR.

Member-Secretary of the ICSSR

12.51 We recommend that the Member-Secretary of the ICSSR should be appointed by the ICSSR from among a panel of three prepared by a Selection Committee consisting of a nominee of the ICSSR, a nominee of the UGC, and a nominee of the Government of India.

12.52 We recommend that the Member-Secretary of the ICSSR should have the status of the Vice-Chancellor of a University.

Financial and Administrative Powers

12.53 We understand that, at the instance of the Government, the ICSSR has adopted the financial rules and regulations of the Government. In our opinion, these rules and regulations need modifications to meet the requirements of the ICSSR. We recommend that the ICSSR should pursue this matter with the Government.

12.54 We recommend that the ICSSR should have the fullest autonomy to operate within the overall budget approved by the Government and within the broad framework of its policies, rules and regulations.

12.55 At present, 'the procedure, terms and tenure of appointments, emoluments, allowances, rules of discipline and other conditions of service of officers and staff' of the ICSSR require prior approval of the Government of India. We think that this has severely limited the ability of the ICSSR to recruit staff of requisite quality and to function efficiently. We recommend that the ICSSR should be given greater administrative powers.

Financial Autonomy

12.56 In our opinion, for an effective financial autonomy, it is necessary to diversify the financial resources of the ICSSR. We recommend that the ICSSR should try to secure grants from other Central ministries, besides the Ministry of Education.

12.57 We recommend that the ICSSR should build up an endowment fund of at least Rs. 10 crores and, to this purpose, secure donations from public and private sector corporations, trusts and foreign funding agencies. We emphasise that such donations should go exclusively to the endowment fund and not used for any capital or revenue expenditure of the ICSSR.

12.58 In our view, the autonomy of the ICSSR is crucial to the successful and effective discharge of its functions. Hence we recommend that the ICSSR should pursue the above suggestions vigorously.

12.59 In view of these recommendations we estimate that the ICSSR will need funds of the following order during the Sixth Plan period:

Sixth Plan Outlay

		(Rs. in lakhs)
A.	Administration	50
B.	Research Grants	200
C.	Research Fellowships	50
D.	Training	10
E.	Study Grants	10
F.	Regional/State/University Centres	150
G.	Documentation Centres	60
H.	Data Archives	10
I.	Publications	40
J.	Other Programmes	75
K.	Loans to Staff, P.F., etc.	20
L.	Capital Programme (Campus)	100
M.	Equipment, Furniture, Vehicles, etc.	10
N.	Library Books	5

O.	Research Institutes:		
	(a) Recurring	Rs. 425 lakhs	
	(b) Non-recurring	Rs. 150 lakhs	575
		Total:	1365

Conclusion

12.60 In conclusion, we might recapitulate the major thrust of our recommendations. They are: Firstly, the ICSSR must take immediate steps to broaden the base of social science research in the country and to this purpose enlist active cooperation of established university departments and institutes. Secondly, the ICSSR should support particularly such research in established university departments and institutes as is likely to deepen the content of social sciences. Thirdly, the ICSSR should develop essentially as a scientific body and should function in that style. This will require a large measure of autonomy which should be explicitly granted to it. Finally, the ICSSR should aim at building up a sizable endowment fund without which it will not be able to secure a degree of financial independence necessary for its long-term development.

RAILWAY ACCIDENT INVESTIGATION REPORT ON COLLISION BETWEEN 103 UP HOWRAH-AMRITSAR DELUXE EXPRESS TRAIN AND UP CPC SPECIAL GOODS TRAIN AT NAINI STATION ON ALLAHABAD DIVISION OF NORTHERN RAILWAY AT 00.15 HRS ON OCTOBER 10, 1977[1]

One Man Commission Shri B.P. Sastry

Officers Present Shri Inder Sahai; Shri L.C. Vaswani; Shri M.P. Gupta

Appointment

The Commission was constituted under the Ministry of Tourism and Civil Aviation (Commission of Railway Safety) in accordance with Rule 4 of the Statutory Investigation into Railway Accidents Rules, 1973 vide Notification No. RS. 13-T(8)/71 dated April 19, 1973 on October 10, 1977.

Terms of Reference

To investigate into the collision between 103 Up Howrah-Amritsar Deluxe Express train and Up CPC Special Goods train at Naini station on Allahabad division of Northern Railway at 00.15 hrs. on October 10, 1977.

Conclusions

86. *Cause of the Accident*: Having carefully considered the factual, material and circumstantial evidence at my disposal, I have

1. Ministry of Tourism and Civil Aviation, (Commission of Railway Safety), Government of India, New Delhi, 1985, 71 + 47 p.

come to the conclusion that the collision of 103 Up Howrah-Delhi Amritsar Deluxe Express train with the stationary Up CPC Special Goods train at km. 818.67 between the Up Starter and Advanced Starter signals of Naini station at about 00.15 hrs. on the night of 9th/10th October, 1977 was brought about by the Express train having been admitted, on clear signals, in the territory between the Up Starter and Advanced Starter Signals while the territory was occupied by the stationary Goods train, the event having occurred on account of the Switchman mistaking the indications of the Advanced Starter signal and the track clearance light.

87. *Responsibility*: I hold that the conditions of working obtaining at the West Cabin of Naini station prior to 10th October, 1977 were responsible for the accident. I do not hold any individual responsible for bringing about such conditions.

88. *Relief Arrangements*

88.1 Relief arrangements were prompt and adequate. Besides Railway personnel, several other organisations, Government Departments and individuals spontaneously participated in rescue operations and did a good job of it. Within about 90 minutes, the first batch of casualties were on their way to hospital and by about 7 a.m. every one requiring to be hospitalised was transferred to the hospital. Considering the magnitude of damage and the manner in which damaged coaches were piled up, this was a magnificent job deserving praise. This had certainly helped in saving some precious lives which would have, in different circumstances, been lost for want of prompt medical attention. A major factor which rendered this possible was the proximity of the site of accident to Allahabad city where all facilities are available and were ungrudgingly placed at the disposal of the Railway Administration. Restoration of through traffic by the evening of the 11th is also considered satisfactory though it meant considerable dislocation of train services on this busy trunk route.

88.2. Discussions with injured passengers in hospitals have, however, brought to light two complaints.

(a) Removal of the injured to hospitals was not properly regulated. When ambulances or other vehicles arrived on the spot, those less seriously injured but able to walk had filled them in their anxiety to leave for hospital as quickly as possible, while those who were helpless and unable to walk, had to wait till they were carried to the vehicles. This, some of the passengers felt, could have been avoided by a better organisation.

(b) The number of casualties transferred to S.R. Medical college hospital was much more than could be satisfactorily handled there while other hospitals, particularly the Military Hospital, which had capacity were given fewer patients. The result was that at S.R. Medical college hospital injured persons had to wait for several hours before they were shifted from the emergency department to their beds in the wards.

88.3 In regard to item (a) my inquiries revealed that arrangements were generally good but there must have been a few cases of injured persons having been lifted late due to the enormity of the problem particularly in the early stages, but gradually the arrangements were systematised and casualties were shifted on the basis of their condition and the opinion of the medical personnel as to priority to be accorded in shifting.

88.4 In regard to item (b) there appears to be some justification for the complaint. The Commandant of the Military Hospital told me, when contacted, that he was advised of the assistance needed by the Railways by about 4 a.m. He made arrangements to receive about 50 injured persons by about 6 a.m. but only 9 had actually been sent. This appeared to be due to a slip made by an Assistant Surgeon who was entrusted with the task of alerting hospitals in the city. In this respect the Railway officials appeared to be under the impression that where Civil Hospitals were available the injured must only be transferred there irrespective of the needs of the situation. With this in mind, only Civil Hospitals were alerted in the first instance and when it was realised that those hospitals were unable to accommodate all the injured, the Military Hospital was advised after about 3½ hrs. of the accident.

88.5 In this context, it may be added that even when the Divisional Railway hospital with a bed strength of 150 was in a position to accommodate some more, very few non-Railway casualties were shifted to that hospital, presumably keeping in view Railway Board's instructions on the subject. I think that in the matter of medical aid required as a result of a serious Railway accident, the Railways need not be so particular about the rules of admission and casualties should be sent to hospitals based on their capacity to render medical aid expeditiously. If any, Railway hospitals should take a greater load than their resources permit but not the reverse. Such a flexible attitude would have avoided hours of agonising waiting to the already shocked and injured passengers in the emergency Department of the Civil Hospital while the Railway and Military hospitals could have accepted some of them. It would be good even from the Railway's point of view if injured passengers go with a feeling that they were properly cared for in Railway Hospitals when suddenly they met with an accident during a Railway journey in unfamiliar surroundings for away from their kith and kin. It is hoped that Railway Board would review their current instructions and revise them suitably advising the Railways to adopt a more flexible attitude in the matter of medical aid to persons injured in Railway Accidents.

88.6 One of the complaints which was voiced in the local News papers during the period was about identification of missing persons and fake claimants of dead bodies with a view to receive the exgratia amount. The Divisional Superintendent and the Superintendent of Railway Police with whom I had discussions in this respect assured me that all that was physically possible was done and there was no substance in the complaints. Even if what had been reported in the Press had happened in one or two odd cases, it is unfortunate that it should have been so, but I am satisfied that it was not due to any negligence on the part of Railway authorities or State Government Departments connected with the matter.

88.7 Another complaint which got prominence in the local news papers was about the difficulties experienced by the friends and relatives of missing passengers whose names did not appear either in the list of injured or among the dead. A letter in this connection was also received by me in respect of one Sri Zadoo stated to have travelled by the ill-fated train along with his son from Howrah, bound for Delhi. Having watched the relief operations at close range during my stay at Allahabad between the 10th and 14th October, I am satisfied that the Railway Administration had done their utmost in this regard but unfortunately one or two cases of missing persons including Mr. Zadoo remained untraced so far. Although the photographs of all those who lost their lives in the accident were taken before disposing of the bodies, it is possible that due to mutilation, it had not been possible to identify the body of Mr. Zadoo. It may be mentioned that 12 bodies remained unidentified even after 72 hours of their death and had to be finally disposed of by the Government.

88.8 A third complaint which appeared in the News papers was about missing belongings of the passengers of the ill-fated Express train. Shri Devendra Pratap Singh Inspector-in-charge of Naini Police station, who was the First Police Officer to have reached the site with 15 policemen at about 1 a.m. assured me in his deposition that the first step taken by him was to encircle the whole area and provide security from pilferage, etc. The Fire Station Officer, Allahabad, Shri Parash Nath, who reached the site at about 01.14 hrs. confirmed this arrangement. The District Magistrate and the Senior Superintendent of Police, Allahabad were on the spot by about 01.30 hrs. The entire area was lit up and rescue operations went on systematically thereafter. In view of these facts I consider that all that was possible had been done by the officers responsible for law and order and if some stray cases had taken place (some of these had also been mentioned by passengers who deposed before me) it is only unfortunate that there should be some persons in society who would, even in a calamity of this nature, indulge in anti-social acts.

Recommendations

89.1 The territory between the Starter and Advanced Starter signals at a station where the conventional Absolute Block System of train working changes into Automatic Block System is a weak link in the system. It is essential that the entire territory up to Advanced Starter signal is track circuited with a view to ensure that a train cannot be despatched beyond the Starter unless the earlier train has completely passed the Advanced Starter signal and continues its journey in the Automatic Signalling territory. It is heartening to note that this detection facility has been provided at Naini station within 3 weeks of the accident by track circuiting the area. I recommend that similar facilities be provided urgently at similarly placed stations on all the Railways.

89.2 Pending provision of this facility, run-through speeds at such stations should be regulated so as to not to display the green aspect of Home and Starter signals to an approaching train. The speed of through trains should be checked by keeping the Starter signal at danger (which would necessitate the Home signal to display yellow) till the train enters the station section. The Starter signal may be approach-lighted so that it displays a clear aspect when the train is sufficiently slowed down while approaching the signal and runs at a speed not exceeding 15 kmph.

90.1 Detection facility in the territory between Starter and Advanced Starter signals is also essential in Absolute Block System of train working on Double and multiple lines and should be gradually provided on a time bound programme, priority being given to sections where trains run through stations at the maximum authorised speed and visibility from the Cabin is not satisfactory.

90.2 Where provision of track circuiting at any such station is delayed for any reasons, adequate safeguards should be provided as an interim measure to ensure safe working conditions at the station and for proper compliance of General Rule 37(a)(iii) by persons operating signals.

91.1 A positive and fool-proof arrangement should invariably be available to the person operating a stop signal at a station enabling him to comply with the requirements of General Rule 36(a) and (c). The means by which compliance of the rule is to be ensured should be specifically mentioned in the Station Working rules of the station.

91.2 Where such a facility is not available for any reason, run through speeds of trains passing through a station should be so regulated as not to exceed the limit by which a standing vehicle could be sighted by a following train in the focus of the engine head light during night and brought to stop short of the signal when necessary. Such speeds should be specified and notified in the working time tables.

91.3 In view of advances made in interlocking arrangements at stations, the rule itself, which came into existence long before such advances could be visualised, appears to be needing a review. Where adequate alternative safeguards are available, the rule could perhaps be relaxed but any such relaxation should be clearly specified and spelt out in detail in the respective station working rules.

92. The stand taken by the Civil Engineers of Allahabad Division in defence of their not having completed their portion of the track circuiting work at Naini expeditiously, even after being aware of its urgency, displays a negative attitude of looking out for some plea for not processing even works connected with safety in a spirit of accommodation. Similar was the delay caused to the processing of the estimate, which in spite of its being a high priority safety work, specially approved by the Railway Board "out of turn", was required to shuttle between the Executive and Accounts branches several times taking about nine months for sanction. This indicates lack of co-

ordination between various branches and lack of sense of urgency among certain officers even in matters relating to safety. This aspect of working at the Executive level appears to be requiring re-orientation.

93. The present practice of quoting only the minimum required distance between signals in signalling plans should be replaced by recording actual distance to facilitate proper scrutiny at the time of sanctioning.

94. Track indicator lights provided at Cabins as an aid to the person operating the signals should be so devised as to display red when a train occupies them and not to get extinguished as provided at Naini prior to October, 1977. This will enable the Cabinman to distinguish between track occupation and power failure.

95.1 At the West Cabin of Naini station, the indicator light of Up Advanced Starter signal changes to red when there is a power failure in the Automatic Signalling territory beyond. This gives exactly similar sequences as when a train passes the Advanced Starter signal. Some device to prevent such misleading indication to the Switchman should be provided.

95.2 Similar locations elsewhere on the Railway should also be checked up and adequate safeguards provided.

96. The Goods train which was involved in the accident was subjected to a perfunctory train examination at Chheoki yard from where it had originated. This forcefully brings to light the need for toning up the compliance of train examination rules in yards as causes of many of the accidents to trains are traced to inadequate attention at the depots.

97. Non-availability of a vacuum gauge on the Brakevan of the Goods train involved in the accident is a feature which is frequently noticed during inspections. There should be a stricter watch in this regard and Goods trains should be prohibited from leaving a depot without a vacuum gauge in working order on the brakevan.

98. Despite Railway Board's directive that speed recorders should be provided in the locomotives hauling Express trains the ill-fated Deluxe Express did not carry a graph paper on its recorder and valuable information about the action taken by the Driver after sighting the obstruction has been lost. This indicates the scant regard given to this directive at lower formations. Steps should be taken to avoid similar situations.

99.1 The work load at the West Cabin at Naini is rather heavy.

The Switchman is required to deal with 30 to 35 trains in a shift of 8 hours, each train movement involving several elements of operation by him. This can be tiresome to a person who is required to discharge such repetitive work monotonously hour after hour. A review of the work load at the Cabin should be undertaken and suitable relief afforded. I note with satisfaction that a Leverman has since been provided to help the Switchmen.

99.2 It came out during the inquiry that there was no procedure on the Railway to undertake periodical reviews of the work load of such important categories of staff as Switchman, Assistant Station Masters, etc., responsible for train operation. It appears desirable that the work load at each such point is subjected to fatigue conditions when engaged on train operating duties. It is understood that the National Commission on labour recommended as early as 1971 a quinquennial review of the classification of all Railway servants under Hours of Employment Regulations and that the Railway Board asked the Railway Administration in their letter No. E (LL)/71/NCL/1 dated 6-1-71 to take steps towards its implementation but so far no headway has been made by the Northern Railway Administration. It is recommended that such a review should, without delay, be made in respect of staff concerned with safety in train operation.

100. It came to light during the inquiry that the present procedure for following up implementation of important recommendations made by departmental inquiry committees or by the Commission of Railway Safety and accepted by the Railway Administration, is not effective. It is desirable that a suitable procedure is evolved to ensure that such recommendations are vigorously followed up. Where necessary, the lessons learnt as a result of departmental inquiries into accidents on individual Railways should be passed on to other Railways also for which Railway Board may consider devising a procedure.

101. The present policy of the Railway Administration is to direct Railway passengers injured in train accidents to Civil Hospitals even when Railway Hospitals are available close by. It is an admitted fact that working conditions in many of the Civil Hospitals are not as good as in Railway hospitals and passengers express their unhappiness when directed to such hospitals. It appears desirable that when Railway passengers suddenly find themselves injured in an accident on a Railway journey they are preferably treated in Railway hospitals

which consideration earns for the Railways the good-will of their valued customers besides giving the persons concerned the much needed relief in unfamiliar surroundings far away from their kith and kin. The Railway Ministry may review their current directives in this regard and order a more flexible attitude to be adopted by the Railways.

102.1 The kerosene-lit tail lamp in use on Indian Railways is of a primitive design with restricted luminosity and visibility. Observations made on an average tail lamp in use on goods trains indicate that its luminosity is not more than 2 lux and the range of visibility does not normally exceed 400 metres under day-to-day working conditions. Absence of specifications for the design and upkeep of the device has resulted in its not being properly maintained by Guards and any deterioration in its condition not being taken notice of by supervisory officials.

102.2 The earlier concept of the tail lamp being considered as only a means of proving the complete arrival/passage of a train at/through a station in night time should give place to its being treated as a device to provide visual conspicuity of the trailing end of trains, particularly in the context of the incidence of rear end collisions of trains with serious consequences, and the ever increasing distances of signal for a departing train on a double line section is required to comply with General Rule 36(a) and (c) with the help of a tail lamp fixed to the last vehicle of a train, the range of its visibility should be at least one kilometre, if not more. Similarly if a Driver of the following train who is wrongly admitted on the same line as the preceding one is expected to check the speed of his train and prevent a collision after sighting the train ahead, the range of visibility of the tail lamp should be around 1.5 kms. equivalent to the emergency braking distance of a full length train at its normal speed. Further, the tail lamp should also have some lateral and vertical range of visibility to enable a Cabinman view it properly from his Cabin located laterally at a distance from the main line or a Driver of the following train passing through a mild curve or on a gradient while approaching the preceding train.

102.3 To meet these requirements it appears essential that the design of the tail lamp should be modernised. Any attempt of modernisation of a tail lamp with a view to increase its range of visibility would necessarily involve giving up of the kerosene-lit lamp in favour of its electrical counterpart. If it could be a flashing type instead of a steady lamp, it would be the most ideal solution to our problems. It is equally important that its luminosity and range (longitudinal, lateral and vertical) should also be specified in precise terms. Only then will it be possible to ensure proper maintenance and up-keep of the lamp to serve the intended purpose. The Railway Board may consider asking the RDSO to study the matter in all its aspects and evolve suitable designs and specifications for tail lamps to be used on different types of trains on the Indian Railways.

103. Supervisory officials whose normal duty includes inspection of work establishments like Cabins should be made to realise that it is their duty to check up on their own whether adequate facilities exist for the observance of rules by the workmen whose work they inspect and not to carry the impression that they should go into the matter only when a representation is made to them by the workmen.

104.1 In terms of Railway Board's directives contained in their letter No. 76-chg. II/14/1 dated 4-6-77 on the issue of marshalling of coaches, anti-telescopic or steel bodied SLRs must be marshalled as the last coach at both ends of the train formation on an Express train. It is surprising that an important train like 103 Up Deluxe Express did not have any SLR next to the engine. Again as per the orders, coaching vehicles which do not carry passengers should preferable be marshalled as outermost vehicles at either end to absorb the impact of collision energy in the event of an accident. In the case of 103 Up Express there was a Generator Car on the train formation. Had Railway Board's directive been observed in respect of this coach the casualties could perhaps have been less than what they actually were. Correct marshalling of coaches of such trains should be impressed on all concerned.

104.2 The coach next to the engine was a BEML coach. While this coach has anti-telescopic characteristics of an integral coach its anti-telescopic strength in relative terms appears to be not more than 60 to 67 per cent of that of the Integral coach. As such, marshalling of coaches of BEML make or other steel bodied coaches of rivetted construction should be prohibited on Mail and Express trains as the outer most vehicle of the train.

105. The log of events after the accident as furnished by the Divisional Superintendent indicates that Accident relief Medical van was ordered by the Divisional control 10 minutes after information about the accident was received in the control office, that is at 00.35

hrs. The Medical van from Allahabad left only at 01.25 hrs. that is, 50 minutes after it was ordered and 60 minutes after information was received. While it is a fact that ambulances and teams of Doctors reached much earlier by road and took charge of the situation and the utilisation of the Medical van was nominal in view of the proximity of the accident to Allahabad, it is all the same a disturbing feature that an accident relief medical van could not have been despatched in less than 60 minutes. It appears necessary that procedural snags, if any, in movement of Medical vans at Allahabad are located and removed.

106. The chain of events leading to the collision on the night of the 10th October, 1977 had their origin in a copper wire theft of electric Traction Return Conductor by unsocial elements. Thus the law and order problem in the locality had a direct bearing on the accident. This may be brought to the notice of the concerned authorities responsible for law and order with a request to take adequate measures to keep the unsocial elements in check.

Comments of Railway Board on Various Paras of the Report

COPY OF O.M. No. 77/SAFETY (A&R)/1/26, DATED 28-8-1980 FROM MINISTRY OF RAILWAYS (RAILWAY BOARD), NEW DELHI, ADDRESSED TO THE CHIEF COMMISSIONER OF RAILWAY SAFETY, LUCKNOW.

SUBJECT: *Collision between 103 Up Howrah-Amritsar Deluxe Express and up CPC Special Goods train at Naini station of the Northern Railway on 10-10-1977.*

The undersigned is directed to refer to Chief Commissioner of Railway Safety's letter No. RS. 21-T (15)/77, dated 10-11-78 on the subject noted above and to furnish the views of this Ministry as under:

Findings

The cause of the accident as established by the CRS in para 86 of the report that the accident was brought about by the Express train having been admitted on clear signals in the territory between the Up Starter and the Advanced Starter signals while the territory was occupied by the Stationary Goods train, the event having occurred on account of Switchman mistaking the indications of the Advanced Starter signal and the track clearance light, is accepted.

As for responsibility brought out in para 87 of the report, the CRS has not indicated precisely the conditions of working at Naini cabin which according to him were responsible for the causation of the accident. It is presumed from his report that the CRS has based his observations on the arguments which are given below alongwith the remarks of this Ministry in juxtaposition:

CRS's Observations

1. It was not possible to comply with the provisions of G.R. 36 (a) and (c), thus justifying the use of the aids available in the Cabin by the Switchman. Although the problem was known to the supervisory Station Master and also the AOS/DOS who were aware about the working conditions of the cabin, nothing was done to rectify the deficiency. The officers who prepared the working rules had a specific responsibility to see that facilities for compliance of the rules were available.

"36. *Fixed signals generally.* —(a) Fixed signals shall always be kept "On" except when taken "off" to allow a train to pass and shall be replaced to "on" immediately such train has passed complete.
(b) A signal which has been taken "off" for the passage of a train shall not be placed "on" until the whole of the train which it controls has passed it, except—

(i) in case of emergency,
(ii) where automatic reversers are in use in which case the lever operating the signal shall not be restored till the whole of the train has passed."

Remarks of the Ministry of Railways

As for provision of aids/indicators in the cabin, it may be clarified that track indicators were provided to indicate when the track beyond the Advance Starter is free to admit a train into the block section. When the track is free, a white light is shown in track indicator which means that the the Advanced Starter can be taken 'off'. However, when the light is extinguished, it means that conditions for taking 'off' the signal are not satisfied. In so far as the indicator of the Advanced

Starter is concerned, in colour light signalling territories, the signal aspect are repeated in the cabin. They indicate whether a signal is lit and whether a signal aspect corresponds with the position of signal lever. The Switchman is to be guided by the indicators of the track circuit/Advanced Starter strictly in accordance with the said explanation, and is not to be misled by deducing wrong conclusions. In fact the track indicator light getting extinguished did not necessarily imply complete passage of the train beyond the Advanced Starter, as the passage of even a part of a train would also give the same indication. In this case, the Switchman made an erroneous interpretation of the indicators. When a train passes the Advanced Starter signal and goes into the next track-circuited area and beyond, the following would be the sequence of changes in the aspects of the Advanced Starter signal and that of the indicator of the Advanced Starter in the cabin:

(i) The signal aspect of the Advanced Starter signal (which is clearly visible to the switchman from the cabin) will change from green to red yellow, double yellow and then finally green again in that sequence.
(ii) The indicator of the Advanced Starter in the cabin will change from green to red and then again green, indicating that the train had gone beyond the next track circuit and the signal had assumed its full permissive aspect.

In this case, because of power failure, the aspect of the Advanced Starter changed only from green to red and the indicator of the Advanced Starter only changed to red and stayed red. These changes are very much different from the changes that would have taken place if a train had passed and was going through.

As for compliance of G.R. 36(c), the normal method for compliance of the said G.R., is by personal observation of the tail lamp, unless it is laid down to the contrary. The distance between the cabin and the Advanced Starter is 867 metres. It has been conceded by the Switchman that it was possible for him to see that last vehicle of an Up train passing the Advanced Starter during night, it was possible to see the last vehicle of the train up to a distance of 427 metres. In any case, if he had any difficulty in compliance of GR 36, he could have represented the matter to his immediate supervisors. It is only the official concerned with the implementation of the rules, who can point out the difficulty, if any, with regard to observance of rules. In this connection remarks of the Chief Commissioner of Railway Safety against CRS's recommendation in para 103 of the report that checks by supervisory officials can only be in the nature of sample checks, are relevant.

The pity of the matter is that in this case, the Switchman had not at all looked out to check the tail lamp of the Goods train, as otherwise the brakevan, which became stationary at a distance of 220 metres from the cabin could have been noticed by him, and he would have realised that something was amiss. As already indicated, the Switchman made wrong deductions of the indications given by the indicators provided in the cabin. These omissions on the part of the Switchman cannot be simply brushed aside.

CRS's Observation

2. The facilities available in the cabin for compliance of G.R. 37 were inadequate.

"G.R. 37 (a) The Station Master shall not give permission to take signals 'off' to admit a train until—

(iii) the line over which the train is to pass is clear and free from obstructions.

Remarks of the Ministry

There was no difficulty whatsoever, for compliance of G.R. 37 during daylight hours. Regarding hours of darkness, it has been confessed by the Switchman that the practice was to look out up to the goods shed. Out of a total distance of 1150 metres (the distance between the Starter and Advanced Starter) which was to be verified by the Switchman for the purpose of compliance with G.R. 37, the first 690 metres of the track was clearly visible during night. As would be noticed from para 59 of the report, the actual visibility for a well maintained electric tail lamp was of the order of 800 metres to 1.5 km. In any case, the doubtful visibility conditions during night hours of the remaining 460 metres of the track up to the Advanced Starter is not materially relevant to the accident. Even if, for the sake of argument, it is accepted that the clearance of the remaining 460 metres of the track could not be verified from the cabin, it does not mean that the Switchman should not have verified the first 690 metres of the track, or *that he should not have looked out at all*. This was a gross negligence on the part of the Switchman, as GR 37 clearly envisages that the Station Master should not give permission to take 'off' signals to admit a train until the line over which the train is to pass is clear and free from obstructions. It may be clarified that in terms of GR 1(37), a Switchman on duty in a cabin is the Station Master for the territory controlled by him. It would thus be seen that the Switchman chose to disregard the provisions of G.R. 37, by not looking out at all.

3. The work load at the cabin was more intensive than that warranted by the classification of the Switchman as "continuous".

Remarks of the Ministry

The observations the CRS were proved incorrect after the Job analysis conducted by the Northern Railway at Naini and a few other representative stations. It was established that the work load, under the existing hours of Employment Regulations, was not all excessive (being on an average 14 hours and 17 minutes as against 18 hours per day which is the maximum classification of 'continuous' for providing three men on an 8 hourly roster indicating that there was no justification to revise the existing 'continuous' classification of the Switchman at Naini.

The result of the job analysis conducted by the Northern Railway from 1-4-1977 to 4-12-1977 was discussed by the CRS during his visit to Allahabad, when he had suggested certain items to be taken as 'streneous' nature of work instead of light character. Taking into consideration the views expressed by the CRS, certain items of work of light character were treated as of 'strenuous' nature of work, but even than the total time of 'strenuous nature being less than 18 hours, did not justify the upgradation of the classification from 8 hourly duty of 'continuous' worker to 6 hourly duty of an intensive worker.

It has been alleged by the Commission that the copy of the job analysis was not supplied to them by the Railway. This does not appear to be convincing, for there should be absolutely no difficulty in giving a copy to the Commission, if asked for.

It is noticed that the Commission has now desired that a fresh job analysis should be conducted, by associating an officers of the Commission and also by simulating conditions that existed prior to the occurrence of the accident to the extent possible. The request for a fresh job analysis has been agreed to by the railway administration who have asked for certain clarifications on the subject from the CRS on 3-2-1979.

CRS's Observation

4. If the Railway Administration had reacted effectively and promptly to the warning sounded by the collision of November 1975, the present accident would have been avoided.

Remarks of the Ministry

It is not correct to say that the administration had not reacted to the warning sounded by the previous accident which occurred in Nov. 1975. In this connection, it may be mentioned that the Committee which inquired into the earlier accident had made two recommendations, viz., (a) provision of track circuiting in Naini yard, and (b) pending the completion of track circuiting posting of an experienced Switchman in the West Cabin.

Regarding item (a) of the recommendation, provision of track-circuiting was given top priority and the work was sanctioned as an 'out of turn' work, and its execution was taken up ahead of the earlier sanctioned works. It may be noted here that period of 18 months taken for completion of works of track circuiting included 7 months of summer and monsoon during which period there is prohibition on changing of sleepers and deep screening of ballast, which was involved in this work. In any case, the other recommendation an experienced Switchman in the cabin had been implemented.

Culpability of the Switchman

The lapses on the part of the Switchman stand substantiated in that he intimated the departure of the Goods train to the ASM on duty at Allahabad East Cabin, before the engine of the goods train had passed the Advanced Starter, and he put back the lever of the signal before the goods train had completely passed it. Further, he did not verify the condition of the track between the Starter and the Advanced Starter before taking 'off' signals for 103 Up Deluxe Express. His statement that after waiting for 3-4-minutes, he put back the lever of the Advanced Starter after physically verifying the clearance of the track by looking out from the cabin, is evidently incorrect because if he had looked out at all, he would have spotted the obstruction which was very close to the cabin. His culpability for the accident, therefore, gets established beyond doubt.

Although the lapses on the part of the Switchman amounted to gross negligence, but the real conspiracy of circumstances was the failure of power due to an act of vandalism by unsocial elements. Even the CRS in para 85 of the report has accepted that the origin of this unfortunate collision could be traced to this unsocial act. He has observed that if there had been no such theft to copper wires from traction power lines on that fateful night, there would have been no occasion for the chain of events culminating in the tragedy.

This Ministry consider that while judging the gravity of the offence committed by the Switchman, the following could be taken as extenuating circumstances:

(i) temporary failure to power due to acts of vandalism leading to the sudden change in the aspect of the Advanced Starter and consequent stoppage of the goods train short of the signal;

(ii) difficulty in re-starting the goods train due to hose-pipes getting disjointed and inadequate train examination at at Cheoki; and

(iii) 103 Up arriving immediately after OHE failure.

Regarding the delay in executing track circuiting works, attention is invited to the remarks against para 92.

Para 89: Accepted. Instructions have been issued to the railways to ensure that at those stations where Automatic Block signalling ends and Absolute Block signalling commences, the portion of the line/lines between the last manual stop signal/signals and the first semi-automatic signal/automatic signal should be track-circuited at that end at which the automatic block signalling commences. Where, however, a station falls in automatic signalling territory, the entire inter-locked portion of the yard should be track circuited.

The Railways have been advised to execute the above work of track circuiting on top priority basis.

Para 90.1: Instructions have been issued to the Railways to provide track circuiting on the portion of the track between the

Starter and Advanced Starter signals, in a phased manner, at such of the stations on double lines/multiple lines, where:

(a) trains run through the station without stopping at the maximum permissible speed;
(b) frequent shunting involving the main line is carried out at this station; and
(c) the layout of the station permits a train to be kept waiting at the advanced starter, clear off the trailing point in rear permitting reception on the main line from rear.

Paras 90.2 and 91: The general question of bringing the Advanced starters closer to the stations is under examination and suitable instructions will be issued to the railways, as soon as a decision is taken in the matter.

Regarding the review of GR 36; it may be mentioned that this rule has been revised only recently after taking into consideration the latest technological changes and conditions of working. The revised general Rule 3.36(1) and (2) reads as under:

"3.36. Fixed signals generally:

(1) Every fixed signals shall be so constructed that, in case of failure of any part of its connections, it shall remain at, or return to its most restrictive aspect.
(2) A signal which has been taken 'off' for the passage of a rain shall not be placed 'on' until whole of the train which it controls has passed it, except:

(a) in case of emergency, or
(b) where arrangement is provided to restore the signal to 'on' automatically, the control operating the signal shall not be restored to its normal position, till the whole of the train has passed it."

Para 92: It is true that there was some time lag in the processing and completion of the work of providing track circuiting, at the Divisional level. The delay was mainly due to the completion of various processes. It may be pointed out here that the period of 18 months taken for completion of the track circuiting included intervention of 7 months of summer and monsoon during which there was prohibition on changing of sleepers and deep screening of ballast which were involved in this work. But for the unfortunate accident on 10-10-1977, the work would have been completed by the target date set down by the Railway. Since the other recommendation of the Committee who inquired into earlier accident of 1975, viz., posting of an experienced Switchman in the Cabin, had already been implemented it cannot be accepted that the delay in the completion of the track circuiting at Naini had contributed to the accident.

The Railway Administration has, however, been asked to investigate the reasons for unavoidable/excessive delay at different stages of completion of various processes *vis-a-vis* the responsibility for the delay on the part of any individual/department.

Para 93: The minimum distance at which signals are placed from fixed structures in case of signalling plan is, in order to cater for the various overlaps/distances required as per G.Rs. Since the exact distance would depend on local conditions and may vary on account of visibility curves, it is not necessary to indicate exact distance. So long as the plans submitted for sanction indicate compliance with the statutory dimensions, the same should be accepted. The actual distances would be available in the Divisional office for purposes of record. Since it is basically necessary to comply with this statutory requirements, signalling plans prepared for execution of work need not sow the actual distances which will be only minor variations of the statutory dimensions on the permissible side and the are incorporated in the completion plans.

Para 94: Instructions have been issued to the Railways as under:

Where track indicators are provided, the following arrangement shall be made:

(i) Stations not provided with Panel Interlocking:

Normally the indicator should show Yellow/White light when the line is unoccupied and Red when occupied. When there is a power failure, the track indicator would get extinguished.

(ii) Panel Interlocked/Route Relay Interlocked Stations:

In such cases normally the track indicators would show no light when the line is unoccupied. When action is initiated to set the route for taking off a signal and the concerned route is set, the track indicator light for the route shows Yellow/White, if unoccupied. However, if any portion of the Track Circuited yard is occupied, a 'RED' indication is shown on the Panel Diagram, irrespective of the route being set or not. The track indicators would show White/Yellow when the track is cleared after the intended movement is completed till the route/signal button or switch is restored to normal unless the panel interlocking/Route Relay Interlocking is provided with Automatic Route release facility. For the point zones, however, if the supply is from a battery, the same may show even in normal circumstances White/Yellow light when unoccupied and red when occupied.

Paras 95.1 and 95.2: Instruction have been issued to the Railways that means must be provided for distinguishing between normal occupation of the track beyond the Advanced Starter/Semi-automatic Signal and in case of power supply failure in the Automatic Block section where the power supply to the Automatic Signals in the block section and to the Advanced Starter/Semi-automatic signal is from different sources.

Para 96: Instructions have been issued to all the railways for toning Up the compliance of train examination rules and ensuring pre-testing of trains wherever such facilities are available.

Para 97: This has been accepted by the Railway Administration for implementation. It is seen that CCRS is satisfied with the action taken by the Railway.

Para 98: Instructions have been issued again to the Railways to carry invariably a graph paper on the Speed Recorders in Electric Locomotives. Railways have been asked to review the stocking limits and provide for adequate stock of graph papers, etc.

Para 99.1: The observation that the work load at the West Cabin at Naini is rather heavy is based on a rough assessment and is not borne out by two job analyses conducted by the railway administration at Naini and a few other representative stations. The results of these job analyses have established that there is no justification to revise the existing 'continuous' classification of Switchman at Naini.

It is also pertinent to point out that result of the job analysis conducted at Naini from 1-12-77 to 4-12-77 was discussed by the CRS during his visit to Allahabad and he suggested certain items to be taken as 'strenuous' nature of work instead of light character. Taking into account the view expressed by the CRS, certain items of work of light character were treated as 'Strenuous' nature of work but even then the total time of 'strenuous' nature being less than 18 hours in a cycle of 24 hours did not justify upgradation of the classification under the Hours of Employment Regulations.

As for CRS's suggestion that the very basis of job analysis requires review, it may be mentioned that the procedure for job analysis has been been laid down keeping in view the Hours of Employment Regulations. Any change in the system can be considered only on specific suggestions being given by the Commission.

Para 99.2: The observations made under this para seem to be based on some misunderstanding of the information given to the CRS during discussions with the Divisional Officers at Allahabad on 20-12-77. The Railway Board had merely asked the Railways to let them known as to what would be the additional requirements in th form of organisation and financial implications involved, in case the recommendations of the National Commission on Labour for quinquennial review of the classification of all railway servants was accepted. The said recommendation of the Commission was never accepted by this Ministry. This was also specifically clarified to the Northern Railway in October, 1972 and again on 4th May, 1978. In the latter communication Northern Railway was further advised that they should continue to conduct job analysis to review classification of those categories about which there were representations or about which the administration suo mote considers it necessary to conduct the analysis in order to clear any doubt about the present classification. The Railway has confirmed that they are already conduction job analysis as per the said directive.

Para 100: This is already in accordance with the extant policy. Instructions on the subject have, however, been emphasised on the railways.

Para 101: This matter was also raised by the Commission of Railway Safety vide para 64 of the inquiry report on the collision which took place at Bachwara station of N.E. Railway on 24-2-77. As already advised in this Ministry's O.M. No. 77/Safety (A&R)/1/5 dated 18-5-79 the practice followed on the railways with regard to treatment of the persons injured in railway accidents is set out in para 711(7) of the Indian Railways Medical Manual, which reads as under:

-(7) The injured persons other than Railway beneficiaries should be shifted, as far as possible, to the nearest non-railway hospitals except in the following circumstances:

(i) Non-availability of non-railway hospital,
(ii) Want of accommodation in the non-railway hospital,
(iii) Unsuitability of the non-railway hospital to render efficient aid
(iv) Difficulty of transport,
(v) Serious condition of the patient,
(vi) In other circumstances considered justifiable by the attending medical officer.

It would be seen from the above that the interests of the injured have been well guarded even in the provisions of the existing rules.

The provisions that the injured persons, other than railway employees, should preferably be taken to a non-railway hospital, have been followed over the years because in train accidents, there is a general feeling that the railways are a guilty party. In the past, there were also allegations that railways deliberately destroyed evidence of the correct number of injured or dead. Even now, once in a while, such allegations are made. If the treatment is undertaken in a railway hospital as a rule and in preference to a non-railway hospital, it will expose the railways to avoidable criticism that the best possible treatment was not made available. In this background, this Ministry consider that the provisions contained in the Indian Railways Medical Manual need not be changed.

Insofar as subject accident is concerned, the best medical aid had been provided to all the patients who were admitted in the Medical College Hospital, Allahabad. This is borne out by the fact that except 6 critically ill cases who expired during the first 24 hours, no other dangerously ill person had died in that hospital, and they improved with the treatment given by the concerned specialists. It is also relevant to mention it here that on the morning of 10-10-1977, the occupancy in Railway Hospital, Allahabad was 159 against the capacity of 150 beds.

Paras 102.1, 102.2 and 102.3: The matter is already receiving the attention of the RDSO. For use on Mail/Express and Passenger trains, electric tail lamp of 24 V auto bulb or reflector assembly, (which uses power from the train battery) has been developed by the

RDSO. This would give much better visibility and is expected to give sufficient warning to the drivers of approaching trains to enable them to control their trains in time. The tail lamp developed has given a good account in preliminary trails. Further trials under various adverse conditions are being planned and it would be possible to arrive at the decision after these trials are completed.

As for Goods trains, the development of a suitable tail lamp by drawing energy from the portable lead acid rechargeable bettery is in progress. It may be mentioned that the development of flasher unit for tail light is also under consideration.

Para 103: As explained by the railway administration, inspection of work establishments like cabins, etc., by supervisory officials can only be in the nature of sample checks. Whether adequate facilities exist for observance of the rules is for the concerned staff to see. If a rule cannot be implemented due to local conditions at a particular station the officer who is required to implement the rule, is expected to bring the lacuna/deficiency to the notice of his immediate supervisor so that steps can be taken to rectify the lacuna.

It is seen that CCRS has noted the position explained by the railway administration.

Para 104.1: Instructions with regard to safety marshalling of trains contained in Board's letter No. 76-Chg II/14/1 dated 4-6-77 have been re-iterated to the Railways for strict compliance.

The Eastern Railway is being asked to fully investigate the reasons for failure to comply with the prescribed marshalling order on 103 Up Deluxe Express and take action to avoid recurrence thereof.

Para 104.2: The issue with regard to anti-telescopic features of the BEML coaches was raised by the Commission of Railway Safety in para 45 of the inquiry report on the collision which took place at Vedayapalem station of S.E. Railway on 9-2-78. As advised in this Ministry's O.M. No. 78/Safety (A&R)/1/1, dated 24-2-79, BEML coaches have anti-telescopic features and are designed to withstand the following loads as per RDSO's specifications:

(i) Vertical load of 2.165 tonnes/metre run uniformly distributed measured stress in this test shall not exceed 14.2 kg./sq.mm.,
(ii) Horizontal compression load of 102 tonnes at each side buffer,
(iii) A horizontal compression load of 61 tonnes applied uniformly

at 305 mm above the centre line of the buffers,

(iv) Combination of loads specified in clauses (i) & (ii),

(v) A horizontal compression load of 31 tonnes uniformly distributed over the body ends.

The strength of the end wall of BEML Coach is, however, less than that of ICF Coaches. Modifications to the end wall construction of BEML coach, have therefore, been evolved in consultation with M/s BEML to bring its strength at par with that of ICF Coaches and one prototype Coach with the modified ends wills has already been built and undergoing strain gauge tests by RDSO before finalising any further modifications that may be required. Meanwhile BEML has also been advised by RDSO to switchover to modified ends pending the results of tests.

Para 105: As accepted by the CRS, adequate medical relief had already reached the site by road. The medical relief van was, however, sent to the site only by way of abundant precaution. The delay in reaching the medical van at the site was due to the obstruction by the over hanging OHE wires.

Instructions have, however, been issued to the Railways vide Board's letter No. 77/Safety (A&R)/29/26 dated 7-6-78 to conduct mock drills for turning out the relief trains and medical vans at prescribed intervals. Such a course would go a long way to ensure that these vans reach the site with utmost expediency. It is seen that CCRS has taken note of the instructions issued by this Ministry.

Para 106: As desired, the observations of the CRS have been brought to the notice of State Government Authorities. The Railway Administration also hold periodical meetings with the senior State Government Officials to discuss the law and order problem.

Additional Recommendation of the CCRS:

Accepted. Necessary instructions have been issued to all the railways.

Relief Measures—Para 88

Observations of the Commissioner of Railway Safety that relief arrangements and restoration of through traffic were prompt, adequate and satisfactory, are noted. Regarding disposition of the casualties to various hospitals, remarks of this Ministry against para 101 may kindly be seen.

In this connection, it may be worthwhile mentioning that lists of the injured and the dead were displayed and information booths were opened at important stations. Information about the accident was conveyed to the relatives of the victims through railway and P&T telephones. Telegrams were issued for conveying information to the families of the affected passengers, and passes were also issued in favour of the relative of the affected persons.

30

STUDY GROUP ON WAGES, INCOMES AND PRICES, 1977 – REPORT[1]

Chairman Shri S. Bhoothalingam

Members Dr. Dharam Narain; Shri Arvind Buch; Shri Hiten Bhaya

Secretary Dr. G.C. Katoch

Appointment

Serious distortions have crept into the structure of pay, dearness allowance and other compensatory allowances of employees in public and private sectors. These distortions have been largely the result of a *ad hoc* approach followed in the past to the problems of periodical revision of emoluments in public enterprises and in organised private industry. Moreover, a major part of the employment in the country is in the rural sector. The incomes of the vast majority of the people in agricultural sector are low and are also liable to serious fluctuations. Any rationalisation of the existing pattern of wages and incomes in different sectors can however be attempted only as an element of Integrated Policy on Wages, Income and Prices.

The Government of India, has, therefore, decided that a comprehensive study on wages, income and price policy should be undertaken immediately. Consequently the Government of India in the Ministry of Finance, Bureau of Public Enterprises sets up a Study Group on Wages, Incomes and Prices vide its Resolution No.2(66)/77-BPE (GM-I) dated October 13, 1977.

Terms of Reference

The Study Group will prepare a draft policy on wages, income and

---

1. New Delhi, Ministry of Finance, Bureau of Public Enterprises, 1978, 146 p.

prices, in framing this draft policy, the Study Group will consider the following issues:

(i) What should be the minimum wage and what should be the norms with reference to which the minimum wage should be determined?

(ii) Whether the minimum wage should be uniform or could be different as between—

(a) Agriculture, industry and services,
(b) Organised and unorganised sectors,
(c) Urban and Rural sectors,
(d) Between different States/Regions,
(e) Between different employers in the organised sector.

(iii) What should be the relevant criteria for determining the differentials between minimum wage and maximum wage and whether the ratio between minimum-maximum wages should be uniform, or could be different in the sectors referred to in (ii) above?

(iv) What should be the criteria for determining maximum income and what relationship should exist between maximum income and maximum wages?

(v) What should be the linkage between wages, incomes and prices, and to review in this connection the existing arrangements for regulation of dearness allowance in private and public sectors?

(vi) What fiscal, economic and other policies should be adopted for achieving objectives of the proposed policy on wages, incomes and prices?

(vii) Whether any legislative changes would be required for implementing the proposed policy on wages, incomes and prices?

Contents

Preface; Summary of Conclusions and Recommendations; The Report:—(i) The objectives, (ii) The Structure of Incomes, (iii) Minimum Wages, (iv) The Rural Sector, (v) High Incomes and Top Salaries, (vi) Wages in the Organised Sector, (vii) Dearness Al-

lowance, (viii) Bonus, (ix) Prices, (x) Miscellaneous, (xi) Implementation; Tables; Appendices from A to C.

Recommendations

Minimum Wage

1. The real minimum wage can only be the absolute national minimum, irrespective of sectors, regions or States, below which no employment would be permitted.

2. In determining such a national minimum wage several considerations have to be kept in view. For instance, it has to be consistent with factors like (1) the per capita national income adjusted after applying the participation rate, (2) average national income per consumption unit, and (3) per capita rural consumption expenditure. It cannot also deviate too much from prevalent earnings in the small scale sector. Above all, its impact must not be such as to inhibit generation of employment.

3. Taking all relevant considerations into account, the national minimum wage to be aimed at should be Rs. 150 per month at current prices. Efforts should be made towards achieving this goal as soon as possible, at any rate within a period of about seven years. But immediately it may not be practicable to adopt this figure without seriously jeopardizing employment and dislocating the tiny and small scale sector. To begin with, therefore, we recommend that the national minimum wage below which no employment will be permitted be fixed at Rs. four per day of eight hours unskilled work, inclusive of any part payment in kind where customary; or at a monthly rate of not less than Rs. 100. The very announcement of this policy and its wide dissemination will itself have tonic effect and make workers conscious of their right.

4. We further recommend that the quantum of the national minimum wage should be revised every two years till the recommended level of Rs. 150 per month (at 1978 prices) is reached; thereafter, it should be mandatory to revise the minimum wage every three years in relation to the trend increase in per capita national income.

5. The proposed minimum wage will be applicable throughout the country for unskilled work for every adult of 18 years or above, irrespective of sex. The present statutory minimum wages, wherever they are lower than the proposed national minimum, will be brought

up to this level. It will not adversely affect any category of employees already in receipt of higher minimum wage. State Governments will continue to have the freedom to fix higher minimum wages for any categories of employment under the Minimum Wages Act.

6. Employment with a reasonably stable employer-employee relationship is an essential condition for the application of the minimum wage. This will therefore not apply to work given out to be done in households, as there will then be no clear employer-employee relationship.

7. We consider that in respect of agricultural sector a desirable minimum rural household income would be a more meaningful concept because of the irregular and seasonal nature of employment and unstable and varied sources of income.

The Rural Sector

8. The minimum desirable rural household income to be aimed at should be such as to enable the bottom 30 per cent to come up roughly to the level of the next higher decile group. We suggest adoption of Rs. 1,800 per annum for the present for planning purposes. Policy measures should be directed towards creating conditions in which the households of those who work part time or sporadically, as well as landless labourers and marginal farmers, are enabled to earn this minimum within a period of seven years.

9. The Draft Sixth Plan has suggested various measures for the eradication of poverty and unemployment in the rural sector which include redistribution of land surplus, implementation of tenancy reforms, organising the poor masses and creation of additional jobs mainly in the agriculture and allied sectors and in the small scale and cottage industries.

10. It is necessary to support and accelerate the employment effects of the programmes contained in the Draft Plan by several types of parallel action. Such action should reach the very poor, viz., the landless labour or those with small bits of land, and those without any worthwhile assets. Our policy should thus aim at (a) improving the productivity and thereby increasing the return from small holdings, and (b) increasing the opportunities for work and ensuring that such work brings in better returns.

11. The first objective is likely to be served by the Plan programmes designed to improve the productivity of marginal

farmers and making available the necessary inputs. In this connection the instrument of contractual guaranteed price can be deployed to induce a shift in the product mix of small and marginal farmers in favour of crops which are at once labour intensive and high value crops. This would call for: (a) effective provision of credit for those farmers essentially through cooperative banks and societies; (b) assured provision of foodgrain supplies at prices which may induce them to shift a part of their holdings to high value crops; and (c) assured arrangements for purchase at guaranteed price so that farmers are protected against the uncertainties of marketing and price fluctuations.

12. The scheme may start with a few selected commodities like potatoes, onions and dry chillies, and with an assurance of a price for those small and marginal farmers who may be willing to participate. Details of the scheme can be worked out to keep leakage and abuse to the minimum. The price to be guaranteed may be an approximation to the trend value of the price of the commodity by taking an average of the post-harvest prices in the previous five years.

13. We recognise the role of local level institutions like cooperatives, Small Farmers Development Agencies, etc., in the planning and operation of such schemes. The work of collection, transportation, storage and disposal could be done by all-India agencies like the Food Corporation of India or NAFED. As experience is gained and success achieved, the range of commodities can be enlarged over time.

14. As regards creation of employment opportunities, wider opportunities for employment would come through the implementation of Plan programmes, but this would take considerable time and their economic effects may not be felt in the short run. Therefore, these efforts need to be strengthened by directing employment programmes to areas where other developmental activities are by themselves now insufficient. Such a scheme of coordinated employment should satisfy the following conditions: (i) the daily wage offered should be, for unskilled labour, not less than the national minimum at daily rates; (ii) those who offer their work should be required to work continuously at least for a week; (iii) they should be required to do whatever they are asked to do, although efforts should be made to give them the kind of work they know; (iv) when there is no work, or not enough work, they should still be paid, but to prevent abuse they should be required to remain in attendance; (v) after the week, the worker

should be free to be leave whenever he likes; (vi) administrative effort should be directed to the preparation and development of such schemes; (vii) every scheme should have provision for the required minimum of material inputs; and (viii) there should be no limitation of number of grounds of finance or lack of schemes.

15. While the orientation of the employment programme will be towards development work, non-seasonal jobs as well as jobs according to the needs of different locations may also be included. These may include spinning and weaving, poultry, milk and milk products, cattle breeding, etc.

16. We believe that if conditions such as we have indicated the incorporated in the scheme, there will be no uncontrolled flood of offers for employment.

High Incomes and Top Salaries

17. We have not proposed any freeze in wages. On the contrary, we believe that wages should gradually increase by obtaining an appropriate share in the growth of gross national product and productivity. Such a growth should take place in a smooth and orderly fashion and not as a result of continuing tension and trials of strength. This should therefore be planned for, and such planning would involve a certain measure of restraint. For such restraint to be generally accepted, we think it is necessary that those earning higher incomes should also be subjected to restraint.

18. One such restraint should be on the distribution of dividends. Obviously, the limitation should not be expressed in terms of a percentage of paid up share capital. The amount distributed as dividend should be limited to a percentage of equity capital and reserves which together represent the investment of the shareholder. This percentage may be fixed at two or three per cent below the rate of earning regarded as necessary to attract enough investment to secure the growth of the industry. Thus, if 12 per cent of capital and reserves is regarded as an appropriate return for the cement industry, the distribution as dividend should be limited to eight or nine per cent. This would incidentally strengthen the capacity of the industry to grow through the use of internal resources.

19. Salaries of government servants and those employed in the public sector are already subject to considerable restraint. The ration between the post-tax salary income of the lowest and the highest in

these sectors is now around 1 : 9. However, if perquisites of government servants were taken into account, this range might widen slightly. On the other hand, higher salaries and perquisites accrue generally to older persons with greater length of service. When comparisons are made between the more experienced persons in the lowest and the highest categories, it will be seen that the range is considerably narrowed. Thus, the differential is already a little narrower than what has been generally envisaged as the goal ten years hence. The question whether there should not be some upward revision of salaries in these ranges, in order to continue to attract persons of the requisite calibre to these posts, needs examination. We recommend that this problem may be referred to the National Pay Commission, the early appointment of which we recommend.

20. In the private sector, however, the differentials are wider mainly because, unlike the government sector, higher salaries have also been revised upwards from time to time following inflation. The differentials in after-tax emoluments vary from industry to industry, and sometimes go up to 1 : 16. Risks and uncertainties in entrepreneurial management being greater, and managerial talent of the requisite calibre being still relatively scarce, the differentials can be higher than in the government sector or the public sector. They still need to be narrowed. High salaries in the private sector are often supplemented by commissions and by tax free or near tax free benefits, which encourage and make possible affluent and even ostentatious ways of living. Further, generous retirement benefits reduce the need for current savings permitting thereby a higher level of consumption during service and after retirement. We think, therefore, the total value of perquisites must be fully taken into account in determining the appropriate level of compensation. These should not normally exceed 25 per cent of basic pay. Further, the method of valuation of perquisites for tax purposes should be uniform for all sectors. Normally, there should also be limit to the total of salary and commission and this limit should apply not only to Directors but others as well. In order to prevent disruption and emergence of new abuses, the limit should not represent too drastic a change. Taking current circumstances into account, the think that Rs. 6000 per month for all new contracts would be a suitable limit for the next five years. Provision may have to be made for certain exceptional cases of high or rare skills such as oil exploration, haute cuisine, etc. Some special arrangements will have to be made for this.

21. We also consider that payment of commission as a mode of remuneration is an outdated concept and a hangover from the old managing agency system. It should, therefore, be phased out within the next three to five years. Simultaneously, a suitable system may be evolved for incentive payments for exceptional performance in the productive sector — both private and public — coupled with penalties for negative or unsuccessful performance.

22. We also think that individual fixation of salaries by government or other external authorities should be avoided because of the complex and varying situations in business and industry. In particular, differentials *inter se* among the higher paid employees of the private sector should be left to be settled through the normal process of negotiated contracts by the managements, subject only to the overall limits prescribed.

23. The only method of trying to enforce a ceiling on incomes is by 100 per cent personal income-tax on the excess over the ceiling. However, recent experience has shown that this does not work. Agricultural incomes continue to be totally exempt from all personal taxation; many other incomes, though legally subject to tax, are not brought within the tax net. Moreover, the threat of a limit on incomes will be a disincentive to work and enterprise. In order to avoid this dilemma, at least in part, we recommend imposing a ceiling not on income but on the two main purposes for which incomes are sought, namely, consumption and private investment. This can be achieved by imposing a high penalty over a certain limit of total income from all sources including agriculture. An individual may be allowed to opt out to paying such a penalty by depositing the whole of the excess income with the government into a special account. This special account will bear interest at rate to be determined by government from time to time. Government will have use of these funds, but they will remain the property of the individual and will pass on to his legal heirs after his death. The individual will also have the freedom to withdraw any desired amount at any time, but the amount so withdrawn would be added to the year's income and taxed. Provision may have to be made for withdrawing from the fund for certain approved purposes, such as investment in own business or other desire lines. But these can be worked out after some experience is gained.

24. An alternative to depositing the excess income with the government into a special account will be to have the income earners channelise the excess income into approved forms of saving which

may be prescribed by government from time to time. Here again, whenever such savings are withdrawn, they would be treated as part of the taxable income of that year.

25. The advantage of such a scheme is that it would not erode the incentive for work and enterprise to the same degree as personal taxation. It will also solve the difficult problem of high incomes which are fluctuating or are of limited duration.

26. The alternative is to have a ceiling on incomes and impose penal marginal tax rates without any facility for deduction of savings. As both these can be regarded as dysfunctional in terms of their average impact on incentives and savings, it would be better to give the option of high income earners to accept much steeper tax rates than those prevailing at present or escape them by stepping up their savings and reducing current consumption. The resultant savings must however be channelised into approved forms which may aid public investment eventually.

27. One of our Members Shri Arvind Buch feels that while the measures recommended may assist to a limited extent in dealing with the question of wide disparities between the lowest and the highest income, these do not go far enough. He has, therefore, suggested several additional measures which are detailed in para 5.41 of the Report.

Wages in the Organised Sector

28. The determination of homogeneous national wage structure is very difficult. We are not beginning with a clean slate and the burden of history is with us. Disparities, anomalies and irrationalities exist and have come to be regarded as 'rights'. Further, there is no reasonable method of determining what should be the absolute level of wage for each category of workers and what is a right differential between one category of workers and another.

29. Even if a national wage structure is determined, which is doubtful, or the historically determined structure accepted, which is improbable, several adjustment in wages or earnings are required from time to time. These are, for instance:

(a) A periodic increment in earnings which is merely related to time, and which has become part of our culture so to say.
(b) Some protection of earnings against changes in the value of

money.

(c) A correction for changes in the productivity of workers which may take various shapes.

(d) A correction in the relative wages of one set of workers, with certain degree of skill and certain onerousness of work, relative to the much higher wage of another set of *similar* workers with the same degree of skill and onerousness of work.

(e) A correction in the relative wages of one set of workers with certain degree of skill and onerousness of work, relative to a much higher wage of another set of *dissimilar* workers with different degrees of skill and onerousness of work.

(f) A set of corrections to reduce the disparities across industries/sectors and within industries/sectors.

30. We have tried to provide appropriate guidelines and principles (a) to get such corrections and adjustments within the framework of collective bargaining, (b) to reduce disparities, and (c) to raise gradually the areas of unduly depressed wages. We only suggest them as the first steps.

31. Wage disparities exist between the Central and State Governments and among the State Governments themselves. Standardisation is not practicable, but some harmonisation is necessary in respect of certain common categories. The minimum wage determined by the Third Pay Commission may be commended to States for adoption within about five years. Model scales for certain common categories (identified by the Sixth Finance Commission) may be worked out by a National Pay Commission which should be appointed soon in consultation with States.

32. The problem of quasi-government and municipal employees is more complex and should be left to the States themselves of tackle.

33. Wage disparities exist in public sector undertakings *vis-a-vis* Government departmental undertakings engaged on similar work and among public sector enterprises themselves. The suggestion for standardised pay scales for similar public sector and departmental undertakings has much merit. But it may not be found practicable as it impinges on the process of collective bargaining. We therefore, recommend the appointment of a Pay Committee to go into the emoluments and service conditions of government industrial employees after comparing them in all respects with corresponding employees in the public and private sectors.

34. In the organised private sector, a standardised pay structure is not practicable in our conditions. There is no practicable method except the process of collective bargaining to determine wages and relativities in this sector from time to time. But to prevent future distortions and work towards the long-term objective of rationalisation, collective bargaining should be subject to certain broad guidelines. Some of the suggested parameters which will equally apply to the public sector can be as follows:

(1) The spread between the highest and the lowest wages in a unit should be normally be 4-5 times the lowest wage.
(2) Similar payment for broadly similar categories of workers in leading industries in the same region.
(3) Scarce skills will merit higher differentials, but non-wage benefits should be taken into account when determining differentials.
(4) In future wage settlements, units having relatively low wages should be enabled to come up faster than those already in receipt of wages far above the majority of enterprises.

35. We have recommended a universally applicable system of dearness allowance which would compensate for increases in cost of living of the basic minimum needs for consumption. This element, therefore, should have ordinarily no influence in wage revisions in the future which should be essentially linked to increases in productivity. In sectors where the measurement of productivity. In sectors where the measurement of productivity is difficult or impossible, such as government services, the increase in national productivity should be taken into account. Where productivity in a sector is less difficult to measure, as in most of the industrial sector, wage increases should be governed by the overall rate of growth in productivity disaggregated by suitable groups of industries, on the basis of homogeneity or otherwise, to be recommended by the proposed Bureau of Incomes and Prices. This guideline, being an average for the industry as a whole, cannot be applied rigidly but some flexibility has to be provided by the permissible rate being between the mean deviation limits above and below the average rate of productivity growth.

36. The guideline will apply to the increase in the total wage bill of a unit. However, increases already accrued due to the existence of incremental scales since the last settlement will have to be taken into

account. The spread of benefits among various groups and levels, and adjustment of wage scales, etc., will be determined entirely by collective bargaining. All wage agreements will have effects from a prospective date in future.

37. In order that existing disparities are not perpetuated or further widened, there has to be a further guideline for "high-wage Islands" allowing for a lower rate of growth than elsewhere in the industry. This may mean that, in some cases revised wage scales may become necessary, excesses being treated as personal pay for existing employees.

38. Overtime payment should be carefully adjusted to needs and should not be allowed to become systematic.

39. All wage settlements through collective bargaining will be operative for 4-5 years. Similarly, Pay Commission/Committees for pay revisions of government employees should be appointed every five years or so.

40. A permanent non-statutory body called the "Bureau of Incomes and Prices" may be set up to undertake continuous review of relevant data and to determine each year the guidelines for the industry or for groups of industries, within which collective bargaining will operate. Its recommended guidelines, on acceptance by Government, will regulate all wage settlements, as well as Wage Boards awards, etc. There will also be higher policy-making Council consisting of 30-40 members representing concerned interests including trade unions, employers and State Governments.

41. If individual units or industries, whether in public or private sector, are unable to reach wage settlements within the norms laid down by the Bureau, the matter should be referred to an independent appellate body whose award would be legally binding.

42. One of our Members Shri Arvind Buch has made several further suggestions which have been reproduced in Para 6.44 of the Report.

Dearness Allowance

43. The existing dearness allowance arrangements vary considerably with reference to the linkage base, mechanism of linkage, degree of linkage, periodicity of revision and the degree of neutralisation both inter-sectorally as well as intra-sectorally. This heterogeneity has resulted in distortions, anomalies and narrowing of dif-

ferentials in all sectors. In certain sectors this has been aggravated by linking dearness allowance to wages. There is, therefore, need for a single national corrective formula to compensate for the rise in cost of the essential consumption basket.

44. It would be appropriate to link future dearness allowance increases to cost of living on a uniform basis. In the absence of better alternative, the index to be used may continue to be All-India Average Consumer Price Index for Industrial Workers, which is widely used. Since there is considerable divergence in the use of the Consumer Index itself, the latest available series should be used. With this proviso, therefore, there would be no objection to the use of the all-India or a regional index. The switch-over to the latest series could be made at the next wage revision. In cases where the Index for Urban Non-manual Employees is in use, it may continue to be used for regulating dearness allowance unless the employees and the employers decide by mutual agreement to switch over to the All India Consumer Price Index for Industrial Workers.

45. The periodicity of dearness allowance revision should be on a quarterly basis for all sectors with reference to the average of the preceding quarter.

46. The two main systems of dearness allowance at present in use are based on either a wage-linked slab system or a value per Index point system. The "per point" system is preferred being more logical, simple, with ease of universal understanding and application. It has also the merit of delinking dearness allowance from wages. It has an in-built progressive edge and does not unduly affect existing relativities in wage structure. We recommend adoption of the per point formula uniformly for future revisions, the value per point being around Rs. 1.30. This is already prevalent in about two-third of the public sector enterprises as also in cement and steel industries. The per point formula with varying point values is also in use in a number of other industries like cotton textiles, jute engineering (West Bengal) and sugar, which may continue till the next wage revision. This formula would ensure full neutralisation at the lower levels. Since D.A. under this system is not related to salary, it will be admissible to all irrespective of salary drawn. In no case will there be a reduction in the dearness allowance at present being drawn.

Bonus

47. Logically, bonus related to profit, of the kind which has

prevailed in India for a long time now, is suitable only in industries producing for the market in reasonably competitive conditions. It is not suitable in the case of organised activities, industrial or other, where the profit motive does not operate at all or where the profits are induced, influenced or otherwise affected by public policy and largely used for the community welfare. Thus, it is unsuitable in government services and similar activities, including the Railways, Posts and Telegraphs, and public utilities, financial and other institutions.

48. On this reasoning, it would not be desirable to extend the system of bonus related to profit to new areas. Further, where the bonus system prevails in unsuitable areas, it should be phased out, if necessary by replacing it with other payments related to more suitable measures of performance.

49. In Railways, Posts and Telegraphs, and Ordnance Factories, etc., fairly large numbers are engaged in activities closely similar to those in industry in the private and public sectors. They are better off in some ways and worse off in others. If, after a comparative study of their emoluments and non-wage benefits, it is found that there real wages are clearly out of line with similar workers in the private and public sectors, corrections must be made through an appropriate revision of the structure and rates of remuneration, and/or suitable incentive payments. We have recommended the appointment of a Pay Committee to under take this study.

50. Even in the industrial sector, both private and public, bonus related to the profits of individual undertakings tends to perpetuate and accentuate disparities in the earnings of workers who do the same work or put in the same effort. It tends to create tensions between workers themselves, between government and workers, between managements and workers and even between managements. In the long run, it would be desirable to replace it by a system which would enable labour to get a fair share of the benefits of productivity without causing such distortions. Meanwhile, it has to be recognised that the bonus system has become a part of the industrial way of life in India. It will not be practicable to give it up until the economy reaches a higher level of productivity and well-being. Until it is replaced by general agreement, we recommend the continuance of the existing system.

51. Government of India may initiate talks with trade unions and managements paying bonus under the Payment of Bonus Act to

replace it by long-term benefits like retirement pensions to all the categories of employees, and some scheme of unemployment relief to those who have once been employed and who have become temporally unemployed due to closures of firms and factories, mines and plantations, etc. Under this scheme low-paid workers may also be exempted from payment of subscriptions under the Employees' State Insurance Act. Wherever bonus is not paid such benefits may also be extended provided national consensus of covering bonus into the above-mentioned long-term social security measures is arrived at through tripartite dialogue.

52. It would also be desirable, at that stage, to provide that a portion of the allocable surplus in high profit industries should be diverted to financing schemes for rural employment recommended elsewhere in this Report.

53. We also recommend that discussions for a gradual change-over towards the new system may be initiated early. There are several choices available and further thought and discussion may indicate even better methods. One such choice is outlined in the Report. Further consideration of this may be the first step in the process of change.

Prices

54. The main thrust of our economic policy has necessarily to be anti-inflationary and towards maintenance of reasonable price stability. Price policy has also to be integrated with policies relating to incomes and wages and thus stabilisation of the cost of living has to be one of its basic objectives. Price stability does not however mean a policy of price freeze. On an average whose-sale prices may move up to 213 per cent per annum and within this the relative prices may also go up or down. Such a movement is warranted by the need to direct investment, production and distribution patterns on desired lines.

55. The Agricultural price policy should lend support to the efforts to increase overall agricultural production, and to induce changes in the cropping pattern in accordance with changes in the composition of demand, besides ensuring that the rise in prices associated with periodic shortages does not push basic necessities out of the reach of the common man. In order to benefit the small and marginal farmers, encouragement should be given for the production

of selected cash crops with a labour intensive bias. Other measures suggested are multiple points of procurement in order to minimise the role of middlemen and simplifying bureaucratic organisation and procedures. The village level organisation will have to be reorganised to ensure that the benefit of concessional inputs passes to the small and marginal farmers, and not to the richer ones. Effects may also be made to reduce the costs of procurement, storage, transportation and distribution of foodgrains.

56. We are recommending a wide network of public distribution system covering the essential goods. Such a scheme should be strengthened by maintenance of adequate buffer stocks and proper distribution, planning and imports whenever necessary. For the distribution of mass consumption goods generally a variety of outlets should be organised and encouraged. These should include consumer cooperative societies, fair price chain stores under the auspices of public authorities and the use, where suitable, of existing outlets such as petrol stations, post offices, licensed self-employed vendors, etc. The benefit of subsidising the items covered by the distribution system should largely flow to the lower income groups. In this connection, an indepth study should be undertaken of the incidence of indirect taxes on the prices of essential goods and the inputs that go into their production.

57. As regards intermediate and capital goods, price controls and the systems of administered pricing will work only in respect of a few homogeneous products like steel and cement. Machinery, plant and equipments and their components often vary in their specifications, quality, etc., and direct control over pricing may be difficult to administer. Thus the answer lies in increasing the competitiveness of the capital and intermediate goods and using the import mechanism to augment supply and ensuring that the domestic prices are not permitted to exceed international prices except by a modest percentage. The protection provided to indigenous industries should be reviewed periodically and import duties wherever necessary may be reduced in a phased manner.

58. Other strategies that may be suggested are :

(i) The system of dual pricing could be operated selectively in the case of commodities afflicted with chronic or recurring shortages. In a longer term content, where the production of the commodities concerned is subject to sharp fluctuations, the successful working of the system pre-supposes a stocking policy on the part of the government as an accompaniment of the public distribution system;

(ii) In view of the comfortable foreign exchange situation and in order to increase competitiveness on the manufacturing sector, we suggest a uniform import a duty of about 20 per cent, particularly on capital goods and intermediates in short supply. Beyond this limit, a specific justification may be required. The policy of banning the export of essential consumer goods has merit during period of serve shortages;

(iii) There is a need to review the system of price controls and subsidies. While the newly set up Dagli Committee would review the present arrangements, the conditions call for setting up of a permanent machinery to examine and monitor the behaviour of prices and to suggest suitable changes in the prices of agricultural products as well as raw materials and manufactured items on a continuing basis; and

(iv) Steps should be taken to encourage and foster the consumer movement. Although other interests are often represented in bodies concerned with pricing and distribution, consumer interests have not been adequately represented. We recommended that this lacuna should be expeditiously filled in by giving adequate representation to consumer interests in the appropriate bodies.

Miscellaneous

59. The need for social security benefits in all sectors as an adjunct of an income policy must be recognised. A long-term objective would be to work towards extending the pension system to all wage and salary earners. For this funds could be drawn from contributions paid by the employers and employees in suitable proportions.

60. There is equal need for devising some social security measures on a contributory basis for the self-employed sector which forms about 62 per cent of the working population. These will include artisans, small shop-keepers and even marginal farmers.

61. Old age pension has been introduced in certain States, but the rates and the criteria for eligibility differ. A suitable model should be evolved and accepted in principle for adoption all over the country in due course.

62. Pensioners are particularly vulnerable to increases in the cost of living. In our view, the minimum pension of wage and salary earners should in no case be less than the national minimum wage we have proposed in Chapter III.

63. The level of pensions of the middle and lower level government servants is low. If these cannot be raised, at least the pensioners should be paid dearness allowance on the same basis as serving employees. In addition, schemes like the Army Group Insurance Scheme may be introduced to enable the pensioners to augment their post-retirement incomes.

64. Similarly, the Extra Departmental Employees in the P&T Department would need to be protected against price rise to the same extent as others working for government.

65. Housing inadequacy in India has both quantitative and qualitative dimensions. Quantitatively the acute backlog in housing is on the increase from year to year as the rate of construction has not kept pace with the growth of population. At present, employees have to pay exorbitant rents even for small tenements, particularly in large cities. The problem really is one of national shortage of housing. It has been estimated that an investment of Rs. 2790 crores per year will be required for the next 20 years to make up the shortage.

66. In the context of incomes policy, a major area of concern is housing in view of the considerable cost involved to the employee. In this regard, we suggest that a beginning be made by formulating expanded ownership housing schemes, increased public financing for such schemes, facilities for transfer and mortgage of houses and suitable tax incentives to encourage individuals to invest in housing. A scheme may also be worked out for allotment of houses constructed by government and semi-government bodies to members of Provident Funds against their long-term accumulations.

Implementation

67. Many of our suggestions and recommendations can be implemented by executive orders while others require legislative action or institutional mechanisms.

68. The practice in other countries which have tried to implement incomes-prices policy has not been uniform. In our democratic set-up, implementation has to be a combination of voluntary acceptance through consensus and statutory backing.

69. We, therefore, recommend a process of consultation and discussion leading to a broad consensus for the main outlines of the policy. This would entail consultations with trade unions, employers' representatives, State Governments and consumer interests as well as representatives of groups like small farmers, workers in the non-organised sector and the self-employed. We expect that such interaction will in due course create the necessary environment for mutual adjustments and constructive cooperation.

70. By way of illustrations, we have indicated the more important policy measures for which legislative changes may be required. The particular laws effected by our recommendations and the nature of changes required will have to be examined in detail by legal experts.

71. As the main instrument for implementation of policies, we envisage a permanent non-statutory body designated as the Bureau of Income and Prices, composed of senior economists and experts in labour, management, etc. The Bureau may function under the Ministry of Finance with a fair degree of autonomy. It would recommend guidelines which, on acceptance by Government, will regulate all wage settlements. It will also coordinate collection of data and under take continuous monitoring of price trends. The detailed functions to be entrusted to the proposed Bureau have been mentioned in the Report.

72. The Bureau will be guided by a coordinating inter-Ministerial group of Secretaries. The broad policy goals to be followed would be formulated by a higher policy-making Council of 30 to 40 members giving wide-based representations to concerned interests including trade unions, employers, State Governments, agriculture and consumers.

73. As independent appellate body with all-India jurisdiction may also be set up to deal with cases where there is failure of collective bargaining to reach settlements within the Bureau's guidelines.

74. We have also recommended the appointment of: (a) a National Pay Commission for harmonising the pay structures of the Central and State Governments; (b) a Pay Committee to examine the pay structure of industrial employees of the Railways, P&T, Defence Production, and other departmental undertakings; and (c) a Pension Commission to look into the problems of pensioners and evolve suitable pension policy for all sectors of employment.

75. We have indicated several areas in which for want of time we have been unable to undertake detailed examination. In all these cases, further studies will be necessary to work out detailed schemes and their financial and other implications before policy-decisions can be taken.

31

WORKING GROUP ON FLOOD CONTROL, 1977 – FINAL REPORT[1]

Chairman Secretary, Department of Irrigation

Members Joint Secretary (Indus); Joint Secretary (Ganga Basin); Financial Advisor, Department of Irrigation; Member (Engineering) J.R.C.; Joint Secretary (L) Department of Agriculture; Representative of Planning Commission; Chief Engineer, Irrigation, Haryana; Chief Engineer, Irrigation, Orissa; Chief Engineer, Irrigation, U.P.; Engineer-in-Chief and Ex-Officio-Secretary, Irrigation and Waterways Department, West Bengal; Chairman Brahmaputra Flood Control Commission, Gauhati; Chairman, Ganga Flood Control Commission, Patna; Chairman, Central Water Commission; Member (WR), Central Water Commission

Convener Member (Floods) Central Water Commission.

Appointment

On the advice of the Planning Commission the Department of Irrigation, in the Ministry of Agriculture and Irrigation constituted Working Group on Flood Control vide Resolution No. 4/4/77-DW. II, dated October 15, 1977.

Terms of Reference

(i) "To make a critical review of the progress made in flood control, drainage and anti-sea erosion in terms of physical targets, viz., the areas provided with reasonable protection and financial tar-

---

1. New Delhi, Department of Irrigation, Ministry of Agriculture and Irrigation, 1978, 59 p.

gets under the Fifth Plan since 1973-74. Particular reference should be made to the problems and constraints faced in achieving the main objectives in physical and financial terms and deficiencies experienced in the implementation of the programme.

(ii) To suggest measures for collection of improved statistics of the areas vulnerable to floods and areas benefited.

(iii) To recommend the strategy, policies and the programme for this sector for the five-year period (1978-79 to 1982-83) with particular reference to the requirements in respect of organisational and administrative set up.

(iv) Measures for stabilisation of the existing benefits resulting from flood control and anti-sea erosion schemes and proper operation and maintenance of these works.

Contents

Introductory; Brief Review of the Flood Control Programme; Area Prone to Floods and Areas Protected; A Brief Review of the Programme and Areas Protected; A Brief Review of the Programme and Achievements in the Fifth Plan: [Term of Reference No. (i)]; Measures for Collection of Improved Statistics of Flood Damage and Area Benefited [Term of Reference No (ii)]; Strategy, Policies and Programme for the Five Year Period 1978-79 to 1982-83 [Terms of Reference Nos. (iii) & (iv)]; Summary of Conclusions and Recommendations; Annexures from I to VII.

Recommendations

Area Prone to Floods and Area Protected

Earlier, it was roughly estimated that an area of about 25 million ha is prone to floods. As a result of floods in the recent years, the area prone to floods is now estimated at about 34 million ha Up to the end of March 1978, an area of about 9.8 million ha has been given reasonable protection.

A Brief Review of the Programme and Achievements in the Fifth Plan Outlays and Expenditure

Against revised Fifth Plan outlay of Rs. 345 crores, the actual expenditure in four years of the Plan is Rs. 286 crores. Thus the financial target has been achieved.

Area Protected

Against a target of 1.8 million ha of area to be protected, the area protected during the four years of the Fifth Plan would be about 1.90 million ha.

Deficiencies Experienced

A number of important schemes take up in the Fourth Plan have not yet been completed. The spillover cost of the schemes taken up in the Fourth and Fifth Plans is of the order of Rs. 500 crores as on March 1978.

Although the Central Flood Control Board as well as Ministers' Committees and the Fifth Plan document have stressed the necessity of early measures for flood plain regulations, no progress has been made in this regard so far.

The Fifth Plan document had stressed the need for long range planning and preparation of Master Plans. No appreciable progress in this direction has been made so far.

No progress has been made in regular and scientific collection and analysis of hydrological and other data.

Funds made available for maintenance by the various States has been considerably inadequate.

Measures for Collection of Improved Statistics of Flood Damage and Area Benefited

Various Committees have brought out that the existing methods are neither scientific and rational nor reliable. Recommendations of Rashtriya Barh Ayog on measures for improved methods of collection of statistics should be awaited. In the meantime recommendations made in Para 5 should be implemented urgently.

Strategy, Policies and Programme for the Five Year Period 1978-79 to 1982-83

Strategy and Policies

Review and Expeditious Completion of On-going Schemes: All the on-going schemes should be reviewed in detail to determine which of the schemes are still considered technically necessary and economically justifiable at present day costs. Schemes satisfying both the above criteria should be got approved immediately. Such approved schemes should be completed during the five year period in a time bound programme. Funds for such schemes should be earmarked.

Inter-State Schemes: Matching and earmarked provision of funds as per agreed programme should be made in the annual plans of each state, so that inter-State schemes are completed in a time bound programme.

Stabilisation of Existing Benefits

State Governments should critically examine all the major existing works and put up proposals to stabilise existing benefits. Such schemes should also receive high priority. Drainage schemes should be reviewed on the basis of criteria circulated by Central Water Commission and the ISI.

Flood Forecasting

The work of flood forecasting should be extended to other Inter-State rivers and should be continued with added emphasis on modernisation of the systems.

Preparation of Master Plans

Special organisations entirely devoted to this work should be set up in flood affected states. These should prepare basin-wise plans in close co-ordination with irrigation and other departments. A specific amount should be earmarked for this work in each annual plan. The Centre should provide matching grants for this work. The outline of Master Plans should be finalised by each flood affected State by

March 1980. Detailed Master Plans should be finalised by March 1982 after examination by CWC/Ganga Flood Control Commission.

Flood Plain Regulation and Management

The conclusion reached by the United States as prescribed at the United Nations Water Conference in 1977 is "The United States and other urbanised countries are already putting the price of their failures to wisely manage the economic and urban development of their riverine and coastal flood plains. Others have the opportunity to benefit from the experience." The basic work of detailed surveys and preparation of contour maps should be carried out in the Central Sector. Thereafter, the State Governments should demarcate areas liable to floods of different frequencies and intensities both on maps as well as on the ground and enforce necessary land use regulations on the basis of the guidelines approved by the Central Flood Control Board in 1977.

Maintenance

It is absolutely necessary that proper norms and standards of maintenance are laid down by each State Government on the basis of the guidelines approved by the Central Flood Control Board. It should also be ensured that funds on the basis of these norms are made available.

Embankments

While embankments constructed so far have by and large given the desired protection to large areas at comparatively low costs, their consequent long-term effects on river regime are yet to be evaluated. Recommendations of Rashtriya Barh Ayog on this aspect should be awaited. Meanwhile approved embankment schemes under construction should be completed after carrying out the review as suggested earlier. New embankment schemes should be taken up with caution after carrying out detailed studies.

Anti-Erosion Works

These should normally be taken up for protection of towns and a group of thickly populated village abadis, railway lines and roads where re-location is not feasible on techno-economic ground and for protection of portions of embankments benefiting large areas where retirement is not feasible.

Storage Reservoirs

All storage reservoir projects in the catchments of flood prone rivers should be given priority for construction during next 5–7 years. All such projects planned for irrigation/power should be reviewed in detail to examine the possibility of providing specific flood storage. Operation schedules should be drawn up so as to provide flood moderation to the extent possible. Some of the on-going and proposed projects have been listed in the main report.

The Ganga Flood Control Commission and States of U.P. and Bihar should immediately carry out studies with regard to likely benefits of flood moderation by the proposed reservoir projects in Nepal.

Joint investigations should be taken up as early as possible for which a provision has been made in the Central Sector.

Anti-Sea-Erosion Works (Shore-Protection Works)

The Central Water Commission and Kerala should jointly carry out a review of the existing works to determine their effectiveness. Adequate maintenance funds should also be made available.

Evaluation of Flood Control and Drainage Works

It is necessary that a critical evaluation of all the major schemes already completed in each State/river basin should be carried out by the States and reports sent to the CWC/GFCC.

Soil Conservation and Afforestation

No major soil conservation measures have been taken up so far in the catchments of flood prone river basins. Experience in other countries indicated that while these measures do have beneficial effects on reduction of flood peaks of small floods on small catchments, these may not have any significant effect in the reduction of flood peaks in the large damage producing floods. However, these are essential in their own right for proper land management and to retain the top soil mantle. They also help in reduction of silt. In the case of soil conservation programme carried out so far in 30 river valley projects, their physical and economic benefits are yet to be evaluated in detail. The Department of Agriculture should take up the soil conservation programme in some of the flood prone areas under their overall programme. Atleast in a few river basins/sub-basins, treatment of critical areas should be done on a saturation scale. Soil conservation programme would be complimentary to the engineering programme of flood control and should taken up simultaneously. However, economic justification of this programme will have to come largely from other inherent benefits of such a programme.

Monitoring

Regular monitoring of all major schemes should be done by both the States as well as the Centre.

Recommendations of Rashtriya Barh Ayog

The Rashtriya Barh Ayog are examining the problem of floods and their control in depth and in all aspects. Their recommendations should be awaited for making any additional changes in the policy and programme and particularly regarding measures for collection of improved statistics of areas vulnerable to floods, areas benefited and requirements in respect of organisational and administrative set up.

Survey and Investigations

Specific funds should be earmarked in the State Plans for scientific collection and analysis of hydrological and other data. Special cells should be created for hydrological analysis is studies.

Programme for the Five Year Period 1978-79 to 1982-83

Outlays for 1978-79: An outlay of Rs. 126.71 crores has been approved by the Planning Commission.

Proposed Outlays for the Five Year Period: It is recommended that an outlay of about Rs. 1200 crores should be provided. Out of this, about Rs. 500 crores will be required for completing on-going schemes.

Central Participation

Although at present flood control is the responsibility of the State Government, taking into account the fact that the damage caused by the floods is also a national loss as well as to enable the States to implement massive programme to be undertaken in 5 years period, a provision of Rs. 215 crores may be made in the Central Sector for financing some selected Inter-State, international and some critical major schemes.

Even formulation of schemes in the best interest of a region would need Central Intervention and financial assistance which would act as a catalyst for bringing about agreement among the State with regard to planning, joint operation, etc.

Area to be Benefited

With an outlay of Rs. 1200 crores, an additional area of about 6m. ha is expected to be benefited. In addition, benefits in the existing protected area are expected to be stabilised, although exact figures are to be worked out.

Organization

It is considered advisable to await recommendations of Rashtriya Barh Ayog on this aspect. However, in order to carry out effectively the ambitious programme now proposed, immediate strengthening of the organisations in the States as well as in the Central Water Commission is necessary. Similarly, special organisations for collection and analysis of hydrological; and other data, preparation of Master Plans, monitoring and quality control should be immediately set up by the various State Governments.

RAILWAY ACCIDENT INVESTIGATION REPORT ON DERAILMENT OF NO. 107 DOWN 'MADRAS-RAMESWARAM PASSENGER' TRAIN BETWEEN PARAMAKKUDI AND PANDIKANMOI STATIONS ON THE MANAMADURAI-RAMESWARAM SINGLE METRE GAUGE SECTION OF SOUTHERN RAILWAY ABOUT 08.15 HOURS ON OCTOBER 17, 1977[1]

One Man Commission Shri K.N. Kamath, Former Additional Commissioner of Railway Safety

Appointment

The Commission was constituted under the Ministry of Tourism and Civil Aviation (Commission of Railway Safety) in accordance with Rule 4 of the Statutory Investigation into Railway Accidents Rules, 1973 vide Notification No. RS. 13-T(8)/71 dated April 19, 1973 on October 17, 1977.

Terms of Reference

To enquire into the Derailment of No. 107 Down 'Madras-Rameshwaram Passenger' Train between Paramakkudi and Pandikanmoi Stations on the Manamadurai-Rameswaram Single Metre Gauge Section of Southern Railway at about 08.15 hours on October 17, 1977.

Contents

Summary; Inspection and Inquiry; Relief Measures; Composition of

---

1. Delhi, Controller of Publications, 1979, 12 p.

Train and Damage; Local Features; Summary of Evidence; Observations and Tests; Discussion; Conclusion; Remarks and Recommendations.

Conclusions

(a) *Cause of the Accident*

On full consideration of the factual, material and circumstantial evidence, I have come to the conclusion that the derailment of No. 107 Dn. "Madras-Rameswaram Passenger" train on 17-10-1977 between Paramakkudi and Pandikanmoi stations on the Manamadurai-Rameswaram section of Southern Railway was a result of defects in the tender of the locomotive coupled with the effect of dynamic oscillations caused by variations in cross levels and the slack gauge of the track.

(b) *Responsibility*

For the defects in the tender of the track, no individual railway official can be held responsible. The responsiblity has to be borne by the maintenance staff for which the Railway Administration may assess the relative responsibility of individual officials taking into account their duties in regard to the maintenance of the locomotive or the track.

(c) *Relief Measures*

I am satisfied that the medical aid was prompt and the relief arrangements were satisfactory.

Recommendations

Although five coaches of the train had derailed, the casualties were all in the fifth coach which was a wooden body sleeper coach. The three coaches immediately behind the tender were of steel body and the fourth coach was a wooden body postal van. The serious damage to the fifth coach emphasizes the risk to the passengers travelling in wooden body coaches. Since it may not be possible to completely put out of use the existing wooden body coaches, their use on long distance Passenger trains on Main lines should be avoided. Their use may be restricted to short distance Passenger trains running a slow speeds.

The sleeper spacing of the shoulder sleepers at the joints near the site of derailment was excessive. Their spacing may be readjusted.

The Railway Board may consider expeditious action on the reference made by the Commissioner of Railway Safety vide his letter No. RS 25-T(22)/77 dated 6-5-1977 suggesting a thorough study to be made into the causes of derailment of YP locomotive tenders.

33

WORKING GROUP ON BLOCK LEVEL PLANNING, 1977 – REPORT[1]

Chairman Prof. M.L. Dantwala

Members Dr. A.N. Bose; Prof. Ranjit Gupta; Dr. Prodipto Roy; Shri R.N. Azad; Shri V. Venkatesan; Prof. V.M. Dandekar; Shri Ghulam Ghouse

Convenor Shri P.H. Vaishnav

Appointment

In pursuance of the decision to initiate block level planning in the country with a view to achieve full employment during the next ten years, the Planning Commission, Government of India constituted a Working Group on Block Level Planning vide No. PC(P) 9/28/WG/77 MLP dated November 5, 1977.

Terms of Reference

According to the Office Memorandum issued by the Planning Commission constituting the Working Group, the Group was to draw up "Detailed guidelines for block level planning". This being a broad statement, it was decided in the first meeting of the Working Group to seek further clarification from the Planning Commission as to the specific points on which the Working Group was expected to deliberate and give its report. The Working Group, therefore, met the Deputy Chairman and Members of the Planning Commission on 26-12-1977 and discussed the terms of reference. During this discussion, the following points emerged as relevant to the work of the Working Group:

---

1. Government of India Planning Commission, 1978

(i) Definition of the exact sphere of block level planning and the way in which it should be coordinated,
(ii) The method of selection of blocks,
(iii) The essential pre-requisites for block level planning,
(iv) The agency for preparing and implementing block level plans. In this context also, where and how voluntary agencies should be associated with block level planning and/or implementation,
(v) The question of how to integrate, particularly where there were more than one implementing agencies
(vi) The cost involved in preparing a Block Plan,
(vii) The relationship between the agency preparing the plan and the agency implementing it.

Contents

Introduction; Block Level Planning—Goals and Objectives; Block as a Planning Unit; Programme Content and Criterial for the Selection of the Block; Planning Machinery; The Planning Process at Block Level (Resource Inventory), Spatial Planning for Socio-Economic Infrastructures; Institutional Change and Organisation of the Poor; Employment Planning; Institutional Credit Support in Relation to Block Level Planning; Training; Summary of Recommendations.

Recommendations

Objectives of Block-level Planning

1. Though the objectives of national planning and the new Government's shift in emphasis towards agriculture and rural development are fairly well defined, we feel that it would be helpful if the same are clearly enunciated for the guidance of the planning authority at the block-level, for the purpose of formulating the plan as well as its implementation. The set of objectives will also serve as a frame of reference for monitoring the progress and assessing the performance. Since the statement of objectives is very brief, it is reproduced in full below:

1. Optimum utilisation of the growth potential of the area leading to increase in income and employment.

2. Ensuring that a larger than proportionate gains of development accrue to the weaker sections of the population—small and marginal farmers, share-croppers, agricultural labourers, rural artisans, etc.
3. Fulfilment of minimum needs programme—health an medical facilities, drinking water, housing, education and supply of essential commodities through a public distribution system.
4. Building up of social and economic infrastructure to achieve the above objectives.
5. Re-orienting the existing institutions/organisations in order to protect the interest of the poor.
6. Building up of appropriate organisations of the poor especially to protect them from exploitation.
7. Promotion of a progressively more egalitarian structure of ownership of assets.
8. Augmenting the duration and productivity of employment of the poor and the underemployed in their existing occupations *inter alia* through upgrading of technology, imparting of skills and setting up of non-exploitative institutions of credit, marketing and extension.
9. Alleviating chronic unemployment through employment on public works.

Choice of Block as a Unit of Planning

2. The appropriateness of the choice of a block as a planning unit has been questioned. In the Report, the Group has clarified that no rigidity is implied in the choice. First, it is conceded that programmes like those for tribal area or hilly regions and soil conservation and land reclamation will have to have a converge appropriate to the specificity of the operational requirements. On the other hand, for certain other types of programmes such as Minimum Needs and public distribution of essential commodities, establishment of graingolas, proximity with the people for whom the benefits are intended, will be helpful to the planning authority both for ascertaining the felt needs and for efficacious implementation. Even so, for the location of service centres, full use will be made of the knowledge and experience gained from the application of the Growth Centre theory.

3. The experience of Comprehensive Area Development Programme (CADP) in West Bengal, which operates at a sub-block

level also reinforces the case for selecting a small area for planning.

4. In any case, keeping a view the imperatives of vertical and horizontal linkages, the Group has recommended the placement of the planning team at the District headquarters. This will ensure integration of the block plans with the district plan. In fact, the preparation of block and district plans will be a part of the same exercise.

Selection of Blocks

5. The Working Group took note of the proposal of the Government of India (Ministry of Agriculture and Irrigation, Department of Rural Development) to introduce block-level planning in 3500 blocks in the next five years. However, in regard to intensive integrated development of the type visualised in our Report, the Group would recommend "hastening slowly". For one thing, the planning machinery in several States, particularly at the district level, is very weak, if not non-existent and a hasty adoption of the proposal may prove self-defeating.

6. The Group has also noted that in 2945 blocks (out of 5000) one or more of the special programmes (SFDA, DPAP, CAD), are already operating. In about 1500 blocks none of the above programmes is operating.

7. Keeping the above facts in view, the Group would like to recommend that beginning with 100 blocks in the current year, the number of additional blocks to be taken up for block level planning each year may be progressively increased, so as to reach a number of 500 (additional) in the terminal year of the Plan. Depending upon the assessment of the performance, the additional number in successive years may be increased or decreased.

8. In a communication to the State Governments, the Government of India (Ministry of Agriculture and Irrigation, Department of Rural Development) has indicated certain criteria for selecting additional 300 blocks per year for intensive development. These criteria are quite appropriate and we endorse them. However, if a fresh view is to be taken on the choice of blocks, a more systematic procedure will have to be adopted for determining priorities.

9. Since the major objective of block level planning is elimination of poverty and unemployment, the priority will have to be given to those districts/blocks in which the intensity of poverty and un-

employment is more acute. However, data on both these parameters are available only at the level of National Sample Survey Regions. We learn that an exercise has been undertaken in the Planning Commission, as a result of which "groups of regions" have been ranked in terms of the intensity of backwardness. We have suggested that the exercise should be carried further and a priority list of districts may be prepared in the Planning Commission through application of some of the other relevant criterial (including those mentioned in the Ministry's communication) for which data are available at the district level. We have recommended that the responsibility for the selection of blocks from among the priority districts should be left to the State Governments. We have also recommended that during the next two years, at least one block should be taken up for intensive development in every district in the country.

10. The Group also considers it essential that the components of all special programmes operating in the selected blocks should be merged in the block level plan recommended in the Report and funds allotted to special programmes should be placed at the disposal of the block level planning authority.

Planning Machinery

11. The Working Group has stressed the need to strengthen the planning capability at the district level.

It is recommended that the planning team at the district level—which will have the responsibility of preparing block plans—should consist of a core group consisting of: (i) Chief Planner with adequate experience and quality of leadership to provide the right type of orientation to block-level planning, and inculcate team spirit to be able to coordinate with other members of the team, (ii) Economist/Statistician (Project formulation and evaluation), (iii) Cartographer/Geographer, (iv) Agronomist, (v) Engineer (Irrigation/Civil), (vi) Credit Planning officer. In addition to the above core-staff, specialists may have to be engaged according to the needs of the area or the programme. For example, in a district where dairy farming is important, a dairy technologist may be needed. Therefore, it will be necessary to make adjustments in the composition of the planning team to suit the requirements of a particular situation and the need of the area to be covered.

12. The leader of the planning team, i.e., the Chief Planning Of-

ficer has to be a person with a fairly high status which should enable him to play his planning role effectively. In the district hierarchy he should be next to the Collector.

Panchayati Raj Institutions

13. Another issue which needs careful consideration pertains to the authority under whose immediate control, guidance and supervision the Planning Team should work. More specifically should that authority be the Panchayati Raj Institutions (Zila Parishad, for example) or the District level administrative authority. While the Working Group full endorses the philosophy of decentralisation in decision-making, for our immediate purpose there are two problems which need to be sorted out. First, in a large number of States Panchayati Raj Institutions are either non-existent or are in a moribund state. This reality has to be reckoned with in making any recommendation which is meant for immediate implementation. Secondly, there is a widespread feeling, which we share, that by and large the Panchayati Raj Institutions do not reflect the interests and needs of the weaker sections of the rural community. An extreme view is that they in a fact obstruct the flow of benefits to the weaker sections. Given the structure of ownership of land and other assets, in the rural (and urban) areas, powerful ideological commitment would be needed for implementing a plan deliberately biased in favour of the poor. We assume that such commitment does exist at the level of national leadership. We are, however, not sure in what measure it has percolated deep down to the district or block level. Therefore, all that we can say is that the decision in this regard should be taken after a proper appraisal of the genuinely representative character of the Panchayati Raj Institutions. We would hasten to add that we do not visualise block-level planning as a purely bureaucratic or expert dominated exercise and we have devoted an entire section in the Report to the importance of public participation both at the stage of plan preparation and that of its implementation. Incidentally, a Committee under the Chairmanship of Shri Asoka Mehta has been constituted to look into the working of the Panchayati Raj system to suggest measures to strengthen them *so as to enable a decentralised system* of planning and development to be effective (emphasis added). In view of this, were should like to refrain from taking a definitive stand on this issue.

Voluntary Agencies

14. An allied issue is that of the role of voluntary agencies. The Working Group shares the view that the country's social and economic problems are so vast and multifarious that the Government's administrative machinery alone cannot tackle them. The establishment of a self-reliant society implies progressive curtailment of people's dependence on the Government. From times immemorial voluntary agencies in our country have played a significant part in promoting people's welfare. Planning at any level, however, has a significant technical component—as we have pointed out, even in a sphere of minimum needs programme—and very few voluntary agencies have the requisite competence to provide the technical input needed for planning. We are aware of the existence of a few voluntary organisations which have developed—or can develop—technical competence to successfully plan and implement programmes in *specific sectors* of the economy. Yet, we think the responsibility for preparing an integrated area plan cannot be "handed over" to a voluntary agency, however, competent. This responsibility must be squarely borne by the Government. The planning team at the district level should consult and actively seek the assistance of the voluntary agencies in their area while preparing the plan and selectively entrust to them, the implementation of some sectoral plans in which they may have requisite expertise and experience. It can even be joint venture but the ultimate responsibility will be that of the planning team. In any case, the Planning Commission to whom we are submitting this Report should, in our view, desist from assigning the responsibility for the preparation of block level plans to a voluntary agency. The State Governments, if they wish, may entrust the task of preparing a certain number (2 to 3 in total) of block plans to a voluntary agency, whose *bona fide* and competence are well established, preferably in collaboration with the planning team.

Professional Institutes

15. We have mentioned before that planning has a significant technical content. There are in the country today a few professional institutes who have developed considerable competence in some specific aspects of planning—as is the case with some voluntary organisations. Even in their case, the Working Group holds the view

that as a general practice, it would not be appropriate to entrust the preparation of block plans to the professional institutes, for the same reasons as have been submitted in the previous section. In matters which require a high degree of technical competence and which is not likely to be available within the Government, their assistance may be sought. In fact, we believe that in several instances their assistance would be very valuable and the planning team should have the humility to seek it. The professional institutes on their part may advise the planning team about the type of service they are in a position to render. In brief, short of accepting the total responsibility for the preparation of the plan, the professional institutes can get actively associated with the planning exercise.

In the section on Training, we have recommended that the Planning Commission in consultation with State Governments may select a few professional institutes for imparting training in planning techniques and associated problems (e.g., resource inventory) to the planning personnel and also to volunteers and local leaders. It has been argued that for making such training realistic and gather teaching material from real life conditions, it may be necessary for the professional institutes to "soil their hands", so to say, with actual planning. If this is considered essential and the State Governments are agreeable, preparation of a couple of block plans may be entrusted to them.

Public Participation

16. The Group has emphasised the necessity and importance of public participation at all stages of planning. At the same time it has drawn attention to certain limitations in the process of such participation. I particular, it has pointed out that since the rural community is not homogenous, it would be necessary to make special endeavour to ensure the participation of the weaker sections in the planning process. Secondly, the public will have to be familiarised with the problem of financial and technical constraints of planning so that it may recognise the need to exercise restraint in presenting the manner restraint in presenting the planner with a catalogue of demands and get used to the inevitability of mutual adjustment.

The Planning Process and Resource Inventory

17. For the purpose of integration of the block and district level

plans with the overall State plan, the State Planning authority will have to hold a briefing session with the district/block level planning teams to given them a broad indication about (1) the total State Plan and its priorities, (2) the financial parameters within which to plan, and (3) the continuing schemes to which a part of the plan expenditure is committed.

18. Usually the planning exercise begins with the compilation of a resource inventory. We have suggested that this may be deferred till the planning team and the subject-matter specialists, through mutual consultations, know exactly what they want for the purpose of inventory and why. We have emphasised that the resource inventory should not be simply a catalogue of statistics. It should be more in the nature of a series of what we call Status Papers containing an analysis of past performance—the successes and failures, and the factors responsible for the same—identification of constraints—of natural endowments, technology, organisation and institutions—and developmental potential. Of particular importance would be a Status Paper on the position of the weaker sections, their needs and disabilities.

19. We have not recommended, for reason implicit in what is stated above, any specific model of proformae and schedules. Several such models are available to which attention has been drawn. The planning team is advised to adopt any one of them with suitable adjustments (with higher level assistance if necessary indicated by their specific situations).

Spatial Planning for Socio-Economic Infrastructure

20. Infrastructure planning is not merely useful for the production of goods and services but also for achieving equity in the distribution of such goods and services to all villages. It is a procedure of making the most rational locational decisions bringing together infrastructures of economic development with social services for integrated rural development. The final integrated area spatial plan will depict the re-organised spatial location of all sectoral infrastructures and demonstrate the economies which would result in : the total *movement* of men and materials; better *utilisation* of facilities; and lower *costs* of total infrastructure investment. Finally, infrastructure planning can be viewed dynamically as a basic prime mover in employment generation not only in agriculture and rural industries but also in the provision of basic needs.

Structural and Institutional Change

21. The Group attaches very great importance to the reform of the agrarian structure and institutional set-up especially for serving the needs of the rural poor and protecting their interest. It is convinced that in the absence of adequate structural and institutional support, the proposed step up in the allocation of financial resource for elimination of destitution and augmenting employment opportunities will not achieve the desired objectives.

22. The Working Group has drawn attention to the fact that absence of basic record of rights in land in many districts has proved a major obstacle in the implementation of land reforms, extension of irrigation facilities, supply of inputs and deployment of credit. It has, therefore, recommended that in those blocks where such record of rights in land does not exist, or is in arrear its preparation should receive a high priority in the block-level plan. It is equally necessary to radically reorient the existing institutions for provision of credit, marketing and supply of the needs of the rural poor, and also establish certain new types of institutions specifically for the poor. One such institution is Grain-goals to overcome what we have termed as "the subsistence constraints". We have described at some length the working of Graingolas established in some of the Comprehensive Area Development Projects in West Bengal. The 'lean period' or the off-season, when the stock of food with the poor gets exhausted, is the time when they get into the clutches of the moneylender and the trader. If some arrangement can be made to help them to tide over this critical period, emergence of destitution can be considerably reduced. If properly organised, the Granigoals can become an effective channel for public distribution of essential commodities at the village level.

23. The Group has also made some suggestions for improving the viability of rural industries, which would help augment the employment and income of the artisans.

Employment Planning

24. The Working Group has recommended that data on employment/unemployment at the block level should be built up, over a period of time, through a proper record of employment generated as a result of the employment augmenting programmes recom-

mended in the Chapter. This will give a more accurate information on the demand for work, its seasonality, responses of the unemployed/underemployed to different types of projects (investments), and the directions in which employment generating investment need to be augmented. Past experience shows that information recorded on the basis of subjective judgements of respondents to hypothetical queries about there need for additional work is not sufficiently reliable to serve as a basis for detailed planning.

25. A two-pronged strategy is needed for employment generation. First, since under-employment constitutes a large component of the total unemployed mandays (non-availability of work to those who are seeking and/or available for work), it is suggested that development projects and planned investment should be directed towards augmenting the duration of employment of the under-employed in their existing occupations. Measures which would help to achieve this objective are well-known : intensification (multiple cropping) and diversification (animal husbandry, horticulture, forestry) of agriculture and rehabilitation of rural industries. Secondly, there is a hard core of the wholly unemployed persons who possess neither assets nor skills to get assimilated in the main stream of economic activities. For them a massive programme of public works, somewhat on the lines of Maharashtra Employment Guarantee Scheme, would be an appropriate strategy of employment planning.

Institutional Credit

26. The Working Group has argued that institutional credit should be tapped to augment the scope and coverage of the development programme. A major obstacle in this is the lack of proper liaison between the development agencies and the institutional credit system. Recognising this lacuna, the Group has suggested that a credit planning officer should be included in the planning team for block level development. Other measures needed for improving the liaison have also been indicated.

27. Though during the last decade there has been a marked expansion, diversification and innovative approaches in the provision of credit to rural areas, a feeling persists that credit institutions are still hesitant and conservative in providing the necessary support to the rural economy. In this connection the Group has taken note of the Committees/Working Groups recently appointed by the Reserve Bank of India to suggest improvements in the structure, operations

and procedures of credit institutions and has expressed the hope that their recommendations would help to remove many of the deficiencies in the flow of credit to rural areas.

28. The Group has simultaneously stressed the need for positive action on the part of the State Government and their administrative agencies for the removal of obstacles in the flow of credit to rural borrowers. The major obstacle in this is lack of accurate and up-to-date record of rights and the delay in issuing occupancy certificates. The States Governments should also appreciate that a project for which credit is sought has to be bankable in the sense that it has to be capable of generating incremental incomes adequate enough to bear a reasonable rate of interest and the type of assistance which the credit institutions should provide to the development agencies have been spelt out. Attention is drawn to the fact that the bankability of several projects can be greatly improved through complementary public expenditure on infrastructure, such as link roads, storage facilities, electrification, etc. Projects designed exclusively for the benefit of the weaker section would need to be subsidised as is done under SFDA and other schemes. The State Governments should also display willingness to take stern action to curb the growing tendency of wilful default in repayment.

29. The guidelines for training focusses on the strategy of establishing in every district of India a small core district planning cell or unit which would work directly under the District Collector or Zilla Parishad but would enjoy some degree of autonomy. Two types of trainees and training programmes are envisaged: the officers recruited (or deputed) to the core staff of the district planning cell; and other senior officers of the district, non-officials and voluntary organisations concerned with block plans in the district. The period of training and type of course curriculum for the former will be for about 3 months and will be directed towards imparting skills in practical planning. In the case of the latter the period of training may be only for 2-3 weeks and will be in the nature of an orientation course in block planning. A third category of training which is only tangentially touched upon is the consciousness raising, motivation and organizational skills of target group of populations who will be beneficiaries of various projects and programmes.

WORKING GROUP ON EMPLOYMENT OF WOMEN, 1977 – REPORT[1]

Chairman Prof. Asok Mitra

Members Shri T.S. Sankaran; Shri K.D. Madan; Dr. K.C. Seal; Dr. R. Thamarjrakashi; Shri. I.C. Puri succeeded by Dr. Ram K. Vepa; Miss Shanti Chakraborty; Shri P.S. Krishnan; Smt. Padma Ramachandran; Smt. Nirmala Buch; Smt. Kalawati Tripathi succeeded by Smt. Kishori Devi; Smt. Devaki Jain; Dr. Sulabha Brahme; Dr. Nirmala Banerjee; Mrs. Sathi Nair succeeded by Sheela Bhide; Smt. Ela Bhatt; Smt. Tai-Bastikar; Dr. Raj Arole; Prof. Kanta Ahuja; Dr. Mrs. Veena Mazumdar

Convener Shri Ghulam Hussain

Appointment

In the context of the preparation of the next Five Year Plan, the Government of India, Planning Commission, Employment and Manpower Planning Division constituted the Working Group on Employment of Women vide its Office Memorandum No. EMP-23/32/75-MP(Vol.II) dated November 7, 1977.

Terms of Reference

(i) Examine ways to increase the employment (including part-time employment) of women in the organised and unorganised sectors both in rural and urban areas.

(ii) Identify groups of un-organised self-employed women and

---

1. New Delhi, Department of Social Welfare, Women's Welfare and Development Bureau, 1978, 89 p.

suggest what steps may be taken to strengthen their employment by resolving difficulties relating to marketing, availability of raw materials, etc., and eliminating middle-men wherever necessary and possible.

(iii) Study the possibility of initiating viable pilot projects groups of women for generation of economic activity.

(iv) Examine the possibility of organised/unorganised women labour into associations/unions on the lines of the Self-Employment Women's Association in Ahmedabad.

Contents

Preface; Introduction; Training and Employment Opportunities for Women; Financing of Programmes for Promotion of Women's Employment; Administration Structure; Promotion of Social Objectives; Central Responsibility in Promoting Women's Development Corporations in the State and for Training of Cadres; Collection and Analysis of Data relating to women; Annexures I and II.

Recommendations

1. The draft Sixth Five Year Plan has recorded that the "labour market as it is operating is not neutral as between men and women" and that there are sectoral imbalances in the opportunities available for women for regular employment, training and promotion. The Plan also emphasises the need for measures to expand employment opportunities for women and special programmes to prepare them for such expanded opportunities.

2. The draft Plan identifies four strategies for increasing employment for women. These are:

(a) Diversification and expansion of education and training opportunities for women;
(b) Manpower budgeting of the female labour force in all comprehensive area development plans and designing of appropriate programmes to offer a variety of training and work opportunities to women;
(c) Promotion of self-employment and small industry employment among women by ensuring a reasonable share of credit and other inputs for them; and

(d) A higher rate of investment in "women preferred" industries and occupations.

The Working Group wholly endorses the strategies at (a), (b) and (c) above and notes that these are in line with the approach suggested in the National Plan of Action for women as reproduced below:

(a) Increased participation of women in occupation where women can be more than or as 'productive' as men;
(b) Encourage participation of women in occupations where they can be as productive as men but where participation has been negligible; and
(c) Encourage participation in certain types of occupations where such increased participation will provide the impetus for change in women's status.

3. With regard to (d), the Working Group would like to caution that a policy of increasing investment in the so called "women preferred" industries is not an unmixed blessing. A perusal of the list of such industries given on the page 102 of the Draft Plan 1978-83 would show that the these industries include:

(a) activities which are generally unorganised and in which women are receiving low incomes/wages and the conditions of work are bad, such as domestic services, sanitation, gathering of fodder by exploitation of forests, etc., and so an expansion *per se* of these activities would mean trapping of more and more women into such physically exhausting jobs often at below subsistence level often under noxious environs.
(b) on the other hand, activities such as manufacturing of dairy products, canning and preservation of dairy products, canning and preservation of fruits and vegetables and rearing of silk worms, production of cocoons and raw silk, etc., the further promotion of which would be desirable.

4. The approach in respect of the "women preferred" industries should therefore be selective—ensuring additional investment only in industries belonging to category (b) above and further ensuring that the proportion of women to total employment in these industries also increases. In respect of the industries in category (a) above it should

however, be ensured that the current proportion of women to total employment in these activities does not decline from the present levels, while steady effort should proceed for the improvement of wages, working conditions and regulation of working hours.

5. The Working Group is of the view that the problem of women's employment is characterised by: (i) their inability, like other weaker sections, to reach for services and assistance programmes offered by Government and Semi-Government institutions, which spring from their basic weaknesses *vis-a-vis* the more powerful sections of society; (ii) a lack of awareness among these institutions about the need to promote employment of women; (iii) the tendency of economically powerful organisations to obtain financial and other assistance in the name of women but diver it to other areas of investment, once obtained; (iv) the fact that technological modernisation in several industries has not resulted in the protection and expansion of women's employment opportunities, nor has it resulted in the widening of skill training opportunities or upward mobility of women workers through better technological attainments.

6. The Working Group is of the view that social objectives of reduction of inequality, poverty and mass unemployment calls for particular caution in promoting entrepreneurial development among women and a greater emphasis on collective organisations of women to achieve these objectives.

7. In the light of the difficulties faced and the lack of interest of promotional organisations like credit institutions and other agencies, the Working Group is convinced that *without a deliberate policy and a specialised agency to identify, Promote and assist individual women and women's groups to develop necessary information and skills to undertake income generating activities, and to actively promote their support by the major supporting agencies, mere directives to the existing promotional agencies will not help.* One of the tasks of the specialised agencies that we recommend would be create better understanding and concern for women's economic and other needs among the various agencies created by Government for development and employment generation so that the gap that now separates the aid givers from the potential beneficiaries may be gradually reduced.

8. The impression has so long been that any programmes for development taken up would automatically benefit both men and women. Experience has revealed that this is not so and it is felt that *unless there is a special plan for women with specific earmarking of*

funds in sectoral plans women will not benefit. Funds that are earmarked for women's programmes should be non-divertible and utilisation should be monitored. In order to achieves this, it is essential for Government to accept the responsibility of creating adequate and properly trained machinery and cadres in each of these areas. *It is essential for Government to adopt a well defined policy for women's development, clearly stating the economic and social objectives so that it receives due and continuous attention and support, both of finance and personnel, and not reduced to marginality within the complex framework of development administration as in the past.*

9. Women's development in the directions set before the nation by the Fathers of the Constitution requires development of opportunities that would enable the large majority of women to participate in the decisions that affect their own lives and that of their family. Access to and control over the income generated by their own labour is the first step in this direction. However, a policy of promotion of women's employment has to go hand in hand with the broader social policy of strengthening women's participatory roles and their ability to exercise their rights with autonomy and dignity. Unless supportive services like creches/child care centres, lighter house work through access to processed food, etc., is ensured, the increased employability of women will only further increase the load on women and reduce them to mere beasts of burden.

10. We are firmly of the opinion that by increasing the employment of women and by a consequent increase in women's participation in decision-making a number of additional benefits will accrue:

(1) As women have a greater interest in limiting the number of children, this will indirectly promote the national objective of a small family norm.

(2) Studies have proved that where a woman earns her income it goes indirectly to improve the nutrition and health of her children, while this is not always so in the case of man's earnings.

(3) Actual equality between men and women which will result from making women economically independent will have a healthy impact on the psychology of children and make them accept both mother and father as equally useful individuals. Employment for women will therefore ensure a nation of children healthy both in mind and body.

11. Keeping in view these general observations, our recommendations are given below under the following heads:

(a) training and employment;
(b) financing of programmes for promotion of women's employment;
(c) administrative structure;
(d) promotion of social objectives;
(e) Central responsibility for promoting Women's Development Corporations in the States for training of cadres; and
(f) collection and analysis of data relating to women.

Training and Employment Opportunities for Women

12. Training and Employment opportunities for women are necessary—

(a) to increase their employability;
(b) to prevent their crowding into low paid, unskilled employment in limited occupations; and
(c) to promote upward mobility and improvement in the status of the women workers.

13. Existing training institutions, e.g., ITIs, Polytechnics, Agriculture and Veterinary Training Institutions and higher technical and professional institutions have no special focus on the training of women. The requirement of minimum educational qualification prescribed and lack of information regarding job prospects and facilities prevent women's access to much of the training offered by these institutes particularly in the trades hitherto considered unconventional for women.

14. The Working Group feels that with the exception of a few trades like,

1. Bricklayer (Refractory)
2. Millwright (Rolling Mills)
3. Rigger
4. Shipweight (Steel)
5. Pipe Fitting (Ship Building)
6. Boiler Attendant

7. Mechanic (Earth Moving Machinery)

and possibly one or two more, which may be considered as injurious to the health of women and therefore deleterious to the interests of the family and the nation, training of women in all other trades needs to be encouraged by positive measures. The Group, therefore, recommends:

(1) Reservation of a percentage of seats for women in all training institutes and in apprenticeship/in-service training and given by employers. Existing reservations for SC/ST, etc., should be woven into the reservation now suggested.

(2) In addition to training in productive skills, introduction of supervisory and entrepreneurial training in the shape of management and marketing skills.

(3) Provision of special incentives and facilities like stipends, hostels, etc., for women in these institutes.

(4) In order to assist women to reach the required minimum educational qualifications for admission to job-oriented middle and lower level technical institutions and arrangements for non-formal education at convenient house will have to be made for condensed course/special courses in required subjects. This will have to be a specific responsibility of the Education Department/Ministry in collaboration with the technical training institutes as well as general educational institutes.

(5) Special recognition in the shape of prizes, citations, etc., to institutions and employers who train women in excess of the reserved number or who produce the best results.

(6) Special recognition for employers who appreciably increase the employment of women (both in numbers and percentage) and impart literacy or non-formal education to women.

(7) Provision of incentives to employers who employ and train more women, particularly for higher supervisory and productive jobs by introducing them to process entailing higher levels of technology, by granting tax rebates (as in the case of labour intensive industries).

For the rural sector, such institutional arrangements will not be adequate. The Group, therefore, makes the following recommendations:

(8) The District Industries Centres entrusted with the programmes of rural industrialisations should be directed to develop special entrepreneurial training and promotional programmes for women.

For this purpose, the D.I.Cs. should have amongst the team of Managers at least one Manager (preferably a woman) to develop programmes for women and assist women entrepreneurs and supervisors and woman cooperatives. Similar emphasis and staff allocation should be made within other organisations like the Design and Technical Development Centres and Services Extension Centres of the Handicrafts Board, Small Industries Services Institutes, Weavers Service Centres and State Government Units at State and District levels.

(9) The training programmes for rural women may have to be provided by mobile training units sponsored by these agencies or other training institutes located nearby, after identifying suitable trades on the basis of local skills, viability, availability of market, plan investment, etc. Such institutions should be associated with the project for a period of time to provide needed assistance in follow-up training, supervision and monitoring. This will call for some orientation of the staff of the existing training institutions to make them responsible to local employment needs, so that new trades can be developed. To ensure continuity in training, rural women should be trained both as organisers and as instructors in locally viable trades.

(10) In view of the fact that the agricultural sector employs the largest number of rural women, it is necessity to ensure proper training facilities for them to improve their skills and demand a better wage as well as to improve their productive capacity. The existing agencies engaged in the training of farmers should be properly equipped to take care of the training needs of rural women in agricultural and allied sectors.

(11) Special incentives to corporation and marketing agencies in the shape of reservation of stalls in Government/Municipal Markets, working capital loans at low rates of interest, etc., may be given if they set up special shops/emporia or expand their present selling outlets so that atleast 25 per cent of their turn-over consists of products made by women. Wherever Government of Municipal Agencies buy goods or services, preference should be given, other things being equal, to goods and services provided by women's cooperatives, associations of workers and entrepreneurs.

(12) Give wide publicity to all these measures for promotion of training and development of employable skills among women through schools, employment exchanges, panchayats, women's associations, the mass media, etc.

Financing of Programmes for Promotion of Women's Employment

Policies for promotion of women's employment will remain merely pious wishes without specific allocation of funds. The Group recommends:

(13) (a) Every sectoral plan (including area plan) should have a special component plan for women and for this purpose Government should earmark a substantial share of their Funds in certain Ministries and departments. In the sectors of agriculture (including allied sectors), industries, education, health, labour and employment, and social welfare, atleast 25 per cent of plan allocation should be earmarked for development programmes for women. In the other sectors where the pattern of expenditure is not amenable to such allocation, the plan should contain specific targets for generating employment, training and other benefits. This should be made a condition for the acceptance of the sectoral plans of both Central and State Governments. A similar approach should be adopted as a condition for release of share capital and other funds to Central and other State public sector organisations.

(b) Such funds should be non-divertible and their satisfactory utilisation should be made a condition for further allocation of resources.

(c) Provision for additional Central assistance to the States should be made to assist and implement women programmes.

(14) Directives should be issued to all financing institutions including Commercial Banks to ensure that a reasonable share of their investment and promotional activities are directed towards women. They should also stipulated as a condition of their financial assistance to individual schemes and projects that a reasonable share of their benefits such as employment flowing from the schemes/projects should go to women.

(15) Several States have made substantial allocations for weaker sections of the population. Since the majority of working women belong to socially or economically weaker sections, funds out of these should be earmarked for women, belonging to these weaker sections. Availability of loan and other inputs provided under special schemes, e.g., Small and Marginal Farmers Development Agency (SMFDA), Drought Prone Areas Programmes, etc., should be directed towards these women as they are already engaged in such work.

(16) Women's projects particularly from the weaker sections

should not be required to give third party surety and should not be denied optimum funds necessary for the success of the project.

(17) Banks and other financial institutions should be requested to establish Women's Cells in the Head Office to look after the interests of women and undertake promotional programmes and programmes for research and development.

Administrative Structure

While the Group recognises that a strong and well informed women's movement articulated through non-official voluntary organisations, specially in the rural sector is necessary to secure a full consideration of the needs of the women and to ensure that dialogue and mutual monitoring that is essential to ensure a proper reciprocity and understanding between voluntary effort and governmental programmes, it feels that one of the major reasons for the neglect of women's problems is the absence of an administrative machinery responsible for identifying these problems and for ensuring effective action by various Government and non-Government agencies for their resolution. We have separately stated that the responsibility for the formation and implementation of the special component for women in every sectoral plan should be placed on each Department. It would still be necessary to have an agency to coordinate and liaise with the various agencies at all level and to act as an administrative catalyst.

The Group, therefore, recommends that:

(18) A compact Directorate for Women's Development be established in every State. This Directorate should have officers at the district to provide a direct channel for communication and promote organisation and mobilisation of women for development programmes.

(19) In every State and Union Territory, a Women's Development Corporation should be set up for promotion and strengthening of women's employment and development. The Group notes that such Corporations already exist in Andhra Pradesh and Maharashtra and is in active consideration in some other States. This Group would prefer the provisions of the Andhra Pradesh model. This Organisation will identify women entrepreneurs (individuals as well as Cooperatives, Associations, etc.), do feasibility and market studies, make credit available through banks, advance margin money, arrange for training and marketing through agencies, dealing with such mat-

ters, e.g., the ITIs, Polytechnics, Handicrafts and Handloom Boards, SISIs, KVIC, S.W.A. Board, etc. They should also perform a catalytic role in developing understanding and interest among other development agencies and assist in channelising their support to programmes/projects for expanding women's employment. They should also stimulate research, development and training in different areas for women's economic advancement. Above all they should help to promote organisations of women workers for economic activity and self-reliance. In order to give the necessary impact to women's development in the short-term as well as in the long-term it will be necessary for the Corporation to undertake commercial as well as promotional activities. Therefore, its capital structure from both the States as well as the Centre should consist of a share capital component for commercial activities and grant-in-aid for promotional activities. To ensure that the benefits of these schemes go to the more needy women, the corporation should direct its efforts essentially to the lower Socio-Economic Groups. (A Model constitution of the Corporation is being prepared and will be submitted separately.)

(20) To ensure effective integration between the Directorate and Women Development Corporation, it will be desirable if the Director for Women's Development is also concurrently the Chief Executive of the Development Corporation. This will also ensure that the staff of the Directorate and the Corporation will supplement each other at all levels so that an infrastructure can be established from the State level down atleast to the District level.

(21) The involvement and representation of different State Departments, financing and specialised agencies, and beneficiary groups on the Corporations/decision-making and advisory bodies at all levels should be ensured.

(22) In major developments departments at the State level, a senior officer should be made responsible to oversee and monitor the special programmes for women.

(23) For better enforcement of labour laws relating to women, specially the Equal Remuneration Act, the number of women labour Inspectors should be increased.

(24) At the Central level, there should be special cells to look after women's programmes in all Departments/Ministries. Such cells already exist/have decided upon in the Ministries/Departments of Social Welfare, Labour, Agriculture, Rural Development and In-

dustries. Such cells are specially needed in the Ministry/Department of Health and Family Welfare, Education, Finance (Banking), the Planning Commission, etc.

(25) The coordination of the activities of these different Central Government Ministries/Departments may rest with the women's Welfare and Development Bureau of the Social Welfare Department.

Promotion of Social Objectives

To fulfil the social and economic objectives mentioned in the preamble, the Group recommends:

(26) Promotion of organisations of women by the agencies mentioned earlier. In wage employment, this will mean strengthening women's participation in trade union activities; for the self-employed sector this could be pursued through the formation of cooperatives and associations on the lines of SEWA, in Gujarat. In this connection, the Group endorses the recommendations of promoting village level organisations for women made in the Report of the Working Group on Development of Village level Organisations of Rural Women of the Department of Rural Development.

(27) Promotion of services like health, education (including workers education and social education), child care, etc., to women workers in an integrated fashion.

(28) (a) Provision for comprehensive child care facilities, as has been mentioned in the production, is an essential condition for promoting women's employment, education and skill development both in urban and rural areas. Therefore, the Group strongly recommends that child care centres should be set up as part of the Minimum Needs Programmes throughout the country. Such Centres should be located within walking distance and could be attached to schools, health centres, mahila mandals and similar institutions. Present Statutory obligations requiring employers to provide creches/day care centres and maternity benefits for workers act as a disincentive to the increase of women's employment. It has also been observed that child care facilities where provided are often unutilised for various reasons. The Group, therefore, suggests that the present obligation on employers to provide these facilities may be replaced by a contribution of employers to a common fund, to be

operated at the State level for child care services. The contribution should be made per employee, men as well as women and should be compulsory for all employers including Government. This will bring child care service within the reach of all women including those in the rural sector and will not merely cater to women in the organised sector as at present. The Group recommends the highest priority for this provision which should be inaugurated in the International Year of the Child; (b) A similar found for maternity benefits may also be started.

(29) In the organised sector, the maximum age for entry or women in employment should be increased to 35 years.

(30) For women already in service, provision should be made to allow them to take leave for a period of a total of 5 years, either in instalments or in lump, to enable them to fulfil their family obligations and for their re-entry into service with the benefit of continuity of service. Active efforts should be made to promote this practice in the private sector.

(31) In order to prevent displacement of women labour through introduction of new technology in all sectors of the economy, it will be necessary to change the existing structure of fiscal law which at present tends to support capital intensive rather than labour intensive technology. It also tends to increase demand on scarce national resources like power. The Group, therefore, recommends that special studies be undertaken to examine the employment impact and relative relative cost efficiency of alternative choices in technology in both agricultural as well as the industrial sector.

(Two typical illustrations in this area are the replacement of labour particularly female labour by power in the textile industry and of hand weeding, predominantly a women's occupations by chemical weed killers in agriculture).

(32) The largest group of working women are wage labourers in the agricultural sector. They are substantially under-employed and under-paid. To improve their employment and increase their bargaining power to raise existing wages, it is necessary to provide alternative and additional employment through Rural Works Programmes and other economic activities throughout the year including the agricultural season. Priority may be given to areas where agriculture wages are the lowest. Selection of the works should be carefully planned to a contribute to overall development programmes. For this purpose the Group recommends provision of a matching grant from

the Centre to the States. These programmes need to be carefully monitored on a continuous and concurrent basis.

(33) Production of inexpensive pre-cooked and semi-processed food in the small and cottage sector should be encourage to generate more employment for women as well as to reduce the drudgery of household work, which will release women for more productive work.

Central Responsibility in Promoting Women's Development Corporations in the States and for Training of Cadres

(34) The Group recommends that the Central Government should assist the development of these Corporations by providing a part of the share capital and grant-in-aid.

(35) The Centre should also assist financially and otherwise training of cadres, both Government and non-Government, entrusted with developing special programmes for women.

(36) The Group feels that unless the Centre takes the initiative as it did in the early stages of the Community Development Movement and later, in family planning and nutrition, a nation-wide network may not grow within a short-time horizon which seems extremely desirable. It suggests a central provision of a modest amount of Rs. 15 crores for both the above purposes, to start with.

Collection and Analysis of Data Relating to Women

(37) There is a need to improve the coverage, flow and analysis of the quantitative and qualitative data on women's employment. Existing gaps in information especially in the unorganised sector should be filled up. All agencies taking up surveys and studies should be directed to collect data sex-wise whenever information relating to individuals is collected.

(38) The conceptual limitations which led to under-reporting of women's employment/work force particularly in the rural areas should be avoided in the next census through appropriate conceptual modifications.

(39) While the policy centre for employment may be located in the Women's Welfare and Development Bureau in the Department of Social Welfare in the Ministry of Education, Social Welfare and Culture, the statistical monitoring centre for coordinating purposes

with special emphasis on the measurement of changes in employment, wages, working conditions and amenities and enforcement of labour laws and conventions should be strengthened in the Ministry of Labour and the Manpower and Employment Planning Division of the Planning Commission should exercise the overall supervisory and coordinating role between the concerned Ministries.

(40) The Planning Commission should undertake continuous analysis of data relating to women, with a view to monitoring the impact of various policies and programmes on women.

ANNEXURE I

Suggestions made by Smt. Devaki Jain, Member, Working Group on Employment of Women

1. There should be representation given to women on the highest decision-making bodies concerned with economic development with special reference to employment; e.g., The Central Planning Commission, State Planning Boards, Financial Institutions such as IDBI, IFC, LIC and Development Boards such as NDDB, KVIC, Silk Board, etc., should have representation of women.
2. The linkage between State and the Central Planning Commission/Boards with the State and National Committees on Women and or Social Welfare Boards should be formally established by having joint Committees monitoring women's employment.
3. In the Ministry of Labour in the Standing Committee to be constituted for unorganised labour, a very strong set up of representatives should be included to develop organisations of female labour. Training programmes on this kind of organisation can be incorporated within the Ministry of Labour and additional funds should be given for the task. All large employers of women both in the centralised and decentralised sectors should be included in the activities undertaken by the Ministry of Labour on unorganised labour.

NARMADA WATER DISPUTES TRIBUNAL WITH ITS DECISION IN THE MATTER OF WATER REGARDING INTER-STATE RIVER NARMADA AND THE LOWER VALLEY THEREOF BETWEEN – REPORT[1]

1. The State of Gujarat
2. The State of Madhya Pradesh
3. The State of Maharashtra
4. The State of Rajasthan

Chairman Shri V. Ramaswami

Members Shri A.K. Sinha; Shri M.R.A. Ansari; Shri G.C. Mathur; Shri E. Venkatesam; Shri V.P. Gopalan Nambiar.

Appointment

On the 6th October, 1969, the Government of India constituted the Narmada Water Disputes Tribunal by Notification No. S.O. 4054 dated 6th October, 1969. Vacancies in the offices of Members of the Tribunal were filled by fresh appointments made by the Government of India vide Notification No. S.O. 1628 dated 2nd May, 1970 issued by the Government of India, Ministry of Irrigation and Power and Notification Nos. S.O. 620 (E) dated 23rd October, 1974 and S.O. 754(E) dated 7th November, 1977 issued by the Government of India, Ministry of Agriculture and Irrigation (Department of Irrigation).

On 6th October, 1969, the Government of India, Ministry of Irrigation and Power referred to the Tribunal for adjudication of the

---

1. Delhi, Controller of Publications, 1978.

water dispute regarding the inter-State river Narmada and the river valley thereof vide Reference No. 12/6/69-WD.

On 16th October, 1969, the Government of India, Ministry of Irrigation and Power, made another reference of certain issues, raised by the State of Rajasthan under Section 5(1) of the Inter-State Disputes Act, (Act 33), 1956 by their reference No. 10/1/69-WD.

On 24th November, 1969, Madhya Pradesh filed a demurrer before the Tribunal with regard to the action of the Government of India in issuing Notification No. S.O. 4054 dated 6th October, 1969 and making a reference of the complaints of Gujarat and Rajasthan to the Tribunal by their reference No. 12/6/69-WD dated 6th October, 1969 and 10/1/69-WD dated 16th October, 1969 were *ultra vires* of the Inter-State Water Disputes Act, 1956.

In CMP No. 13 of 1971, Maharashtra prayed that certain issues should be tried as preliminary issues. In CMP No. 12 of 1971, Madhya Pradesh made a prayer of a similar character. After hearing the Counsel for all the party States, the Tribunal decided by its Order dated 26th April, 1971 that issues 1(a), 1(b), 1(A), 2, 3 and 19 should be tried as preliminary issues of law.

The Tribunal heard the arguments of all the party States and also the Attorney General on behalf of the Union of India on these preliminary issues. On 23rd February, 1972, the Tribunal delivered its judgement holding in the main that the Notification of the Central Government No. 10/1/69-WD dated 16th October, 1969 referring the matter raised by Rajasthan by its complaint was *ultra vires* of the Inter-State Water Disputes Act, 1956. The Tribunal further held that the action of the Central Government constituting the Tribunal by its Notification No. S.O. 4054 dated 6th October, 1969 and making a reference of the water dispute raised by the complaint of Gujarat by Notification No. 12/6/69-WD dated 6th October, 1969 were not *ultra vires* of the 1956 Act and the Tribunal had jurisdiction to decide the dispute referred to it at the instance of Gujarat.

Against the judgement of the Tribunal on the preliminary issues dated 23rd February, 1972, Madhya Pradesh and Rajasthan appealed to the Supreme Court by special leave and also obtained a stay of the proceedings before the Tribunal to a limited extent. The Supreme Court directed that the proceedings before the Tribunal should be stayed but discovery, inspection and other miscellaneous proceedings before the Tribunal might go on. The Supreme Court also permitted the State of Rajasthan to participate in the interlocutory proceedings.

The Orders of the Supreme Court granting special leave to Rajasthan and Madhya Pradesh are dated 1st May, 1972 and 6th June, 1972.

Contents

Volume I – *Section A:* Constitution of the Tribunal–References made by the Central Government and subsequent proceedings; *Section B:* Trial of preliminary issues and judgement of the Tribunal dated 23rd February, 1972; *Section C:* Agreement of party States dated 12-7-1974 and subsequent proceedings; A Historical Review of the Dispute; Narmada River System; Hydrology–Discharge observations and Run-off; Determination of the cultivable commanded area of Gujarat and Madhya Pradesh; Water Requirements of Madhya Pradesh and Gujarat; Water Resources of Mahi and other rivers crossed by Navagam Canal in Gujarat; Law relating to Equitable Appointment of the Waters of Inter-State Rivers in India; Apportionment of Waters of the River Narmada; Tables; Statements; Annexures; Plates.

Volume II – Full Supply Level of Navagam Canal offtaking from Sardar Sarovar, and its bed gradient; Determination of the Height of Sardar Sarovar Dam; Geological and Seismological Aspects of Sardar Sarovar Dam Site; Height of Navagam Dam–Examination of the alternative proposals of Madhya Pradesh and Maharashtra; Distribution of Costs and Benefits; Downstream Benefits–Question of payment by Gujarat to Madhya Pradesh; Directions of Madhya Pradesh, Gujarat and Maharashtra as regards submergence, land acquisition and rehabilitation of displaced persons; Allocation of Cost of Sardar Sarovar Project; Directions regarding setting up of Machinery for implementing the decisions of the Tribunal; Order as to Costs and other incidental matters; Final Order and decision of the Narmada Water Disputes Tribunal; Annexures; Statements.

Volume III– *Appendices* – Decision of the Tribunal dated 26-4-1971 directing that some of the issues may be tried as preliminary issues of law; Decision of the Tribunal dated 23-2-1972 on preliminary issues of law; Order and Decision of the Tribunal dated 8-10-1974 in regard to modification/deletion of certain issues on the basis of the agreement dated 12-7-1974 amongst the Chief Ministers of Madhya Pradesh, Maharashtra and Rajasthan and the Adviser to the Governor of Gujarat; Agreement dated July 22, 1972, amongst the Chief Ministers of Madhya Pradesh, Gujarat, Maharashtra and Rajasthan; *Exhibit C-1:* Agreement dated 12-7-1974 amongst the Chief Ministers of Madhya Pradesh, Maharashtra and Rajasthan and the Adviser to the Governor of Gujarat; CMPs 234 and 261 of 1977 of the Union of India; CMP 180 of 1974 with Exhibit C-2 dated 21-11-1974–Note on Yield Series of Narmada River.

Volume IV – *Part I:* Brief Facts; Culturable Commanded Area of Gujarat; Culturable Commanded Area of Madhya Pradesh; *Part II:* Water requirements of Madhya Pradesh and Gujarat; Determination of water requirements of Madhya Pradesh; Water requirements of Gujarat; *Part III:* Apportionment of water of river Narmada; Law of equitable apportionment; Allocation of Narmada Water between Gujarat and Madhya Pradesh; Equitable apportionment of excess waters and sharing of distress in lean years amongst the Party States; *Part IV:* Full supply level of Navagam offtake From Sardar Sarovar; Height of the Navagam Dam; *Part V:* Distribution of costs and benefits; Directions to Madhya Pradesh, Gujarat and Maharashtra regarding submergence, land acquisition and rehabilitation of Displaced Persons; Directions regarding setting up of the machinery for implementing the decision of the Tribunal; Downstream Benefits–question of payment by Gujarat to Madhya Pradesh; Allocation of costs of Sardar Sarovar Project; Period of operation of the Order of Apportionment; Orders as to the costs and other incidental matters; *Part VI:* Final orders.

Volume V – *Plates :* Index map of Narmada Basin showing Political Division (Exhibit G. 1284); L-Section of Narmada River showing Major Projects (adapted from Plate XIII, Ex. MP-312, volume III); Map showing Commands of major projects and the sites of Hydel Projects in the Narmada Basin (Exhibit MP-1105); Map Showing Zones I to XI and Land Irrigability classification of command under FSL 300 Canal proposed by Gujarat (Exhibit G-1276).

Terms of Reference

1.1.3 *Reference by the Central Government dated 6th October, 1969*

On the same date, the Government made a reference of the water dispute to this Tribunal by their Reference No. 12/6/69-WD which states:

"In exercise of the powers conferred by sub-section (1) of Section 5 of the Inter-State Water Disputes Act, 1956 (33 of 1956), the Central Government hereby refers to the Narmada Water Disputes Tribunal for adjudication of the water dispute regarding the inter-State river, Narmada, and the river valley thereof, emerging from letter No. MIP-5565/C-10527-K dated the 6th July, 1968, from the Government of Gujarat."

1.1.4 *Reference of the Central Government dated 16th October, 1969*

On 16th October, 1969, the Government of India made another reference of certain issues raised by the State of Rajasthan under Section 5(1) of the 1956 Act by Reference No. 10/1/69-WD dated the 16th October, 1969, which states:

"Whereas by Notification of the Government of India in the Ministry of Irrigation and Power No. S.O. 4054 dated the 6th October, 1969, the Central Government has constituted the Narmada Water Disputes Tribunal for the adjudication of the water dispute regarding the inter-State river, Narmada, and the river valley thereof;

"And Whereas the water dispute regarding the inter-State river, Narmada, and the river valley thereof emerging from the Government of Gujarat's letter No. MIP-5565/C-10527-K dated the 6th July, 1968, has been referred to the said Tribunal;

"And Whereas certain matters connected with and relevant to the said water dispute have been raised by the Government of Rajasthan in their letter No. F. 9(1)Irrg/69 dated the 20th September, 1969;

"Now, Therefore, in exercise of the powers conferred by sub-section (1) of Section 5 of the Inter-State Water Disputes Act 1956 (33 of 1956), the Central Government hereby refers the said matters also to the said Tribunal for adjudication".

1.1.5 *Demurrer by Madhya Pradesh*

On 24th November, 1969, the State of Madhya Pradesh filed a Demurrer before the Tribunal that the action of the Government of India in constituting the Tribunal by Notification No. S.O. 4054 dated 6th October, 1969, and in making a reference of the complaints of

Gujarat and Rajasthan by their References No. 12/6/69-WD dated the 6th October, 1969, and No. 10/1/69-WD dated the 16th October, 1969, were *ultra vires* of the 1956 Act. The contention of Madhya Pradesh was that there was no "water dispute" within the meaning of Section 2(c) read with Section 3 of the 1956 Act and also that the Government of India had no material for forming the opinion that the water dispute could not be settled by negotiation within the meaning of Section 4 of the 1956 Act. It was alleged that Maheshwar, Harinphal and Jalsindhi projects were purely power projects and would not diminish the flow of water prejudicially affecting the interests of Gujarat or of its inhabitants. It was said that implementation of these projects would not reduce the irrigation potential to 12 lakh acres or less as alleged by Gujarat. Madhya Pradesh also objected that Gujarat had no right to construct the Navagam Dam above FRL 210. It was asserted that the claim of Gujarat to construct Navagam Dam at FRL 530 was beyond its competence as the construction of such a dam will sub-merge the territories of Maharashtra and Madhya Pradesh and three important projects of Madhya Pradesh at Jalsindhi, Harinphal and Maheshwar would be sub-merged. It was also contended that the State of Rajasthan not being a coriparian State had no legal right to set in motion the machinery of the Inter-State Water Disputes Act. It was claimed that Rajasthan not being a Basin State had no right to share the waters of the river Narmada. The problem had also not been discussed between Rajasthan and Madhya Pradesh and the conditions precedent laid down in Sections 3 and 5 of the Act have not been satisfied.

1.1.6 *Framing of Issues*

After the party State had filed their respective statements of case and their respective rejoinders to each other's statement, the Tribunal framed 24 issues in the first instance at their seventh meeting held on 28th January, 1971. The issues were amended on 26th April, 1971. The issues as finally settled were as follows: –

1. Is the action of Central Government constituting this Tribunal by the Notification No. S.O. 4054 dated 6-10-1969 or in making a reference of complaint of Gujarat by Notification No. 12/6/69-WD dated the 6-10-1969 under the Inter-State Water Disputes Act (Act No. 33 of 1956) *ultra vires* for the alleged reasons:

(a) that there was no "water dispute" within the meaning of Section 2(c) read with Section 3 of the Act; and/or

(b) that the Central Government had no material for forming the opinion that the water dispute "could not be settled by negotiations" within the meaning of Section 4 of the Act.

1 A. Has this Tribunal jurisdiction to entertain or decide the question as to whether the action of the Central Government in constituting this Tribunal under Notification No. S.O. 4054 dated 6-10-1969 and in referring the complaints of Gujarat and Rajasthan by Notifications No. 12/6/69-WD dated 6th October, 1969, and No. 10/1/69-WD dated 16th October, 1969, *ultra vires* of the Inter-State Water Disputes Act, 1956?

2. Is the Notification of the Central Government No. 10/1/69-WD dated 16-10-1969 in referring the complaint of Rajasthan to this Tribunal for adjudication under Section 5 of the Act *ultra vires* for the reasons:

(a) that the complaint of Rajasthan is not a matter connected with or relevant to the water dispute between Madhya Pradesh, Maharashtra and Gujarat already referred to the Tribunal by the Central Government by its previous Notification dated 6-10-1969; and

(b) that no part of the territory of Rajasthan is located within the Narmada basin or its valley?

3. Is the State of Rajasthan not entitled to any portion of the waters of the Narmada river on the ground that the State of Rajasthan is not a coriparian State or that no portion of its territory is situated in the basin of the river Narmada?

4. Has the State of Madhya Pradesh no right to execute and complete the projects for hydro-electric development at Maheshwar I and II, Harinphal and Jalsindhi? Do any or all these projects prejudicially affect the interests of the Gujarat State or its inhabitants?

5. In Maharashtra estopped and bound by the representation of the former Bombay State in its letter dated 16-1-1959 to CWPC dropping the investigation regarding the power project at Keli Dam site?

6. Is Gujarat entitled to construct:

(a) a high dam with FRL 530/MWL 540 or thereabouts or less FRL/MWL at Navagam across the Narmada river; and

(b) a canal with FSL 300 or thereabouts or less at its offtake adequate discharge carrying capacity from the Navagam Dam?

7. What is the utilisable quantum of waters of Narmada at Navagam dam site on the basis of 75 per cent or other dependability and how should this quantum be apportioned among the State of Gujarat, Maharashtra, Madhya Pradesh and Rajasthan?

(a) On what basis should the available waters be determined?

(b) How and on what basis should equitable apportionment of the available waters of Narmada be made between the different States? What should be the allocation of each State?

(c) Should diversion of waters outside the Narmada drainage basin be permitted? If so, to what extent and subject to what safeguards for the concerned States?

(d) Should any preference or priority be given to irrigation over production of power?

(e) Has any State any alternative means of satisfying its needs? If so, what is the effect?

(f) What are the 'existing uses' or appropriation of Narmada waters by each party State and to what extent should they be recognised and protected?

8. Is Rajasthan entitled to allocation of sufficient quantity of water to irrigate 7½ lakh acres or less of culturable command area with minimum intensity of 110 per cent or less through a direct canal from Navagam? If not, how much?

9. What directions, if any should be given for the equitable apportionment of the waters including excess waters of Narmada river and of its basin?

9A. What directions, if any are required to be given regarding the sharing of distress among the concerned States in the event of the waters of the Narmada falling short of the allocated quantum?

10. Is Gujarat entitled to any injunction restraining Madhya Pradesh from constructing the proposed dams at Jalsindhi, Harinphal and Maheshwar I and II?

11. Should a declaration be given that Maharashtra is not entitled to implement the Jalsindhi Agreement or join in the construc-

tion of the proposed dam at Jalsindhi?

12. Is Gujarat entitled to a declaration that it may use 23.49 million acre feet (inclusive of evaporation losses at Navagam Dam) or less of Narmada waters every year?

13. Should any directions be given:

(a) for-releases of adequate water by Madhya Pradesh below Narmada Sagar for the setting up and operation of Navagam Dam FRL 530/MWL 540 or thereabouts or less FRL/MWL;
(b) for specification of FRL and MWL of the storage at Navagam Dam and the FSL of Navagam canal so as not to prejudicially affect the interests of Madhya Pradesh, Maharashtra or the other concerned States;
(c) for releases by the State of Madhya Pradesh below Narmada Sagar for the benefits of the States of Gujarat and Maharashtra; and
(d) for the release by the State of Madhya Pradesh below Narmada Sagar for the benefits of the State of Rajasthan.

14. What machinery, if any, should be set up to make available and regulate the allocation of waters to the States concerned or otherwise to implement the decision of the Tribunal?

15. Should the apportionment of the waters of Narmada be made amongst the concerned States so as to be binding on them for all times or whether any and if so, what period should be fixed for which such apportionment shall remain binding?

16. What directions, if any, are required to be given for timely releases of the Narmada waters from the upstream reservoirs to meet effectively the requirements at and from Navagam on the basis of the allocation of waters made by the Tribunal?

17. Whether the costs and benefits of the Navagam project of Gujarat are required to be shared amongst the concerned States. If so, in what manner and on what terms and conditions? If not, whether Gujarat is liable to pay any, and if so, what compensation to Maharashtra and/or Madhya Pradesh for loss of power?

18. Whether the Navagam project is liable to pay any compensation to any upstream project or projects in consideration of receiving regulated releases of the Narmada waters therefrom? If so, how much and on what terms and conditions?

19(i) Whether the proposed execution of the Navagam project

with FRL 530 or thereabouts or less involving consequent submergence of a portion of the territories of Maharashtra and/or Madhya Pradesh can form the subject-matter of a "water dispute" within the meaning of Section 2(c) of the Inter-State Water Disputes Act (Act 33 of 1956).

19(ii) If the answer to 19(i) is in the affirmative, whether the Tribunal has jurisdiction:

(a) to give appropriate directions to Madhya Pradesh and/or Maharashtra to take steps by way of acquisition or otherwise for making the sub-merged land available to Gujarat in order to enable it to execute the Navagam project with FRL 530 or thereabouts or less;
(b) to give consequent directions to Gujarat on other party State regarding payment of compensation to Maharashtra and/or Madhya Pradesh and/or share in the beneficial uses of Navagam Dam; and
(c) for rehabilitation of displaced persons.

20. Whether Gujarat is entitled to the declarations and injunctions sought in sub-paragraphs (xi), (xii), (xiii), (xiv), (xv) and (xvi) of paragraph 87.1 of its Statement of the Case?

21. To what reliefs and directions, if any, are the parties entitled?

22. How are the costs of the present proceedings and costs incidental thereto to be apportioned among the party States?

Final Order and Decision of the Narmada Water Disputes Tribunal

In Chapters I to XIX of the Report, the chairman of the Tribunal, Shri V. Ramaswami and member Shri M.R.A. Ansari have expressed their opinion on all the important issues arising in this case. Shri A.K. Sinha, another member of the Tribunal, has expressed on certain issues a different opinion which is reproduced in Volume IV of this Report. In accordance with the majority opinion, the Tribunal gives the following Decision and makes the following order under Section 5(2) of the Inter-State Water Disputes Act, 1956 read with Section 5(4) of the same Act:

Final Order and Decision of the Tribunal

Clause I: Date of coming into operations of the order.

This order shall come into operation on the date of publication of the decisions of this Tribunal in the official Gazette under Section 6 of the Inter-State Water Disputes Act, 1956.

Clause II: Determination of the utilisable quantum of Narmada waters at Navagam Dam site.

The Tribunal hereby determines that the utilisable quantum of waters of the Narmada at Navagam Dam Site on the basis of 75 per cent dependability should be addressed at 28 Million Acre Feet. (34. 537.44 M. Cu.m.)

Clause III: Apportionment of the utilisable quantum of Narmada waters.

The Tribunal hereby orders that out of the utilisable quantum of Narmada waters.

(a) Madhya Pradesh is entitled to a share of 18.25 Million Acre Feet (MAF) (22, 511.01 M. Cu. m.);
(b) Gujarat is entitled to a share 9 Million Acre Feet (11, 101.32 M. Cu. m.);
(c) Rajasthan is entitled to a share of 0.5 Million Acre Feet (616.74 M. Cu. m.); and
(d) Maharashtra is entitled to a share of 0.25 Million Acre Feet (308.37 M. Cu. m.)

Clause IV: Order with regard to Excess Waters and Sharing of Distress.

(1) The utilisable flow of Narmada is excess of the 28 Million Acre Feet (MAF), (34, 537.44 M.Cu.m.) of utilisable flow in any water year, i.e., from 1st of July to 30th of June of next calendar year is apportioned in the following ratios of allocation, i.e., 73 for Madhya Pradesh 36 for Gujarat, 1 for Maharashtra and 2 for Rajasthan;

(2) In the event of the available utilisable waters for allocation in any water year i.e. from 1st of July to 30th of June of the next calendar year falling short of 28 Million Acre Feet (MAF) (34, 537.44 M. Cu.m.), the shortage should be shared between the various States in the ratio of 73 for Madhya Pradesh, 30 for Gujarat, 1 for Maharashtra and 2 for Rajasthan;

(3) The available utilisable waters in a water year will include the waters carried over from the previous water year as assessed on the 1st of July on the basis of stored waters available on that date;

(4) The available utilisable waters on any date will be inclusive of return flows and exclusive of losses due to evaporation of the various reservoir; and

(5) It may be mentioned that in many years there will be surplus water in the filling period after meeting the storage requirements and withdrawals during the period. This will flow down to sea. Only a portion of it will be utilisable for generating power at Sardar Sarovar river-bed power-house, and the rest will go waste without even generating power at the last river bed power-house, should be allowed to be utilised by the party States to the extent they can.

Gujarat is, therefore, directed that whenever water starts going waste to sea, without generating power, Gujarat shall inform the Narmada Control Authority (hereinafter referred to as the Authority), with copies to designated representatives of all the concerned States, and Gujarat shall also inform them when such flows cease. During the period of such flows the party States may utilise them as they like, and such utilisation by the party States will not count towards allotment of supplies to them but use of such water will not establish any presumptive right.

Clause V: Period of operation of the order of Appointment.

Our orders with regard to the equitable allocation in clauses III and IV are made subject to review at any time after a period of 45 years from the date of the orders of the Tribunal.

Clause VI: Full Supply Level of the Navagam Canal.

The Tribunal hereby determines that the Full Supply Level of

Navagam Canal offtaking from Sardar Sarovar should be fixed at 91.44 m (+300′) at its head regulator with a bed gradient of 1 in. 12,000 from head to 290 km (mile 180), that is, upto the offtake of Saurashtra branch. From that point to Rajasthan border the bed gradient should be 1 in 10,000. These bed gradients may be changed by Gujarat and Rajasthan by manual agreement.

Clause VII: Full Reservoir Level and Maximum Water Level of the Navagam Dam.

The Tribunal hereby determines that the height of the Navagam Dam should be fixed for Full Reservoir Level +138.66 m (+ 455′) and Maximum Water Level at + 140.21 m., (+460′).

Clause VIII: Sharing of Costs and Benefits.

(1) The Tribunal hereby determines that out of the net power produced at Navagam at canal head and river bed power houses on any day the share of Madhya Pradesh will be 57 per cent; Maharashtra's share will be 27 per cent and Gujarat's share will be 16 per cent.

(2) The Tribunal makes the following further orders:

(i) The power generated in the River Bed and Canal Power Houses at Navagam will be integrated in a common switchyard;

(ii) Madhya Pradesh and Maharashtra will be entitled to get 57 per cent and 27 per cent respectively of the power available at bus bar in the switchyard after allowing for station auxiliaries;

(iii) The entitlement of power and energy for any day can be utilised fully or partly by the concerned states or sold to another participating state under mutual agreement. It cannot, however, be carried forward except under a separate agreement or working arrangement entered into among the affected parties;

(iv) Gujarat will construct and maintain the transmission lines needed to supply the allotted quantum of power to Madhya Pradesh and Maharashtra upto Gujarat State border along an alignment as agreed to between the parties and if there is no agreement, along such alignment as may be decided by the Narmada Control Authority. The transmission lines beyond Gujarat State border shall be constructed and maintained by Madhya Pradesh and Maharashtra in their respective States;

(v) The power houses and appurtenant works including the machinery and all installations as well as the transmission lines in Gujarat State will be constructed maintained and operated by Gujarat State or an authority nominated by the State;

(vi) The authority in control of the Power Houses shall follow the directions of the Narmada Control Authority is so far as use of water is concerned;

(vii) The scheme of operation of the Power Houses including the power required and the load to be catered for to the different party States during different parts of the day shall be settled between the States at least one week before the commencement of every month and shall not be altered during the month except under agreement among the States or under emergencies;

(viii) The capital cost of the power portion of Navagam Complex shall comprise the following:

(a) Full cost of Unit-III electrical works and control works pertaining thereto upto and including the switchyard;

(b) Full cost of transmission lines in Gujarat State constructed for supplying power to Madhya Pradesh and Maharashtra;

(c) 56.1 per cent of the net cost of common facilities such as Dam and Appurtenant works, i.e., Unit I of Sardar Sarovar Project after allowing for credits if any; and

(d) 56.1 per cent of the credit given to Madhya Pradesh for the downstream benefits derived from Narmada Sagar Dam.

(ix) Madhya Pradesh and Maharashtra shall respectively pay to Gujarat 57 per cent and 27 per cent of the capital cost of the power portion of the Sardar Sarovar head-works worked out vide (ix) above. This amount shall be paid in annual instalment until the capital works are completed. Each instalment will be worked out on the basis of the budgeted figures of the concerned works at the commencement of each financial year and shall be set off and adjusted against actual figures at the end of the financial year;

(x) In addition to the payments vide (x) above. Madhya Pradesh and Maharashtra shall also pay to Gujarat 57 per cent and 27 per cent respectively of the operation and maintenance costs of the Sardar Sarovar Power Complex each year. These payments are also to be based on budgeted figures at the commencement of each financial year and adjusted against actual cost at the end of the year; and

(xi) Notwithstanding the directions contained hereinabove, the party States may, by mutual agreement, alter, amend or modify any of the directions in respect of sharing of power and payment for it.

Clause IX: Regulated Releases to be made by Madhya Pradesh for the requirement of Sardar Sarovar Project with regard to the quantum and pattern of regulated releases, the Tribunal makes the following order:

It has been agreed by the party states and decided by the Tribunal in its order dated 8th October, 1974, that the utilisable quantity of water of 75 per cent dependability in the Narmada at Sardar Sarovar Dam site should be assessed at 28 Million Acre Feet (MAF) (34, 537.44 M. Cu.m.). The actual inflow of 75 per cent dependability however, is only 33, 316.29 M.Cu.m. (27.01 MAF) and this is brought up utilisable quantity of 28 MAF (34.537.44 M.Cu.m.) by means of canyover in various reservoir allowing for evaporation losses and regeneration out of 28 MAF (34.537.44 M. Cu.m.), 11,101.32 M.Cu.m. (9 MAF) has to be provided for Gujarat and 0.5 MAF (616.74 M. Cu.m.) for Rajasthan at Sardar Sarovar Dam. The requirements at Sardar Sarovar have to be met by releases by Madhya Pradesh and by inflows from the intermediate catchment, surplus to the requirements of Madhya Pradesh below Narmadasagar and Maharashtra. The releases from Maheshwar work out to 11,015.86 M.Cu.m. (8.12 MAF) as in paragraph 11.9.1 of Chapter XI on Height of Sardar Sarovar Dam. Making uniform monthly releases the amount of water to be released by Madhya Pradesh per month would be 234.65 M. Cu.m. (0.677 MAF). The actual inflow in the river system, however, would very from year to year and therefore, the releases by Madhya Pradesh would also vary.

The inflow during the filling period, July to October, cannot be predicted at the beginning of the season. It is only in October that it would be fully known whether the particular year is a normal year or the extent to which it is a surplus or deficit year. Normally the releases by Madhya Pradesh during the filling period, therefore, would have to be more or less on the basis of the year yielding 28 MAF (34.537.44 M. Cu.m.) utilisable quantity. The month of July and early part of August are crucial for kharif sowing. It is important that during this period regulatory arrangements should ensure that due share of water is made available to all parties.

Having regard to the facts mentioned in the preceding two paragraphs, we order that detailed rules of regulation and water accounting shall be framed by Narmada Control Authority in accordance with the guidelines given below. These guidelines may, however, be altered, amended or modified by agreement between the States concerned.

(i) The 28 MAF (34.537.44 M. Cu.m.) utilisable supplies of 75 per cent dependability in a water year (1st July to 30th June next year) shall be shared by the party states as under:

Madhya Pradesh	–	18.25 MAF (22, 511.01 M.Cu.m.)
Gujarat	–	9.00 MAF (11,101.42 M.Cu.m.)
Rajasthan	–	0.50 MAF (616.74 M.Cu.m.)
Maharashtra	–	0.25 MAF (308.37 M.Cu.m.)
		28.00 MAF (34,537.44 M.Cu.m)

(ii) Surplus or deficit utilisable supplies in a water year shall be shared to the extent feasible by the party States in the same proportion as their allotted shares in (i) above;

(iii) The water available in the live storages of the various reservoirs on 30th June shall be reckoned as an inflow to be shared in the next water year;

(iv) the releases necessary to ensure Gujarat and Rajasthan's share of water in a water year shall be let down by Madhya Pradesh at a reasonably uniform rate, permiting only such variation as the Authority may direct or approve and keeping in view the directions for regulated releases;

(v) The Authority shall ensure by so directing the releases by Madhya Pradesh that there is at all times sufficient utilisable water in Sardar Sarovar to meet the requirements of the next ten days. For this purpose, Gujarat and Rajasthan would intimate their requirements of the 10 daily period well in advance;

(vi) Utilisation in a water year by each party State shall be figured out on the basis of actual daily discharge at canal head on every major and medium project. For minor works, it shall be on the basis of area irrigated under different crops the delta for each crop being approved by the Authority. For pumping schemes, drawing directly from the river its tributaries or reservoirs, whether for irrigation, domestic or industrial use, water drawn shall be reckoned on the basis of the rated capacity of pumps and the number of hours they run. For a cross check, the seasonwise and cropwise area irrigated by each pumping scheme shall also be recorded, and if the figures of water drawn as worked out by the two aforesaid methods differ the decision of the Authority as regards water drawn shall be final;

(vii) Withdrawals from Sardar Sarovar for Navagam Canal for Gujarat and Rajasthan shall be measured at the head of Navagam Canal. The supply to Rajasthan shall be measured at Gujarat-Rajasthan border. The loss in the canal in carrying the supply for Rajasthan shall be determined by the Authority after the canal has been constructed and shall reckon against the share of Rajasthan;

Water let down into the river from Sardar Sarovar through power house turbines shall be measured on the basis of power generated by it and that escaped through the spillway by measurement at the spillway;

Gujarat may let down water from Sardar Sarovar for its and such releases shall reckon against its share. Such releases for downstream use shall be made through the turbines and the power so generated shared between Madhya Pradesh, Maharashtra and Gujarat in the prescribed ratio. Water let down into the river from Sardar Sarovar except at the specific indent of Gujarat shall not reckon against the share of

Gujarat;

(viii) For major and medium projects, water account shall be kept by 10 daily period. The last 10 daily period of a month may have 11 days, 10 days in the month. For minor schemes water accounts shall be kept by crop seasons. Kharif (July to October), rabi (November to March) and hot weather (April to June). For pumping schemes and domestic and industrial uses it shall be monthly;

(ix) The water use by minor and pumping schemes in any ten daily period may provisionally be taken to be the same as in the corresponding period in the previous year on the basis of average use during the crop period. For final water account however, it will be determined as in (vi) above;

(x) Each state shall furnish to the Authority and make available to any party State desiring the same such data and information as the Authority may require and ask for;

(xi) The Authority shall arrange the review of the ten days releases made by Madhya Pradesh at least once a month and after as considered necessary for directing any change in the releases. It may designate a person for doing so;

(xii) The Authority shall direct final adjustment to be made in the following water year of the use in excess of the authorised use, if any by any State or States during the preceding water year by curtailing the share(s) of the State or States concerned which have used water in excess and make over the same to the State or the States which have received short supplies. Water supplies to Rajasthan on any day in excess of 10 per cent over and above its conduct shall reckon against use by Gujarat;

(xiii) The Authority shall furnish the annual water account for the water year to the Governments of the party States by the end of August to the next water year. Each State may make any observation on the account and/or point out corrections in it if any, within one month of its receipt. After making the necessary modifications, the Authority shall furnish to each party State the final annual water account for the water year by 31st October. The Authority shall cause the annual water account to be published each year.

Clause X: Payment to be made by Gujarat should credit to Madhya Pradesh for such regulated releases.

We further order that Gujarat should credit to Madhya Pradesh each year 17.03 per cent of the expenditure on account of Narmadasagar Dam in the financial year commencing from the year of taking up of the construction of Narmadasagar Dam. This will be initially credited on the basis of budget allotment to be adjusted at the end of the year on actual expenditure. The post construction expenditure on maintenance is not to be considered as cost of construction.

Clause XI: Directions Regarding Sub-mergence, Land Acquisition and Rehabilitation of displaced persons.

Sub-Clause I: Definitions.

1(1) "Land" The expression "land" shall have the same meaning as defined in the Land Acquisition Act, 1984 (hereinafter referred to as the Act) which states "the expression 'land' includes benefits to arise out of land, and things attached to the earth or permanently fastened to anything attached to the earth".

1(2) "Oustee" An 'oustee' shall mean any person who since at one year prior to the date of publication of the modification under Section 4 of the Act has been ordinarily residing or cultivating land or carrying on any trade, occupation or calling or working for gain in the area likely to be sub-merged permanently or temporarily.

1(3) "Family" (i) a family shall include husband wife and minor children and other persons dependent on the head of the family, e.g., widowed mother; (ii) Every major son will be treated as a separate family.

Sub-Clause II: Lands which are to be compulsorily acquired.

II(1). Madhya Pradesh and Maharashtra shall acquire for Sardar Sarovar Project under the provisions of the Land Acquisition Act, 1894, all lands of private ownership situated below the FRL + 138.68 m (455′) of Sardar Sarovar and all interests therein not belonging to the respective States. If on the basis aforesaid 75 per cent or more land of a contiguous holding of any person is required to be compulsorily acquired, such person shall have the opinion to compel compulsory acquisition of the entire contiguous holding;

II(2). Madhya Pradesh and Maharashtra shall also acquire for Sardar Sarovar Project under the provisions of the Land Acquisition Act, 1894, all buildings with their appurtenant land situate between FRL+138.68 m (445′) and MWL+141.21 m (460′) including backwater effect.

II(3). The backwater level at the highest flood level in Sardar Sarovar shall be worked out by the Central Water Commission in consultation with Madhya Pradesh and Gujarat.

Sub-Clause III: Liability of Gujarat to pay compensation for Land Acquisition and Rehabilitation, etc.

III(1). Gujarat shall pay to Madhya Pradesh and Maharashtra all costs including compensation, charges and expenses incurred by them for or in respect of lands required to be acquired as aforesaid;

III(2). Gujarat shall pay to Madhya Pradesh and Maharashtra and the Union of India compensation for the respective Government lands and structures on principles similar to those underlying the Land Acquisition Act, 1894. Where any dispute or difference arises between Gujarat, Madhya Pradesh and Maharashtra, and the Union of India with respect to the compensation payable as aforesaid any of the three States of Gujarat, Madhya Pradesh and Maharashtra and the Union of India may refer the matter in dispute to arbitration. The State of Gujarat on the one hand and the States of Madhya Pradesh, Maharashtra or the Union of India (as the case may be) on the other hand shall respectively nominate one Arbitrator each. In the event of disagreement between the Arbitrator such dispute or difference shall be a person appointed in that behalf by the Chief Justice of India from among persons who are, or have been judges of the Supreme Court. The decision of the Arbitrators or as the case may be, of the umpire shall be final and blinding on the parties and shall be given effect to be them.

III(3). Gujarat shall pay to Madhya Pradesh and Maharashtra land revenue in accordance with the respective Land Revenue Codes of Madhya Pradesh and Maharashtra in respect of all lands in their respective territories acquired for Gujarat or conveyed to it;

III(4). Gujarat shall pay to Madhya Pradesh and Maharashtra all costs, charges and expenses incurred by Madhya Pradesh and Maharashtra for the purpose of removal and reinstallation of any ancient or historical monuments, archaeological remains, religious place of worship or idols likely to be affected by sub-mergence under Sardar Sarovar and that in the event of such payment being made, no separate compensation as hereinbefore provided shall be required to be paid in respect of the same having been affected by the sub-mergence.

III(5). Gujarat shall pay to Madhya Pradesh and Maharashtra all costs, charges and expenses required to be incurred by them for rehabilitation of oustees and oustee families in their respective territories in accordance with the directions hereinafter contained; and

III(6). Gujarat shall pay to Madhya Pradesh and Maharashtra costs on account of establishment charges for land acquisition and rehabilitation and other departmental staff which Madhya Pradesh and Maharashtra may consider necessary for the purpose of such acquisition and rehabilitation.

Sub-Clause IV: Provision for Rehabilitation.

IV(1). According to the present estimates the number of oustee families would be 7366 spread over 173 villages in Madhya Pradesh 401 families spread over 27 villages in Maharashtra. Gujarat shall establish rehabilitation villages in Gujarat in the irrigation command of the Sardar Sarovar Project on the norms hereinafter mentioned for rehabilitation of the families who are willing to migrate to Gujarat. For oustee families who are unwilling to migrate to Gujarat, Gujarat shall pay to Madhya Pradesh and Maharashtra the cost charges and expenses for pective territories on the norms at hereinafter provided.

IV(2)(i). According to the present estimates the number of oustee families below RL 106.68 metres (RL 350′) would be 30 spread over 20 villages in Madhya Pradesh and 250 families spread over 20 villages in Maharashtra. Within six months of the publication of the decision of the Tribunal in the Official Gazette, Gujarat,

Madhya Pradesh and Maharashtra shall determine by mutual consultation the location of one or two rehabilitation villages in Gujarat to rehabilitate oustee from areas below RL 106.68 metres (RL+350′). Gujarat shall acquire necessary lands for the rehabilitation villages and make available the same within two years of the decision of the Tribunal. Within six months of the decision of the location of the rehabilitation villages in Gujarat, Madhya Pradesh and Maharashtra shall intimate to Gujarat the number of oustee families from areas below RL 106.68 metres (RL 350′) willing to migrate to Gujarat. For the remaining oustee families Madhya Pradesh and Maharashtra shall arrange to acquire lands for rehabilitation within the respective States.

IV(2)(ii). Madhya Pradesh and Maharashtra shall set up adequate establishments for land acquisition and rehabilitation of oustee families. Gujarat shall deposit within three months of the decision of the Tribunal Rupees ten lakhs each with Madhya Pradesh and Maharashtra in advance towards cost of establishment and rehabilitation in these states to be adjusted after actual costs are determined Madhya Pradesh and Maharashtra shall start land acquisition proceedings for areas below RL 106.68 metres (RL + 350′), within six months of the decision of a Tribunal and convey the lands to Gujarat for project purposes within three years of the decision of the Tribunal. Within 18 months of the decision of the Tribunal, Gujarat shall make an advance payment of Rs. 70 lakhs to Madhya Pradesh and Rs. 100 lakhs to Maharashtra towards the compensation of land, to be adjusted after actual costs are determined.

IV(2)(iii). Regarding the oustee families from areas above RL 106.68 metres (RL + 350′) Gujarat shall intimate to Madhya Pradesh and Maharashtra within six months of publication of the decision of the Tribunal in the official Gazette the number and general location of rehabilitation villages proposed to be established by Gujarat in accordance with the decision of the Tribunal. Within one year receipt of proposal of Gujarat, both Madhya Pradesh and Maharashtra shall intimate to Gujarat the number of oustee families willing to migrate to Gujarat. The three States by mutual consultation shall determine within two years of the decision of the Tribunal, the number and general location of rehabilitation villages required to be established by Gujarat in its own territory. Madhya Pradesh and Maharashtra shall intimate to Gujarat the number of such villages to be established in Madhya Pradesh Maharashtra and for which

Gujarat would be required to make payments to Madhya Pradesh and Maharashtra respectively.

IV(2)(iv). Gujarat shall acquire and make available a year in advance of the sub-mergence before each successive stage, irrigable lands and house sites for rehabilitations of the oustee families from Madhya Pradesh and Maharashtra who are willing to migrate to Gujarat. Gujarat shall in the first instance offer to rehabilitate the oustees in its own territory.

IV(3). Gujarat shall also provide the following grants and amenities to the oustees:

(a) Resettlement Grants (Rehabilitation Grant)—Gujarat shall pay per family a sum of Rs. 750 inclusive of transportation charges as resettlement grant;

(b) Grant-in-aid.

In addition, Gujarat shall pay per family grant-in-aid in the following scale:—

Where total compensations is received	Grant-in-aid
Above Rs. 2000	Nil
Between Rs. 2000 and Rs. 500	Rs. 500 less an amount equal to one third on the compensation in excess of Rs. 500
Less the Rs. 500	Rs. 500

(c) Civic amenities:–

(1) One primary school (3 rooms) for 100 families.
(2) One Panchayat Ghar for every 500 families.
(3) One Dispensary for every 500 families.
(4) One seed store for every 500 families.
(5) One Children's park for every 500 families.
(6) One village pond for every 500 families.
(7) Drinking water will with trough for every 50 families.
(8) Each colony should be linked to main road by roads of appropriate standard.
(9) One platform for every 50 families.
(10) Every oustee family shall be entitled to and allotted a house site, i.e., a plot of land measuring 18.29X27.43 m.

(60′ X90′) free of cost. In addition, a provision of 30 per cent additional area for roads, Government buildings, open space, etc., shall be made by Gujarat under civic amenities.

(ii) The State of Gujarat shall make the following provisions for rehabilitation in Madhya Pradesh and Maharashtra:—

	Rs.
(a) Resettlement	750 per family
(b) Grant-in-aid	500 per family
(c) Acquisition of land for resettlement of families affected @ 0.40 hectare (one acre) for 6 families.	1,500 per acre.
(d) Civic amenities:	
1. One primary school @ 100 families	30,000 each
2. One Community Hall-cum-Panchayat Bhavan @ 100 families	20,000 each
3. One Dispensary @ 500 families	25,000 each
4. One seed store @ 500 families	10,000 each
5. One Children's park @ 500 families	6,000 each
6. One well with trough @ 50 families	10,000 each
7. One pond @ 500 families	20,000 each
8. One tree platform @ 50 families	1,500 each
9. One religious place of worship @ 100 families	1,000 each
10. Construction of approach roads and links roads for Abadies 3 km. per every new Abadi	30,000 per km.
11. Electrical distribution lines and street lights 2 km. per 100 families	11,000 per km.
12. Social amenities for each municipal town going under sub-mergence, viz., water supply and sanitary arrangements layout, levelling of sets, etc.	5,00,000 each town

IV(4)(i). Gujarat is directed to provide for rehabilitation and civic amenities as per directions contained hereinabove in sub-clause IV(3) in its estimate for 13 Land compensation and rehabilitation.

IV(4)(ii). Notwithstanding the provisions hereinbefore contained, Gujarat shall not be liable to pay any compensation for the loss of public properties, facilities or amenities such as drinking water wells, primary school buildings, internal roads, village sites approach roads, dispensaries, Panchayat buildings, rural electrification, highway, bridges, telegraph lines, power lines, etc., if corresponding alternative properties, facilities or amenities are to be provided at the cost of the Sardar Sarovar Project. The party owning the facility shall have the opinion to accept compensation for utilities as existing or ask for their replacement or re-location at the cost of Gujarat.

IV(5). It is made clear that the monetary values in Clause IV(3)(e) are liable to be changed at the time of actual rehabilitation. Where any dispute or difference arises as regards the changed valuation, the matter shall be determined by Arbitration in the manner provided in Clause III(2) above the Gujarat's liability shall stand altered accordingly.

IV(6)(i). In the event of Gujarat being enable to resettle the oustees or the oustees being unwilling to occupy the area offered by Gujarat, Madhya Pradesh and Maharashtra shall make such provisions for rehabilitations civic amenities, etc., on the lines mentioned in Clauses IV(1) to (4) above. Gujarat shall, in that event be liable to pay all such expenses, costs, etc., arising out of or in connection with rehabilitation and provision of civic amenities for the oustees including the cost of all acquisition proceedings and payment of compensation, etc., as per the Land Acquisition Act, for the land allotted to oustees for cultivation and habitation.

IV(6)(ii). In no event shall any areas in Madhya Pradesh and Maharashtra be sub-merged under the Sardar Sarovar unless all payment of compensation, expenses and costs as aforesaid is made for acquisition of land and properties and arrangements are made for the rehabilitation of the oustees therefrom in accordance with these directions and intimated to the oustees.

IV(7). Allotment of Agriculture Land. Every displaced family from whom more than 25 per cent of its land holding is acquired shall be entitled to and be allotted irrigable land to the extent of land acquired from it subject to the extent of land acquired from it subject to the prescribed ceiling in the state concerned and a minimum of 2 hectares (5 acres) per family. This land shall be transferred to the oustee family if it agrees to take it. The price charged for it would be as mutually agreed between Gujarat and the concerned State of the price to be paid for the land a sum equal to 50 per cent of the compensation payable to the oustee family for the land acquired from it will be set off as an initial instalment of payment. The balance cost of the allotted land shall be recovered from the allottee in 20 yearly instalments free of interest. Where land is allotted in Madhya Pradesh or Maharashtra. Gujarat having paid for it vide clause IV (6)(i) supra, all recoveries for the allotted land shall be credited to Gujarat.

IV(8). Any dispute between the States in respect of clauses IV (1) to (7) of these directions shall be referred to and determined by arbitration in the manner provided in Clause III(2) of these directions.

Sub-Clause V: Programme for payment to be made by Gujarat to Madhya Pradesh and Maharashtra.

V(1). As soon as practicable after the publication of the decision of the Tribunal in the Official Gazette, Gujarat shall prepare and furnish to the other party States, a fresh estimate of sub-head 13 Land for the Sardar Sarovar Project as permitted by the Tribunal including in particular, costs of acquisition of lands in Madhya Pradesh and Maharashtra and of rehabilitation of oustee families in Madhya Pradesh and Maharashtra.

V(2)(i). As soon as practicable after the decision of the Tribunal in the Official Gazette and in any case before expiry of three months thereafter, both Madhya Pradesh and Maharashtra shall furnish to Gujarat three sets of Majmuli/Taluka maps of all talukas in their respective territories likely to be sub-merged wholly or partly under Sardar Sarovar. These maps shall indicate village boundaries within three months after the receipt of the Majmuli/Taluka maps Gujarat shall mark thereon the boundary of the area situated below the FRL as also that between FRL and MWL including backwater effect and shall return one respective set so marked to Madhya Pradesh and Maharashtra.

V(2)(ii). As soon as practicable after the receipt of one set of the Majmuli/Taluka maps marked as aforesaid and in any case within six months thereof the Governments of Madhya Pradesh and Maharashtra shall publish notifications under sub-Section (1) of Section 40 of the Act notifying that the lands in their respective territories situated below the FRL and building with their appurtenant lands between FRL and MWL, including backwater effect (to be specified in the notifications) are likely to be needed for the Sardar Sarovar Project.

V(2)(iii). As soon as practicable after publication of the Tribunal in the Official Gazette as hereinbefore referred to and in any case within one year thereof, Gujarat shall intimate to Madhya Pradesh and Maharashtra yearwise programme of construction of the dam.

V(2)(iv). Objections; if any received against the purposed acquisition of lands as notified under Section 4 of the Act shall be heard and disposed of and any reports to the State Government as contemplated by sub-section (2) of Section 5A of the Act shall be made with utmost expedition. The Governments of Madhya Pradesh and Maharashtra shall issue requisite notifications under Section 6 of the Act with utmost expedition and in any case before the expiry of three years from the dates of publication of the respective notifications under sub-section (1) of Section 4 of the Act.

V(2)(v). As soon as practicable, after receipt of the yearwise programme of construction of the Sardar Sarovar Dam from Gujarat both Madhya Pradesh and Maharashtra in consultation with Gujarat shall finalise their respective yearwise programme of completing the proceedings for compulsory acquisition of lands in their respective territories upto the stages of making awards under Section 11 of the Act and of-taking possession of the lands under Section 16 of the Act.

V(3)(i). Gujarat is required to pay to Madhya Pradesh and Maharashtra compensation for compulsory acquisition of lands market value of Governments lands to be conveyed to Gujarat and expenditure to be incurred in connection with the rehabilitation of oustees families to be rehabilitated in Madhya Pradesh and Maharashtra as hereinbefore provided. Madhya Pradesh and Maharashtra shall on or before 30th September of each year intimate to Gujarat the amount required to be paid by Gujarat to Madhya Pradesh and Maharashtra respectively having regard to (a) the extent of lands in Madhya Pradesh and Maharashtra in respect of which awards are likely to be made under Section 11 of the Act, (b) the extent of Government lands likely to be conveyed by Madhya Pradesh and Maharashtra to Gujarat during the next financial year, and (c) the expenditure likely to be incurred by Madhya Pradesh and Maharashtra shall also take into account the differences if any between the payments made by Gujarat in pursuance of this Clause for the current financial year and the amount actually payable during the said financial year.

V(3)(ii). On the basis of these estimates, Gujarat shall on or before the 31st May of the following financial year make payments to Madhya Pradesh and Maharashtra of the amounts estimated as provided in Clause V(3)(i) above.

V(3)(iii). Gujarat shall at each successive stage of sub-mergence intimate to Madhya Pradesh and Maharashtra the area coming under sub-mergence at least 18 months in advance. The inhabitants of the area coming under the respective stages of sub-mergence will be entitled to occupy or use their properties without being required to pay anything for such occupation and use till a date to be notified by the State concerned which date shall not be less than six months before sub-mergence. They must vacate the area by the notified date.

V(4)(i) On payment of the amounts to be paid each year by Gujarat as compensation for compulsory acquisition of lands as aforesaid Madhya Pradesh and Maharashtra shall as expeditiously as possible complete the acquisition and transfer such lands to Gujarat so as to vest the lands in Gujarat to be used only for the purposes of sub-mergence and subject to Clauses V(5) to (8) of these directions.

V(4)(ii) On payment of the market value of Government lands by Gujarat as hereinbefore provided Madhya Pradesh and Maharashtra and the Union of India shall convey such lands to Gujarat so as to vest in Gujarat to be used only for the purpose of sub-mergence and subject to Clauses V(5) to (8) of these directions.

V(5). Gujarat shall pay to Madhya Pradesh and Maharashtra the amount of land revenue payable every year for the lands coming under sub-mergence at the rates prevailing in Madhya Pradesh from times to time.

V(6). Notwithstanding vesting in Gujarat of the lands coming under sub-mergence, Madhya Pradesh and Maharashtra shall continue to enjoy all rights of Sovereignty intact over the sub-merged area in the respective States.

V(7). Madhya Pradesh and Maharashtra respectively shall be exclusively entitled to all rights of fishing, boating and water transportation over the part of lake over the sub-merged land within Madhya Pradesh and Maharashtra respectively provided, however, that such right is not exercised to the prejudice of any utilities of the Sardar Sarovar Project or cause hindrance in the legitimate performance of their duties by the project personnel.

V(8). All residual rights not specifically transferred to Gujarat in respect of the lands coming under sub-mergence shall continue to vest in the Government in whose territory they are situated.

V(9). In the event of the said lands not being used for the purpose of sub-mergence for which it is acquired the State of Gujarat shall re-transfer such land to Madhya Pradesh or Maharashtra as the case may be subject to the condition that Madhya Pradesh and Maharashtra refund to Gujarat the amount of compensation received from Gujarat in respect of such land.

V(10). In the event of any land acquired for rehabilitation of oustee families is not used for the purpose it shall be returned to the original owner on payment, where feasible or otherwise disposed of and due credit given to Gujarat.

V(11). All costs incurred by Gujarat on acquisition of land and rehabilitation of oustees in respect of Sardar Sarovar shall be charged to Sardar Sarovar Project estimate, Unit 1 – Dam and Appurtenant Works.

Sub-Clause VI: Nothing contained in clause XI shall prevent the alteration, amendment and modification of all or any of the foregoing Clauses by agreement between all the party States.

Clause XII: Allocation of cost of Sardar Sarovar Project between Irrigation and Power.

We determine that the cost of Unit 1 – Dam and Appurtenant Works should be apportioned between irrigation and power as follows:

Irrigation	43.9 per cent
Power	56.1 per cent.

Clause XIII: Allocation of Irrigation component of cost of Sardar Sarovar Project between Gujarat and Rajasthan.

(a) The irrigation component of the cost of Unit 1 of Sardar Sarovar Project (Dam and Appurtenant Works) should be shared by Gujarat and Rajasthan in the ratio of 10:1; and

(b) As regards Navagam Main Canal the actual cost should be shared by Gujarat and Rajasthan on cusec-mile basis in the first instance and on completion of the work the share cost shall be adjusted as indicated in chapter XVII. Rajasthan shall credit its share cost each year initially on the basis of budget allotment. This should then be adjusted at the end of the year to actual expenditure. The post construction expenditure on maintenance is not to be considered as cost of construction.

Should any difference arise between Rajasthan and Gujarat on figures of cost in respect of Navagam Main Canal for purposes of sharing the cost, the matter shall be referred to the Narmada Control Authority and on such a reference its decision shall be final and binding.

Clause XIV: Setting up of Machinery for Implementing the decision of the Tribunal.

We make the following orders with regard to setting up of machinery for implementing the decision of the Tribunal.

Sub-Clause 1: Constitution of the Authority:

1(1). An Inter-State administrative authority to be called Narmada Control Authority (hereinafter referred to as the 'Authority') shall be established for the purpose of securing compliance with and implementation of the decision and directions of the Narmada Water Disputes Tribunal (herein after referred to as the 'orders').

1(2). The Authority shall consist of seven high-ranking Engineer Members of whom one each shall be of the rank of Engineer-in-Chief, Chief Engineer or Additional Chief Engineer of the Irrigation Department appointed by the Government of each of the States of Madhya Pradesh, Gujarat, Maharashtra and Rajasthan and three other eminent Engineers of a rank not less than that of a Chief Engineer to be appointed by the Central Government in consultation with the party States. One of the three Independent Members shall be nominated by the Central Government, as the Chairman of the Authority with a deliberative vote at meetings where decisions are taken on any matter affecting the interest of more than one State and he will be incharge of the administrative work of the Authority. The Central or State Government , as the case, may be shall have the power to remove or suspend from the Authority any member who in its opinion is not suitable to continue as member.

1(3). Each Independent member shall be a full time member and be appointed for a term not exceeding five years. The members appointed by the State Governments shall be part-time members. The appointing authority for independent member or that for part-time member, as the case may be, shall determine the terms and conditions of appointment in each case. As far as possible, the first appointment of the seven members of the Authority shall be made within three months from the date of publication of the decision of the Tribunal in the Official Gazette.

1(4). Vacancies of Members;

On any vacancy occurring in the offices of the three independent Members the Central Government shall appoint a person to such vacant office, and on any vacancy occurring in the office of the four members other than the independent members, the State Government by whom the member whose office falls vacant was appointed shall appoint a person to the vacant office.

In case of illness or absence for any cause whatever of a Member the Central Government or State Government by whom he was appointed (as the case may be) may appoint a person as an Acting Member during such illness or absence and such acting member shall while so acting have all the powers and perform all the duties and be entitled to the indemnities of the member (vise sub-Clause 5) in whose stead he so acts, save and except that the next senior independent member appointed by the Central Government and not the Acting Member shall act as Chairman at business meetings of the authority in the event of illness or absence of the Chairman of the Authority.

Sub-Clause 2: Secretary of the Authority;

The Authority shall employ a Secretary who shall be an Engineer. He shall not be a Member of the Authority.

Sub-Clause 3: Quorum and Voting;

Five members shall be a quorum and the concurrence of the majority shall be necessary for the transaction of the business of the Authority except such business as the authority may from time to time prescribe as routine. The Authority shall not prescribe as routine any business in which the interests of any two of the states are likely to be in conflict. For the transaction of routine business three members shall be a quorum and in the absence of the Chairman of the Authority, the Chairman elected at the meeting shall have a deliberative vote and in the event of an equality of votes a casting vote also.

Subject as aferesaid the membes shall have equal powers.

Sub-Clause 4: Disposal of Business by the Authority:

4(i). Subject to the provisions of sub-Clause 4(2) below, the Authority may dispose of any matter before it either by circulation or by holding a meeting. However, it will be open to any member of the Authority to require that a matter shall not be disposed of by circulation but at a meeting.

4(2). On the following matters the Authority shall record its decision by a Resolution at a meeting in which the Chairman and all the members from the party States are present:

(i) Framing of Rules of Business;
(ii) Delegation of functions to a Member or Secretary or any official of the Authority;
(iii) Categorising any part of the business of the Authority as of a formal or routine nature; and
(iv) Any other matter which any of the four party States require that it shall be decided at a meeting where all the members from the party States are present.

4(3). Subject to the foregoing provisions, the Authority shall frame its own Rules for the conduct of its business.

4(4). The Authority shall cause proper minutes or records of all its proceedings to be kept as a permanent record.

Sub-Clause 5: Indemnity of Members;

No Member, officer or employee of the Authority shall be liable for loss, injury or damage resulting from (a) action taken by such member, officer or employee in good faith and without malice under the apparent authority of the orders, even though such action is later determined to be unauthorised or (b) the negligent or wrongful act of omission of any other person, employed by the Authority and serving under such member, officer or employee unless such member, officer or employee failed to exercise due care in the appointment of such other person of the supervision of his work.

Sub-Clause 6: Officers and Servants of the Authority;

The Authority may from time to time appoint or employ such and so many officers and servants as it thinks fit and remove or dismiss them, under the rules and regulations applicable to the appointment, removal and dismissal of the Central Government officers and servants. All such officers and servants shall as such be subject to the sole control of the Authority. The scales of pay and other service conditions shall be as applicable to Central Government employees.

Persons employed in the services of the four States may be appointed or employed by the Authority in such proportions as the Authority may deem fit. The Authority shall arrange with the State Governments to spare the services of the persons employed in the State Governments for whole-time employment with the Authority or for the performance of any work or services for the Authority. The Authority may also make direct recruitment of any personnel or obtain the same from the centre or other source as considered appropriate.

Sub-Clause 7: Administrative and Field Organisation costs;

All expenses of the Authority (including the salary and expenses of the independent members) shall be borne by the State Governments of Madhya Pradesh, Gujarat, Maharashtra and Rajasthan in equal shares. The expenses pertaining to a member representing a State shall be borne by the State concerned. The cost of maintaining, operating and controlling the gauging and other hydrological stations in each State and the telecommunication systems for communicating the date shall be borne by the State concerned. The costs of construction and maintenance of the storages, power installations, division works, head works and canal networks shall be borne wholly by the State Government in whose territory the works are located or shared in case the benefits are shared.

Sub-Clause 8: Powers, Functions and Duties of the Authority;

8(1). The role of the Authority will mainly comprise co-ordination and direction. Normally all bilateral matters should be dealt with mutually by the States concerned and referred to the Authority only if there is a dispute.

8(2). The Authority shall be charged with the power and shall be under a duty to do any or all things necessary sufficient and expedient for the implementation of the orders with respect to;

(i) The storage, apportionment, regulation and control of the Narmada waters;
(ii) Sharing of power benefits from Sardar Sarovar Project;
(iii) Regulated releases by Madhya Pradesh;
(iv) Acquisition by the concerned State for the Sardar Sarovar Project of lands and properties likely to be sub-merged under Sardar Sarovar;
(v) Compensation, rehabilitation and settlement of oustees; and
(vi) Sharing of costs.

8(3). In particular and without prejudice to the generality of the foregoing functions, the Authority shall perform *inter alia* the following functions:

(i) Madhya Pradesh or Gujarat as the case may be shall submit to the Authority the Sardar Sarovar Project Report, the Narmada Sagar Project Report, the Omkareshwar Project Report and the Maheshwar Project Report. The Authority shall point out to the States concerned the Central Water Commission and Planning Commission any features, of these projects which may conflict with the implementation of orders of the Tribunal. Any subsequent changes in the salient features or substantial increase in cost in respect of dams, power houses and canal head works shall be reported to the Authority for taking appropriate action in the matter;
(ii) The Authority shall decide the phasing and shall co-ordinate construction programmes of the Narmada Sagar and Sardar Sarovar Projects with a view to obtaining expeditiously optimum benefits during and after the completion of the construction of the projects, having due regard to the availability of funds;
(iii) The Authority shall obtain from the concerned States peri-

odical progress reports both as to works and expenditure, and shall on receipt of such reports review the progress of construction of different units of the projects and wherever necessary advise the State concerned on the steps to be taken to expedite the work. The States shall submit in respect of Projects in sub-clause 8(3)(i) completion reports to the Authority;

(iv) The Authority shall issue appropriate directions wherever necessary for timely and full compliance by the concerned States with the orders of the Tribunal in th , matter of acquisition for the making available to Gujarat lands and properties likely to be sub-merged under the Sardar Sarovar Project and in the matter of compensation and rehabilitation of oustees thereunder;

(v) The Authority shall cause to be established maintained and operated by the State Governments concerned or any one or more of them, such stream and other gauging stations, equipped with automatic reorders where necessary, discharge, slit and evaporation observation stations and measuring devices as may be necessary from time to time for securing the records required for carrying out the provisions of the orders. It deemed necessary the Authority may require the installation, maintenance and operation by the State concerned of measuring devices of approved type at the head of main canals as also at the offtake of the canal for Rajasthan for measuring amount of water diverted from Narmada river system;

(vi) Concurrent records shall be kept of the flow of the Narmada at all stations considered necessary by the Authority and the records correlated;

(vii) The Authority shall frame rules of regulation and water accounting as per guidelines given in chapter XV of this Report. It shall determine the share of water of each State for every ten-day period for purposes of regulation and water accounting;

(viii) The Authority shall ensure implementation of the orders of the Tribunal in respect of: (a) quantum and pattern of regulated releases by Madhya Pradesh; (b) payment for such regulated releases/sharing of cost;

(ix) The Authority shall collect from the State concerned data of the areas irrigated by Narmada waters in each season of power generated at each hydro-electric power station at and downstream of Narmadasagar of withdrawals for domestic, municipal and industrial or any other purposes and of waters going down the river from Sardar Sarovar Project;

(x) The Authority shall determine the volume of water flowing in the river Narmada and its tributaries in a water year (1st July to 30th June next year);

(xi) The Authority shall determine from time to time the volume of water stored by each State in reservoirs and other storages and may for that purpose adopt any device or method;

(xii) The Authority shall determine at appropriate periodic intervals the use of Narmada waters made by the States, or such of them as necessary, at any place or in any area at any time and for that purpose it may take note of all diversions of obstructions, whether natural or artificial or partly natural and partly artificial from the river Narmada and its tributaries and measure such use by any method as it deems fit;

(xiii) The Authority or any of its duly authorised representative shall have power to enter upon any land and property upon which any project or development of any project, or any work of gauging, evaporation or other hydrological station or measuring device has been or is being constructed operated or maintained by any State for the use of Narmada water. Each State through its appropriate departments shall render all co-operation and assistance to the Authority and its authorised representatives in this behalf;

(xiv) The Authority shall meet as often as necessary and decide on a proper management of waters including in particular the manner and details of withdrawals of water from the storages on the Narmada river system in accordance with the orders. In particular, the Authority shall meet at the end of filling season and review the availability of water in the storages on the Narmada river system and decide upon the pattern of their regulation for the next irrigation season taking into account the carryover storages;

(xv) The Authority shall give directions for a phased programme of construction for generation and transmission of power in fulfilment of the shares of power allocated to the three States of Madhya Pradesh, Maharashtra and Gujarat from Sardar Sarovar and for payments therefore in accordance with the orders of the Tribunal. The Authority shall also ensure that generation and transmission of power from Sardar Sarovar complex are in accordance with the orders; and

(xvi) The Authority shall issue appropriate directions for the establishment maintenance and operation of an effective system of flood forecasting and flood control, including reporting of heavy precipitation, and telecommunication systems. The safety of a structure shall primarily to the responsibility of the chief engineer incharge of the structure and no decision or order shall be binding on him if in his opinion the safety of the structure will be endangered thereby. The Authority shall publish annually and make available to party States the data regarding operation of reservoirs during floods.

8.(4). In the light of its experience, the Authority may modify or add to the functions enumerated hereinabove in sub-clauses 8(3)(i) to (xvi) by a resolution.

8(5). All the concerned States shall submit to the Authority all the relevant information called for by the Authority in connection with the Narmada Valley Development expeditiously and within reasonable time.

Sub-Clause 9: Annual Report of the Authority;

The Authority shall prepare and transmit to each of the four States as early as possible and in any case before the end of the Current Water Year (1st July to 30th June) on Annual Report Covering the activities of the Authority for the proceeding year and to make available to each State on its request any information within its possession any time and always provide access to its record to the States and their representatives.

Sub-Clause 10: Records of the Authority and their Location;

The Authority shall keep a record of all meetings and proceedings, maintain regular accounts and have a suitable office where documents, records accounts and gauging data shall be kept open for inspection by the four States or their representatives at such times and under such regulations as the Authority may determine.

The location of the Central regional and sub-regional offices of the Narmada Control Authority shall be determined by the

Authority.

The headquarters of the Authority shall be at New Delhi till such time as it decides on its permanent location.

Sub-Clause 11: Contracts and Agreement;

The Authority shall enter into such contracts and agreements as may be necessary and essential for the full and proper performance of the functions and duties conferred or imposed on it.

Sub-Clause 12: Financial Provisions;

(1) All the capital and revenue expenditure required to be incurred by the Authority shall be borne by the four states of Madhya Pradesh, Gujarat, Maharashtra and Rajasthan equally. The Governments of the four States shall provide the necessary funds to the Authority to meet all capital and revenue expenditure required to be incurred by the Authority for the discharge of its functions.

(2) On the Constitution of the Authority each of the Governments of the four States shall contribute Rs. 5,00,000 (Rupees five lakhs) to the fund of the Authority in the first instance.

(3) The Authority shall in the month of September of each year prepare detailed estimate of the amounts of money required during the twelve months from the first day of April of the ensuing year, showing the manner in which it is proposed to expend such money. The Authority shall on or before the 15th of October forward a copy of such detailed estimate to the concerned Chief Engineers of the four States and indicate the amounts required to be contributed by each State for the ensuing financial year. Each of the State Governments shall pay to the Authority its contribution as indicated by the Authority on a before the 30th day of April of the ensuing year.

(4) The Authority shall maintain detailed and accurate accounts of all receipts and disbursements and shall after the close of each financial year prepare on Annual Statement of Accounts and send copies thereof to the Accountants General as well as the concerned Chief Engineers of the four States. The form of the Annual Statement of Accounts shall be such as may be prescribed by rules. The Accounts maintained by the

Authority shall be open for inspection at all reasonable times by the four States through their duty authorised representative or representatives.

(5) Disbursement shall be made from the fund of the Authority only in such manner as may be prescribed by the Authority. The Authority may incur such expenditure as it may think fit to meet any emergency in the discharge of its functions.

(6) The accounts maintained by the Authority shall be audited by the Comptroller and Auditor General of India or his nominee, who shall certify subject to such observations as he may wish to make on the annual accounts of the Authority. The Authority shall forward to the Accountants General and the concerned. Chief Engineers of the four States copies of the Report of the Comptroller and Auditor General of India and shall include the same in its Annual Report.

Sub-Clause 13: Decision of the Authority;

The decisions of the Authority on all matters and covered under clause 8 shall be final and binding on the four party States. However, there shall be a Review Committee which may *suo moto* or on the application of any party State review any decision of the Authority.

Sub-Clause 14: Review Committee;

14(1). The Review Committee shall consist of five members including a Chairman as under:

(i) Union Minister for Irrigation as the – Chairman
(ii) Chief Minister of Madhya Pradesh – Member
(iii) Chief Minister of Gujarat – Member
(iv) Chief Minister of Maharashtra – Member
(v) Chief Minister of Rajasthan – Member

The Secretary of the Union Ministry of Agriculture and Irrigation, Department of Irrigation shall be the convener of the Review Committee but shall not have any voting right.

In case there is a Presidents rule in any of the States the Governor of that state or his authorised representative will act as Member of the Review Committee.

14(2). The Chief Ministers of the four States may nominate the respective Irrigation Ministers either generally or specially as the alternate Member with full powers of voting taking decisions, etc.

14(3). The Review Committee may review the decision of the Authority at a meeting or which the Chairman and all the members of the Review Committee are present.

14(4). Advance notice of the proposed meeting of the Review Committee, its agenda and agenda notes will be forwarded by the convener to the party States.

14(5). The decision of the Review Committee shall be recorded in writing and shall be final and binding on all the States.

Sub-Clause 15: Construction outside jurisdiction of the Authority;

The construction of the works and the planning of the Projects will be carried out by each State through its own agencies and in the manner such State deems proper without any interference by the Authority or the other States, save and except to the extent as prescribed in the orders of the Tribunal.

Sub-Clause 16: Nothing contained in this order shall prevent the alternation, amendment or modification of all or any of the foregoing clauses by agreement between all the States concerned.

Sub-Clause 17: In CMP 234 of 1977 and CMP 201 of 1977.

The Union of India has consented to participate in the machinery to be established by the order of the Tribunal, if so directed and to do its bcst to implement the decision of the Tribunal.

In terms of these CMPs, we direct the Union of India to participate in the machinery set up by the order of the Tribunal to implement the directions of the Tribunal specifically under Clauses 1(2), 4, 12(6), 13, 14 and generally to implement all the other directions so far as the Union of India is concerned.

Clause XV: Order as to costs of Proceedings;

The States of Gujarat, Madhya Pradesh, Maharashtra and Rajasthan shall bear their own costs of appearing before the Tribunal. The expenses of the Tribunal shall be borne and paid by the aforesaid four States in equal shares.

Final Orders

In the view I have taken, I pass the final orders as follows:

Clause I: Date of coming into operation of the order

The orders hereunder passed shall come into operation on and from the date of publication of the Report and decision of the Tribunal in the Official Gazette of India under Section 6 of the Inter-State Water Disputes Act, 1956.

Clause II: Apportionment of the utilisable quantum of waters of Narmada River

It is determined that the utilisable quantum of waters of the Narmada at Navagam Dam site on the basis of 75 per cent dependability, is assessed at 28.00 million acre feet (MAF).

Clause III: Apportionment of the utilisable quantum of waters of Narmada River

It is hereby declared that out of the said 28.00 MAF or utilisable quantum of waters,

(a) Madhya Pradesh is entitled to a share of 17.25 million acre feet;
(b) Gujarat is entitled to a share of 10.00 million acre feet;
(c) Rajasthan in entitled to a share of 0.50 million acre feet; and
(d) Maharashtra is entitled to a share of 0.25 million acre feet.

Clause IV: With regard to excess waters and sharing of distress

(i) The utilisable flow of Narmada in excess of 28.00 million acre feet in any water year, i.e., from 1st July to 30th June of next calendar year, is apportioned in the following ratio: –

Madhya Pradesh	69
Gujarat	40
Maharashtra	1

Rajasthan	2

(ii) In the event of available utilisable waters for allocation in any water year from 1st of July to 30th of June next calendar year falling short of 28 million acre feet, the shortage shall be shared between the concerned State in the ratio as under:

Madhya Pradesh	69
Gujarat	40
Maharashtra	1
Rajasthan	2

(iii) to (v)

Orders under these clauses shall be the same as contained in sub-clauses (iii) to (v) of Clause IV of Chapter XX (Vol. II) of the Report.

Clause V: Period of Operation of the Order of Apportionment

My orders with regard to equitable apportionment as contained in Clauses III and IV above and all matters incidental thereto and/or connected therewith shall be subject to reconsideration at any time on the expiry of a period of 45 years from the date of coming into operation of this order.

Clause VI: Full Supply Level of the Canal

The full supply level of the canal off-taking from Sardar Sarovar is fixed at +300 with a bed gradient of 1 in 12,000 from head to mile 180, i.e., upto the off-take of Saurashtra Branch. From that point to Rajasthan Border, the bed gradient shall be 1 in 10,000. These bed gradients may be altered by Gujarat and Rajasthan by mutual agreement.

Clause VII: Full Reservoir Level and Maximum Water Level of the Navagam Dam

It is hereby determined that the height of the Navagam Dam shall be fixed to suit full reservoir level +458 and maximum water level at +463.

Clause VIII: Sharing of Costs and Benefits

(a) It is hereby determined that out of the net power produced in Navagam at canal head and river bed power houses on any day, the share of the respective parties shall be as under:

Madhya Pradesh	57.5%	of power produced at Sardar Sarovar
Maharashtra	27.7%	
Gujarat	14.8%	

(b) Further following orders are passed as under:

(i) The power generated in the river bed and canal power houses at Navagam shall be integrated in a common switchyard;

(ii) Madhya Pradesh and Maharashtra shall be entitled to get 57.5 per cent and 27.7 per cent respectively of the power available at Bus Bar in the switchyard;

(iii) to (viii) and (ix) (a) to (d)
Orders under these sub-clauses shall be the same as contained in sub-clauses (iii) to (viii) and (ix)(a) to (ix) (d) of Clause VIII of Chapter XX (Vol. II) of the Report;

(x) Madhya Pradesh and Maharashtra shall respectively pay to Gujarat 57.5 per cent and 27.7 per cent of the capital costs of the power portion of the Navagam head works, as worked out under sub-clause (ix) above. This amount shall be paid in annual instalments unit the capital works are completed. Each instalment will be worked out on the basis of the budgeted figures of the concerned works at the commencement of each financial year and shall be set off and adjusted against actual figures at the end of the financial year; and

(xi) In addition to the demands mentioned in sub-clause (x) above, Madhya Pradesh and Maharashtra shall also pay to Gujarat 57.5 per cent and 27.7 per cent respectively of the operation and maintenance costs of the Navagam power complex each year. These payments are also to be based on budgeted figures at the commencement of each financial year and shall be adjusted against actual costs at the end of the year.

Clause IX: Regulated releases to be made in Madhya Pradesh for the requirement of Sardar Sarovar Project

By agreement between the concerned party States, the utilisable quantum of water on 75 per cent dependability in the Narmada at Sardar Sarovar Dam Site, has been assessed at 28.00 million acre feet and this has been accepted by the Order of the Tribunal dated 8th October, 1974. The actual in-flow of 75 per cent dependability, however, is 27.01 million acre feet, which has been brought up to utilisable quantity of 28.00 million acre feet, by means of carry-over in various reservoirs allowing for evaporation losses and regeneration. Out of this 28.00 million acre feet of water, 10.00 million acre feet has to be provided for Gujarat and 0.5 million acre feet for Rajasthan at Sardar Sarovar Dam Site. Thus the requirements at Sardar Sarovar will have to be met by releases from Narmada Sagar and by inflows from the intermediate catchments, surplus to the requirements of Madhya Pradesh below Narmada Sagar. If there is any variation of the actual inflow in the river system the releases from Maheshwar shall vary to that extent suitably.

The water available in the live storage of various reservoirs on 30th June, shall be reckoned as an inflow to be shared in the next water year. The releases to be made by Madhya Pradesh for Sardar Sarovar in a year of 75 per cent dependability on the basis of the height of the dam, namely, FRL 458 for allocation of 10.00 MAF to Gujarat works out to 8.936 MAF.

I direct that Madhya Pradesh should make yearly releases of 8,936 MAF with such modifications in any year as Narmada Control. Authority may direct in consideration of the actual inflow available during the year. The releases necessary to ensure Gujarat and Rajasthan's share of water in a water year shall be made by Madhya Pradesh at a reasonably uniform rate permitting only such variation as the Narmada Control Authority may direct or approve. The regulation shall be by ten-day periods.

The total inflow into the river system during each ten-day period shall be computed by aggregating the inflow into the reservoirs of major and medium projects and one third of the use by minor and pumping schemes during the corresponding month in the previous year.

The rest of the orders in Clause IX shall remain the same as contained in the corresponding Clause IX of Chapter XX (Vol. II) of the Report.

Clause X: Payments to be made by Gujarat, to Madhya Pradesh for regulated releases

Gujarat shall credit to Madhya Pradesh each year 21 per cent of the expenditure on account of Narmadasagar Project from the financial year commencing from the year of taking up of the construction of Narmadasagar Project. This will be initially credited on the basis of budget allotments to be adjusted at the end of the year on actual expenditure. The post-construction expenditure on maintenance is not to be considered as cost of construction.

Clause XI: Directions regarding Sub-mergence of land, Acquisition and Rehabilitation of Displaced Persons

The Orders and Directions under this clause shall be the same as contained in the corresponding Clause XI of Chapter XX (Vol. II) of the Report.

Clause XII: Allocation of Costs of Navagam Project between irrigation and power

It is determined that the cost on Unit I – Dam and appurtenant works, shall be apportioned between Irrigation and Power as Follows:

Irrigation	44.6 per cent
Power	55.4 per cent

Clause XIII: Allocation of Irrigation component of costs on Navagam Project between Gujarat and Rajasthan

(a) The irrigation component of costs of Unit I of Sardar Sarovar Dam and appurtenant works shall be shared by Gujarat and Rajasthan in the ratio of their share of water 10:05 or 20:1. In other words 1/21 of the cost has to be borne by Rajasthan.

(b) Orders in sub-clause (b) of Clause XIII shall be the same as contained in the corresponding sub-clause (b) of Clause XIII of

Chapter XX (Vol. II) of the Report.

Clause XIV: Setting up of Machinery for implementing the decision of the Tribunal

The Order for setting up machinery for implementing the decision of the Tribunal shall be the same as contained in the corresponding Clause XIV of Chapter XX (Vol. II) of the Report.

It is further ordered that notwithstanding anything contained in any of the provisions of the directions and orders as contained in Clause XIV – Part A above, all the concerned party States shall be at liberty to modify or make suitable changes thereof, if necessary in future, only by mutual agreement between all the party States, namely, Madhya Pradesh, Gujarat, Maharashtra and Rajasthan for carrying out and implementing or giving effect to the orders and directions herein made.

Clause XIV: Part B – Directions regarding Rules or Regulations and Water Accounting

Detailed Rules and Regulations and water accounting shall be framed by the Narmada Control Authority – hereinafter called, 'the Authority'. For framing these Rules and Regulations, the following terms shall be closely observed: –

(i) The 28.00 million acre feet (MAF) of utilisable supplies of 75 per cent dependability in a water year (1st July to 30th June next year) shall be shared by the party States as under:

Madhya Pradesh	17.25 MAF
Gujarat	10.00 MAF
Rajasthan	0.50 MAF
Maharashtra	0.25 MAF
	28.00 MAF

(ii) Surplus or deficit utilisable supplies in a water year shall be shared to the extent feasible by the party States in the same proportion to their allotted shared in sub-clause (i) above.

(iii) to (xiii) The rest of the orders or directions under these sub-clauses, shall be the same as contained in the corresponding sub-clauses (iii) to (xiii) of Clause XIV, Part-B of Chapter XX (Vol. II) of the Report.

Clause XV: Orders as to the Cost of the Proceedings

The States of Gujarat, Madhya Pradesh, Maharashtra and Rajasthan shall bear their own costs of proceedings before the Tribunal. The costs and expenditure of the Tribunal shall be borne and paid by the aforesaid four States in equal shares.

New Delhi A.K. Sinha
August 16, 1978 Member

RAILWAY ACCIDENT INVESTIGATION REPORT ON THE COLLISION OF NO. 385 DOWN BHUSAVAL-NAGPUR PASSENGER TRAIN WITH COUPLED LIGHT ENGINES OF NO. D-30 UP GOODS TRAIN ON THE DOWN MAIN LINE OF AKOLA STATION ON THE BHUSAVAL-BADNERA DOUBLE LINE BROAD GAUGE SECTION OF CENTRAL RAILWAY AT ABOUT 22.15 HOURS ON NOVEMBER 9, 1977[1]

One Man Commission Shri P.M.N. Murthy

Appointment

The Commission was constituted under Ministry of Tourism and Civil Aviation (Commission of Railway Safety) in accordance with Rule 4 of the Statutory Investigation into Railway Accidents Rules, 1973 Vide Notification No. RS.13-T(8)/71 dated April 19, 1973 on November 9, 1977.

Terms of Reference

To enquire into the collision of No. 385 Down Bhusaval-Nagpur Passenger train with coupled Light Engines of No. D-30 Up Goods Train on the Down Main Line of Akola Station on the Bhusaval-Badnera Double Line Broad Gauge Section of Central Railway at about 22.15 hours on November 9, 1977.

----

1. Delhi, Controller of Publications, 1981, 21 p.

Contents

Summary; Inspection and Inquiry; Relief Measures; The Trains; Local Features; Summary of Evidence; Observations and Tests; Discussion; Conclusions; Remarks and Recommendations; Annexures; Railway Board's Comments on Various Paras of the Report.

Conclusions

42. On full consideration of the available evidence I have reached the following conclusions:

(a) *Cause of the accident*—The collision of No. 385 Down Passenger train with the coupled light engines of No. D-30 Up Goods train on the Down main line of Akola station on the Bhusaval-Badnera Double Line Broad Gauge Section of Central Railway at about 22.15 hours on 9th November 1977, was the result of the Passenger train being driven past the Reception Signals—at least the Home Signal if not both the Outer and Home—of Akola station at danger.

(b) *Responsibility*—(i) The primary responsibility for the accident lies on Shri C.L. Arora, Driver of the Passenger train. He contravened the provisions of General Rules 76 and 122 and Subsidiary Rule 76-2(b), extracted in Annexure IV.

(ii) The Firemen of the train—S/Shri Baban Vithoba and Tukaram Govind who according to their own deposition, were both on the look-out for signals while approaching Akola must share some responsibility for the accident. Their inadequate vigilance is revealed by the events that followed. They contravened the provisions of General Rule 122 (reproduced in Annexure IV).

(A brief bio-data of these officials is at Annexure V).

43. *Relief Measures*—(a) Apropos Section II of the Report, the relief measures were prompt and adequate.

(b) The action of Dr. Jatkar, Railway Assistant Divisional Medical Officer, Bhusaval in putting himself out on medical relief regardless of his own injury (sustained in the accident), is praise-worthy and in the right tradition of public service. The Railway Administration may suitably convey their appreciation to Dr. Jatkar.

(c) Appreciation is also due to the Management of the District Civil Hospital at Akola, whose Doctors promptly responded to the call and reached the site within half an hour of the occurrence.

Recommendations

44. This accident is yet another instance of human failure, where even with 3 persons on the foot-plate one or both Reception Signals were passed at Danger. The Research, Designs and Standards Organisation may be directed to include this case in their study of Drivers disregarding signals, expedite the identification of attendant factors and evolve corrective measures to mitigate such failures—[Refer Railway Board's O.M. No. 73/Safety (A&R)/1/18, dated June, 5, 1974 in connection with the statutory inquiry report on the collision accident at Burhanpur station, Central Railway on 12th December 1973.]

45. Adverting to paras 18, 19, 20 and 37(c) of the Report, the need to ensure meticulous compliance with the Station Working Order through periodic counselling and effective surveillance by supervisory officials is emphasized.

46. Overspeeding by Drivers should be viewed with concern and errant Drivers suitably taken up [Paras 12 and 39(c)].

47. Steam brakes provided on locomotives should be adequately maintained so as to be effective at all times (Para 23).

48. The requirements of General Rule 143(d) regarding dimming of electric headlights may be highlighted to Driving crew (Para 23).

Railway Board's Comments on Various Paras of the Report

Para 44: The question of case studies of the staff involved in the accidents has been under consideration of this Ministry. In view of the fact that such case studies are time consuming and Psycho-technical Cell with their existing resources cannot undertake a large number of such studies, it has been decided that whenever it is felt necessary either by a Railway administration or by CRS to have the case of a particular staff studied by the Psycho-technical Cell, the Railway administration concerned would send the requisite case details to the Psycho-technical Cell, who after examining the case, would decide whether or not the case study is required to be undertaken. Accordingly, the Central Railway has referred the matter to the R.D.S.O. for advice, whereafter action as necessary would be taken by the Railway administration.

Para 45: The observations of the ACRS have been brought to the notice of all concerned by the Railway administration. This has been noted by C.R.S.

Para 46: The instructions with regard to checking of speeds of trains by the inspecting officials already exist. These were recently reiterated vide Board's letter No. 77/Safety (A&R)/1/23 dated 6-11-78, a copy of which was endorsed to CRS also.

As explained by the Railway administration a scrutiny of the speed-recorder chart is made with a view to check whether or not drivers have overspeed. Of late, there has been some shortage of recording papers. Action, has, however, been taken to over-come the shortage.

Para 47: The observations of the ACRS have been noted by the Railway administration who have reiterated the instructions that the steam brakes provided on the steam locomotives should be maintained so as to be effective at all time.

The Railway is, however, being asked to take up with the staff for their failure in this case.

Para 48: The Railway has taken note of the ACRS's observations and has reiterated the extant instructions with regard to dimming of the electric headlights of the locomotives.

The Railway is also being advised to emphasise the requirements of G.R. 143(d) suitably through the safety orientation programmes.

SUB-GROUP ON SKILL DEVELOPMENT OF WOMEN, 1977 – REPORT[1]

Chairman Shri P.S. Krishnan

Members Shri T.S. Sankaran; Dr. Veena Mazumdar; Lt. Col. K.S. Saksena; Shri B.N. Guha Biswas; Shri S. Sadasivam; Shri R.T. Deshmuk

Appointment

In connection with the formulation of the next Five Year Plan a Working Group on the Employment of Women under the Chairmanship of Dr. Asok Mitra was set up by the Government of India, Planning Commission (Employment and Manpower Planning Division) on November 7, 1977. The Group in its first meeting held on 14 November, 1977 decided to set up a Sub-Group on Skill Development of Women.

Terms of Reference

That definite and positive steps should be taken as a matter of deliberate policy, to correct this situation and to create a climate in which more and more women will be encouraged to take training in a variety of trades. Therefore, any action which will result in giving women a more equal share of what is due to her, which will enable her to choose for herself the kind of life she wants, and which will in crease her status and assure her a decent living, needs to be encouraged.

----

1. New Delhi, Department of Social Welfare, Women's Welfare and Development Bureau, 1978, pp. 69-72-74 (Bound with Report of the Working Group on Employment of Women, 1977)

Contents

Introductions; Recommendations.

Recommendations

In the existing system of ITIs, Polytechnics and Apprenticeship Training Schemes, attempts should be made to increase the number of women admitted for training in different trades by offering incentives and facilities like stipends, hostels, etc. In order to attract a greater number of girls, these incentives would have to be in addition to those already existing. Moreover, to do away with the concept of a men's jobs and women's job greater incentives could also be given in trades which have till now not attracted many women.

To get over the initial difficulties of only a few women coming forward to take training in certain trades, arrangements would have to be made to admit girls from adjoining areas and provide hostel facilities for them.

It is very strongly felt that unless a certain percentage of seats are reserved for womcn in thc Industrial Training Institutes and in the different trades designated for apprenticeship training, it would be extremely difficult to make any really tangible improvement in the lot of women seeking employment. Reservation would also ensure that instructors (of institutes) and employers (under the Apprentices Act) do not turn down women seeking such training, on the ground that the trades are not suitable for women, or that on women has ever taken training that particular trade.

A statement showing the trade-wise break-up of trainees on the I.T.I. roll (Annexure I) reveals that in most of the trades, some of the existing capacity goes unutilized. Hence reserving some of the seats for women will not adversely affect the training needs of men. The seven trades where the number of trainees is more than the existing capacity are : Draughtsman (Civil), Electrician, Mechanic (Diesel), Welder (Gas and Electric), Cutting and Tailoring, Cane, Willow and Bamboo work, Stenography (Hindi). Amongst these, the only trades which have a large number of women trainees is Cutting and Tailoring and to some extent Cane, Willow and Bamboo work. Assuming that the higher employment potential in certain trades is the reason for the large number of trainees in these trades, then that would be a statutory justification for reservation of training places in these trades for women in the context of the need for increasing employment opportunities for women.

It was however felt that it may not be necessary to reserve seats or offer incentives in all the trades in which skill training is at present given. Due to physiological reasons, it may be inadvisable for women to train for all the designated trades as some of them might adversely affect their health. Of the existing trades, seven trades designated under the Apprentices Act (listed below) were considered by the groups to be unsuitable for women for these reasons. (None of the list of trades under the ITIs was considered unsuitable for women).

1. Bricklayer (Refractory)
2. Millwright (Rolling Mills)
3. Rigger
4. Shipwright (Steel)
5. Pipe Fitting (Ship building)
6. Boiler Attendant
7. Mechanic (Earth Moving Machinery)

In all other trades, it was felt that training of women should be encouraged by reservation of seats, offering special incentives and facilities as mentioned earlier. In the case of apprenticeship trades, since much of the opposition may be from employers, incentives should be offered to the employers to recruit and train women. A scrutiny of the figures showing the number of apprentices trained as on 25-6-1977 (Annexure II) reveals that in certain States, e.g., Uttar Pradesh and West Bengal even though the total number of apprentices is more than 10,000 the number of women apprentices is a very small fraction of this. Hence reservation for women in apprenticeship training is especially necessary. As an additional measure special incentives/awards may be given to employers and institutes who train the largest number of women and who train women in excess of the reserved number—especially in non-traditional occupations.

The minimum educational qualifications laid down as a pre-requisite for admission into the ITIs and Polytechnics debar more women than men from admission, and therefore a situation might arise where due to lack of an adequate number of women with the requisite educational qualifications, the seats reserved for whom in training institutes might go un-filled. To meet such a situation, there should be a provision for relaxation of the minimum education for women with special classes being held to bring women trainees up to the standard. All these measures should be widely publicized in high schools, through employment exchanges, etc.

It is understood that there is a proposal under consideration in the Ministry of Industry to give incentives to labour-intensive industries in the shape of rebate. If this is adopted, within this scheme, incentives could be given to entrepreneurs who employ more than a certain percentage of women in labour intensive industries. This would substantially increase the employment of women.

Within an industry/employment also, promotion opportunities for women are very limited. This is because women get very little opportunity of improving their skills. Practically no inservice training is given to them. A provision should therefore be introduced for reservation of seats for women in in-service training also. Awards could also be given to employers who show the best results in this regard.

For rural areas, however, this kind of institutional training will not be of very great relevance. The purpose of vocational training is to develop more employable skills and to give women access to technology and organisational knowhow. Several trades exist where training over a short period would be adequate to enable a person to acquire skills to earn a living or to improve skills so as to earn a better wage. Such training could be organised through mobile units. The trades in which such training is to be given would have to be decided upon by the local authorities taking into consideration local needs and resources, production and marketing centres either available or to be set up, plan investments, projects, etc. Since the majority of rural women are illiterate, the training programmes will have to be graded for different literacy/educational groups. This could also be combined with non-formal education. Though some schemes for self-employment have been undertaken by the Khadi and Village Industry Commission and the Small Industries Development Organisation, unless there are more efforts directed specifically towards women, employment of women will not appreciably increase. There exists on the other hand a very real danger of women being pushed out of the employment market, by being replaced in traditional occupations by trained men.

It was felt that as an experiment some pilot projects in such training efforts could be taken up in one or two districts in each State. As the Small Industries Development Organisation have already made separate studies for each district and have reports indicating the possibility of starting small industries, the kind of industries which should be taken up in the district, the infrastructure available, etc., these studies could be referred to before these pilot projects are taken up. These projects would necessarily have to be backed up by the joint efforts of the Ministries/Departments concerned so that the women trained are not left without any scope for employment. The training will also have to be based on the feasibility of developing particular industries, occupations in that area. These may be agro-based, processing or manufacturing. Some skills may already be present, but technological strengthening would improve productivity and reduce the physical burden of women. It was also suggested that these pilot projects could wherever possible, associate a technical institution, e.g., Small Scale Industries Service Institute, Agricultural College, I.T.I., Polytechnic, etc., from the inception of the project so that this technical institute could act as a supervisory body and ensure a fair amount of success (as in the Integrated Child Development Scheme).

Under the Rural Industries Project being taken up by the Small Industries Development Organization, every district is to have one General Manager, seven Managers, and several technical officers (for different trades) for promotion of Small-scale, Khadi and Village industries. It would be worthwhile to have a large number of women either of the managerial or technical officer level, or where this is not possible to have technical officers for those industries which a large number of local women can take up (e.g., rope making, basket weaving, etc).

In order to ensure that this rural training is a continuous process and does not end with the projects, it was also considered necessary to train a few rural women, with potential both is organizers and as instructors in trades which are locally acceptable and viable, so that they in turn could train more women in these trades. This would necessitate making use of the already existing local institutions like Mahila Mandals, etc. It was felt that as one of the suggestions likely to be made by the Working Group on Rural Associations (Mahila Mandals) would be to have a team of persons at the district level to look after various programmes for women to be implemented through Mahila Mandals it would be advisable to have a person on the team who could look into employment opportunities for women and vocational training. The rural women trained under the rural training scheme would work in close liaison with the team member.

This team member will also have to be primarily an organizer who can mobilize necessary resources to organize training in the skills particularly identified for women of that area—a person with enough dynamism to get the project going.

Personnel of the training institutes should be responsive to their surroundings, so that demands of the employment market can be met by a starting new trades in the institutes. These personnel can be given the proper orientation, by holding seminars, meetings, etc.

In brief the Group makes the following recommendations:

I. *Industrial Training Institutes, Polytechnics and Apprenticeship Training Scheme*

(a) Reserve a certain number of seats for women in training institutes and apprenticeship trades. (Paras 9.3 to 9.5)

(b) Encourage women to join these institutes/trades by giving incentives and facilities like hostels, stipends, etc. (Paras 9.1 to 9.2)

(c) Hold special crash classes in ITIs and Polytechnics for women whose qualifications may fall slightly short of basic required qualifications, in order to enable them to join the regular training courses. (Para 9.6)

(d) Encourage employers/institutes to train number of women, by awarding prizes, special citations to employers/institutes who produce the best results/train women in excess of the reserved number. (Para 9.5)

II. *Employers*

(e) Reserve a certain percentage of seats for women in inservice training given by employers. (Para 9.8)

(f) Give special recognition in the shape of national awards, etc., to employers who—

— give inservice training to a large number of women
— appreciably increase the employment of women
— impart literacy or non-formal education, etc. (Para 9.8)

(g) Encourage employers to take in more women by giving a rebate to industries which employ a larger number of women.

This should be lined to the proposals of the Ministry of Industry to give rebates to labour industries. (Para 9.7)

III. *Rural Training*

(h) Hold short-term training courses for rural women through mobile units attached to near by Training Institutes after identifying suitable trades on the basis of local skills, viability availability of market, plan investment, etc. A technical institute nearby should be associated as a supervisory body. (Paras 9.9 and 9.10)

(i) To ensure continuity in training, rural women should be trained both as organizers and instructors in locally viable trades. These women can work in liaison with and be directly supervised by the team of technical officers at the district level proposed by the Working Group on Rural Associations, for promotion of employment amongst women. (Para 9.12)

(j) The Rural Industries Project should have a definite slant towards women. It should have either some women as managers and technical officers or offer training in occupations which a large number of rural women can and are willing to take up. (Para 9.11)

(k) Give an orientation to the personnel of existing training institutes to make them responsive to local employment needs, so that new trades can be started to meet these needs. (Para 10)

(l) Give wide publicity to all these measures in schools, through employment exchanges, panchayats, Women's Associations, etc.

ANNEXURE I

Statement showing Trade-wise Break up of Total Capacity of Students on Roll as on 31-3-1977 in 356 Training Institutes in the Country

Sl. No.	Trade	Capacity	On rolls as on 31-3-1977 Women	Total men and women
1.	2.	3.	4.	5.
A. Engineering Trades				
1.	Building Constructive	416	—	262
2.	Draughtsman (Civil)	3129	94	3205
3.	Draughtsman (Mech.)	4016	31	3897
4.	Electrician	16392	4	16503
5.	Electroplator	432	—	302
6.	Fitter	25516	3	24802
7.	Instrument Mechanic	2436	42	2238
8.	Machinist (Composite)	12152	9	11939
9.	Machinist (Grinder)	2020	—	1922
10.	Mechanic (M and V)	8053	—	6717
11.	Ref. and Air Conditioning Mechanic	1917	14	1530
12.	Mechanic (Radio and Television)	3972	110	3554
13.	Pattern Maker	1184	—	867
14.	Surveyor	1761	19	1543
15.	Turner	16003	10	15784
16.	Watch and Clock Maker	272	6	181
17.	Wireman	10262	8	9492
18.	Electronics	1021	31	976
19.	Tools and Die Maker	940	—	902
20.	Millwright Mechanic	92	—	67
21.	Farm Mechanic	192	—	145
22.	Blacksmith	2420	5	1750
23.	Carpenter	3834	23	2799
24.	Mechanic (Diesel)	2936	—	3042
25.	Mechanic (Tractor)	2473	—	2269
26.	Moulder	3805	24	3624
27.	Painter	780	77	609
28.	Plumber	1225	4	1098
29.	Sheet Metal Worker	2786	73	2387
30.	Upholstry	52	—	24

Contd.

1.	2.	3.	4.	5.
31.	Welder (Gas and Electric)	9706	9	9750
32.	Wireless Operator	150	1	133
	Sub-Total	142325	597	134313
	B. Non-engineering Trades			
1.	Bleaching, Dyeing and Printing	32	17	17
2.	Hand Weaving of Fancy and Furnishing Fabrics	224	37	103
3.	Hand Weaving of Woollen Fabrics	—	—	—
4.	Knitting with Hand and Machine	256	197	214
5.	Hand Weaving of Newar, Tape Durries and Carpets	32	—	17
6.	Manufacture of House-hold Utensils	16	—	—
7.	Manufacture of Sports Goods (Wood)	16	—	7
8.	Manufacture of Sports Goods (Misc.)	—	—	—
9.	Manufacture of Footwear	48	—	21
10.	Manufacture of Suit-case and other leather goods	160	10	81
11.	Book Binding	208	60	135
12.	Manufacture of Sports Goods (Leather)	16	—	7
13.	Hand Composing and Proof Reading	620	91	452
14.	Printing Machine Operator (P.M.O.)	556	—	424
15.	Cutting and Tailoring	2937	2372	3028
16.	Preservation of Fruits and Vegetable including Canning	68	33	50
17.	Embroidery and Needle work	681	607	627
18.	Weaving of Silk and Woolen Fabrics	—	—	—
19.	Cane, Willow and Bamboo Work	16	16	20
20.	Stenography (English)	4274	1090	3918
21.	Stenography (Hindi)	2196	563	2225
	Sub-Total	12356	5093	11346
	TOTAL 'A' and 'B'	154681	5690	145659

ANNEXURE II

Implementation of the Apprentices Act, 1961

Apprenticeship Training Scheme

Consolidated Statement of the Engagement of Apprentices
Position as on 25.6.1977

Sl. No.	Name of the State/Region	Seats located	Seats Utilised	No. of Women apprentices
1.	2.	3.	4.	5.
1.	Andhra Pradesh	5402	5409	85
2.	Assam	1298	1163	23
3.	Bihar	5800	5880	3
4.	Chandigarh	225	225	10
5.	Delhi	4458	4438	10
6.	Goa	283	91	11
7.	Gujarat	7048	5580	78
8.	Haryana	4100	4320	127
9.	Himachal Pradesh	832	546	39
10.	Jammu and Kashmir	405	671	64
11.	Karnataka	7504	7213	583
12.	Kerala	6209	6037	407
13.	Madhya Pradesh	2637	2641	10
14.	Maharashtra	16907	18668	666
15.	Orissa	2897	2532	12
16.	Pondicherry	313	334	34
17.	Punjab	2424	2424	265
18.	Rajasthan	2000	2005	—
19.	Tamil Nadu	9242	9569	278
20.	Uttar Pradesh	11492	11163	85
21.	West Bengal	10599	10687	32
22.	Meghalaya	130	62	22
23.	Tripura	198	78	—
24.	Manipur	40	37	2
25.	Nagaland	—	—	—
	Total: State Private Sector Establishments	102443	101923	3092

Contd.

1.	2.	3.	4.	5.
Central Sector Estts.				
1.	Eastern Region	15309	14219	91
2.	Northern Region	16801	12714	206
3.	Southern Region	16760	16220	310
4.	Western Region	12308	11781	269
	Total: General Sector Establishment	61178	54934	876
	Grant Total of States/Private Sector Estts.	163621	156857	3968

SUB-GROUP ON DEVELOPMENT OF SELF-EMPLOYMENT & ENTREPRENEURSHIP AMONG WOMEN, 1977 – REPORT[1]

Chairman Shri P.S. Krishnan

Members Miss Shanti Chakraborty; Mrs. Sethi Nair; Smt. Ela Bhatt; Dr. (Mrs.) Veena Mazumdar; Shri J.V. Bapu Raj; Shri S.P. Taneja

Appointment

In connection with the formulation of the next Five Year Plan a Working Group on the Employment of Women under the Chairmanship of Dr. Asok Mitra was set up by the Government of India, Planning Commission (Employment and Manpower Planning Division) on November 7, 1977. The Group in its first meeting held on 14 November, 1977, decided to set up a Sub-Group on Development of Self-Employment and Entrepreneurship.

Terms of Reference

To suggest the aims that should guide all agencies dealing with the development of self-employment and entrepreneurship.

Contents

Introduction; Recommendations.

---

1. New Delhi, Women's Welfare Development Bureau, Department of Social Welfare, 1978, pp. 65-68 (Bound with Report of the Working Group on Employment of Women, 1977).

Recommendations

(1) Technical institutions like ITIs, Women's Polytechnics and other vocational institutions as well as specialized agencies like institutes of management should introduce suitable courses of training for women entrepreneurship. Women and girl students of these institutions who have *prima facie* aptitude and interest for self-employment should be identified during the later part of their courses in these institutions.

The design and Marketing Service Extension Centres of the Handicraft Board, Small Industries Service Institute of the Small Industries Organisation, the Weavers Service Centres of the Handloom Organisation and State Government Units at State and District levels should have fully equipped and staffed training wings where women entrepreneurs could be given the necessary training in the disciplines with which they are concerned. The training programmes available at these centres should be broadly of two kinds—one of primary and basic nature for fresh entrants and the other on advanced refresher type for those already in the line and needing socialised knowledge and skills. Women entrepreneurs have to be helped in formulating their projects or schemes carefully. The starting point has to be market date. Unless these are data to show the marketability of the goods or services, at a viable price, the scheme is bound to fail. In gathering the market data, the entrepreneur should be fully associated and this will develop entrepreneurship. This should be supplemented by the data available with the promotional agencies. After a sound or viable scheme has been formulated for an entrepreneur, a procedure should be evolved in accord prompt sanctions which should include credits as well as arrangements for training and post-training production at one point so that she does not have to run from pillar to post. From this point of view, banks should be associated with the process of project formulation right from the beginning. The question of credit has been considered in detail below. So far as training is concerned, in addition to the suggestions mentioned above, it would be useful to have sandwhich type of training with the second-half coming after the trained candidates gather some experience of their industry business. After a scheme is sanctioned, a course of training both technical/professional as well as commercial-cum-management should be a condition for disbursement of credit. In identifying schemes and projects the services of voluntary institutions and organisations with established record of sound work and private and public sectors industries should be utilised.

Government funds should be provided through promotional agencies for margin money as in the case of self-employment scheme. The Social Welfare Board's grants should be dovetailed with the above funds.

A suitable percentage of public funds provided for assistance to small cottage industries should be earmarked for women.

Women's Financial Corporations staffed by women, should be set up in all States and funds for assistance to women should be channelled through these corporations.

There should be an assurance that subject to marketability and viability, there will be no financial limited so far as self-employment programme for women is concerned and third party surety should not be asked for by the lending institutions.

These should be a women's cell at the head office of all banks to look after the interest of women.

Banks and financial institutions should be associated right from the beginning of project formulation.

Facilities for efficient marketing of the products made by the women entrepreneurs is another important assistance to be assured. On this ultimately would depend the success of the entire programme. Hence no project should be started or given any financial assistance without proper market study being first made. The various marketing and service centers of the Handicrafts Board, Small Industries Servic Institute of Small Industries Organisation. Weavers Service Centres of the Handloom Board, the State Directorate of Industries and District Level Units and Cottage and Small Scale Industries Corporations, Central as well as State should have specialised staff to guide and assist women entrepreneurs in carrying out such market studies before taking up any project. Corporation and marketing agencies should be given special incentives by way of reservation of staffs in Government/Municipal markets, working capital loan on low rate of interest, etc., if they set up special shops/ emporia or expand their present selling outlets so as to cover at least 25 per cent of the turnover from products made by women entrepreneurs. Wherever Government or municipal agencies buy goods or appoint contractors for supply of certain services, preference should be given, other things being equal, to goods and services provided by women entrepreneurs and their co-operatives.

The work of providing employment to a large number of women should involve massive effect on the part of all departments of Government. The sub-group is therefore of the view that each department should prepare its own programme for women and ear-mark for that purpose a fair proportion of their budget. All such programmes of various departments should form a sub-plan for women and should be coordinated by a senior women officer of the rank of a Commissioner in the Women's Bureau of the Department of Social Welfare as in the case of Scheduled Castes and Tribes.

The women entrepreneurs will face a number of difficulties and problems at various stages of setting up and running a business enterprise and would need prompt assistance to overcome them. To meet this end, it is suggested that all departments of Government, Central as well as States including municipal authorities, corporations and other government undertakings should set up women's cells headed by senior women officials at the regional and headquarters office to attend to all complaints and problems of women entrepreneurs like the Ombudsman System. Those cells should not only deal with problems brought to them by the entrepreneurs but also act as a monitoring cell which will keep in constant view the programme of the units of the self-employed women as well as group of women entrepreneurs their cooperative, associations, etc., with reference to certain norms of healthy working, so that any difficulties and strains could be identified before they become problems and timely remedies found.

The Sub-Group felt that while promoting self-employment among women, a fair number of Scheduled Caste and Scheduled Tribe women entrepreneurs should be developed among them.

SUB-GROUP ON STATISTICS ON THE EMPLOYMENT OF WOMEN, 1977 – REPORT[1]

Chairman & Convener Dr. K.C. Seal

Members Dr. (Mrs) R. Thamarajkshi (she expressed her inability because of her pre-occupation); Smt. Padma Ramachandran; Shri S.S. Kapoor; Miss Mina Gupta; Shri N. Navanithan, Shri K.S. Natarjan; Shri R.P. Goyal

Appointment

In connection with the formulation of the next Five Year Plan a working group on the employment of women under the chairmanship of Dr. Asok Mitra was set up by the Government of India, Planning Commission (Employment and Manpower Planning Division) November 7, 1977. The Group in its first meeting held on 14 November, 1977, decided to set up Sub-Group on Statistics on Women's employment.

Terms of Reference

To examine the available information on various aspects of employment of women; identify gaps therein and make suggestions for the collection of data for formulating policies/programmes in respect of employment of women.

Contents

Introduction; Sources of Information; Female Work Participation

---

1. New Delhi, Women's Welfare and Development Bureau, Department of Social Welfare, 1978, pp. 16-50 (Bound with Report of the Working Group on Employment of Women, 1977)

Rate; Employment of Women; Unemployment Data; Recent Studies; Conclusions.

Recommendations

An analysis of information of the data-base regarding employment position of women made in the foregoing sections suggests the following conclusions.

During the first half of the present century, female participation rates declined. But the male participation rates were also falling, comparatively at a slower rate. In the 1971 census labour force has been recorded at a lower level than in 1961 census but because of conceptual differences, participation rates are not comparable between the censuses. As indicated in Section III for urban females in the 27th Round, rates are consistently higher than the 1961 census rates for all the age groups. For rural females, the 27th Round rates are appreciably higher than the 1961 Census rates for the broad age group 30-59. The labour force participation rates based on past NSS data using current status approach did not show a definite trend in the participation rates of rural or urban female during the period 1958-73. As the sampling errors of the age specific labour force participation rates of NSS data are not known, it cannot be asserted that the participation rates have shown a significant rise during the sixties. It may not, however, be unreasonable to infer that the change in the female participation rates had been quite slow during the sixties and consequently, the participation rates observed in the 27th Round of the National Sample Survey could be used as the best approximation to the participation rates obtaining in 1971. Thus, applying the participation rates of the 27th Round of NSS to the 1971 census population, a female labour force of 75.34 million (68.27 million in rural areas and 7.07 million in urban areas) has been estimated for 1971.

The annual growth rate in women employment in the organised sector as indicated by the Employment Market Information Programme has been generally higher than in total employment for the period 1971-77.

The Growth rate in women employment was higher than that in total employment in the Public Sector during the period 1971-77 but the situation is reverse in the private sector.

The adjusted 1971 female labour force shows per annum rate of growth of 2.63 per cent over 1961 census, 2.45 per cent in the unorganised sector and 4.0 per cent in the organised sector, as against 1.9 per cent, 1.7 per cent and 2.3 per cent respectively in the case of male.

Sectorally highest growth in women work force has been recorded in transport, storage and communication and lowest in manufacture and repair.

A comparative analysis of unemployment rates among women in rural and urban areas as compared to the unemployment rates of men reveals that chronic unemployment was higher among men in rural areas. On the other hand, unemployment rate among women under the other two concepts – weekly status and daily status – was greater than men both in rural and urban areas. This is despite the fact that women in work force increased at a faster rate than men during the period 1961-71 (59.50 million to 74.60 million in the case of women as against 129.18 million to 152.28 million in the case of men). It would, thus, appears that unemployment rate among women labour higher mainly due to a faster rise in women work force than the number of jobs created for them during the sixties (under the daily and weekly status concepts).

The percentage increase in 1972 and 1976 (over the previous years 1971 and 1975) has been recorded as 30.8 and 9.4 in case of women for job seekers, whereas is works out to 35.8 per cent and 4.3 per cent in respect of the male job-seekers.

The proportion of educated job-seekers (registered)—males and females, has risen during the period 1971-76. In 1971 there were 5.83 lakh women job-seekers of which 3.28 lakhs or 56 per cent were educated (matriculates and above). The percentage increased to 63 in 1976. As regards male job-seekers, the proportion of educated persons has risen from 43 per cent in 1971 to 50 per cent in 1976.

Placement of women job-seekers (registered) has fallen from 61,000 to 58,000 in this period and the percentage of placement to registration from 10.9 per cent to 8.6 per cent in 1971-76. In the case of male job-seekers the placement has declined from 4.46 lakhs in 1971 to 4.39 lakhs in 1976. The percentage of placement to registration of male job-seekers has come down from 9.8 to 8.9 during the period 1971-76.

Judged according to levels of education the number of placement of women job-seekers has sharply declined in the case of matriculate, higher secondary and post-graduate job seekers. The same position holds good in the case of male job seekers.

As per 1972 survey conducted by the Directorate General of Employment and Training, 77.6 per cent of employed female graduates passing in 1968 secured employment within two years as against 81.9 per cent in the case of male graduates. Fifty-three per cent of females graduates were unemployed and seeking job as against 34.6 per cent of all graduates.

But of the total estimated female work force of 67.9 million in 1971 in rural areas, there are 40 million cultivator and 16.9 million agricultural labourers. Employment outside cultivation amounted to about 11 million. Of this 4.8 million workers or about 44 per cent were engaged in 10 industries. The next 10 per cent were engaged in another 10 industries.

With regard to women employment in urban areas, 51 million (out of total of 6.6 million) women were employed in industries of this, 2.9 million (or about 57 per cent) female workers were absorbed to industries.

Defining women proneness as employment of women to the extent of 40 per cent and above of the total employment, 10 industry groups have been identified which are dominantly women prone as indicated above.

Regarding urban females, industries at the three digit level in which employment of women has increased by more than 100 per cent during the period 1961-71 number 115 out of 271 3-digit industries. These are 63 industries at 3-digit level in which the employment declined from the 1961 level.

Suggestions for Improvement

The available information on women employment in inadequate and not regularly available. It is urgent that steps should be taken to improve the coverage, flow and analysis of statistical data on women, employment in India. The need for better coverage of unorganised sector, which employs bulk of women, is particularly indicated. At the 'Blue Print of Action Points' has noted "lack of necessary data in respect of employment in unorganised sector greatly restricts any plan of or employment as unorganised sector is crucial for employment generation."

The National Committee on the Status of Women's Recommendations that National Employment Service should be expanded to cover rural areas and a women's cadre developed in the service to provide employment information and assistance to women requires consideration at different levels. The Committee has also suggested the setting up of special autonomous commissions at the Centre and in the States for the enforcement of various welfare measures and protective laws. The Committee is also of the view that to perform such functions this Commission should call for information on different matters from the concerned agencies of Government and suggest improved methods of data collection. This recommendation deserves examination.

The Equal Remuneration Act, enacted recently, envisages the setting up of State level committees for its enforcement. The enforcement of the provisions of the Act will necessarily generate data which will require to be promptly tabulated and analysed. It will be advantageous if the State Employment and Manpower remain in close touch with the committees for proper analysis and dissemination of employment information.

The Women's Bureau organised recently in the Labour Ministry has significant role to play in putting together, in the form of a fact book. All the available information on the employment, unemployment and wages and bringing out yearly revisions in a systematic manner.

The Annual Employment Review brought out by the Directorate General of Employment and Training contains employment live register data of women but does not give information on the education categorywise, placement and registration of women job seekers. Such information will be very useful. The survey conducted by the D.G.E.&T in 1972 about graduates of 1968 has given value information on women graduates. A survey of the 1971 or 1973 batch of women graduates or of women job seekers will provide further up to date information. Avenues of part-time employment for women should be explored. Statistics of such employment also would prove useful. Furthermore steps should be taken to fill the data gap pertaining to employment and unemployment of women by age-group and marital status.

In the context of any plan and policy formulation and for building up of a detailed employment profile of women base line or bench mark data form a reliable starting point. The role of the National Sample Survey in this connection assumes special importance. A separate enquiry by NSSO on women like the 25th round survey of the weaker sections for providing bench mark data is worth considering.

The Labour Bureau has recently conducted a Rural Labour Enquiry. It is urgent that the data thrown up by the survey, particularly on rural women or households of which women are expeditiously tabulated, analysed and published.

Preparatory work regarding formulation of concept methodology and procedural details for the next (1981) census is underway in the office of the Registrar General. The conceptual limitations which led to the under reporting of the women employment work force particularly in the rural areas should be avoided in the next census through appropriate conceptual modifications.

One of the useful indicators is divising strategy for women employment would be the growth/decline in women employment in various industries preferably at 3-digit level of industrial classification. In view of the non-comparability of the 1961 and 1971 census economic data, it is not possible especially for the rural areas to develop such indicators and identify industries or occupations/where employment of women could be augmented. This will be possible if data to be collected in 1981 census do not suffer from conceptual limitations of 1971 census as referred to in the previous paragraph. In the mean time micro-level studies on a sample basis may be intimated in selected areas/industries.

It is worth investigating as to what extent and in which sectors the present legal restrictions imposed by the Factories Act (viz., prohibiting employment of women in certain types of jobs involving heavy loads, work of more than stipulated heights and work at night) can be relaxed so that there is no undue dissemination in the employment of women.

Various studies/researches particularly at the micro level are necessary for collecting information on: (i) employment conditions, (ii) Unemployment situation, and (iii) skill profile of local women. The Blue Print of Action Points has also suggested researches for filling gap in existing information, quantitative, particularly on employment potential in the unorganised sector. It is necessary that a comprehensive time-bound research plan is drawn up for this purpose in which various research organisations and in universities will collaborate.

NATIONAL POLICE COMMISSION, 1977 – FIRST REPORT[1]

Chairman Shri Dharma Vira, retired Governor

Members Shri N.K. Reddy; Shri K.F. Rustamji; Shri N.S. Saksena; Prof. M.S. Gore

M. Secy. Shri C.V. Narasimhan

Alterations Shri C.V. Narasimhan, former Director of Central Bureau of Investigation, functioned as Member Secretary of the Commission from its inception till 19th April, 1980 when he left to take a posting in his parent cadre in Tamil Nadu on replacement of his services from the Central Government to the State Government. After the departure of Shri Narasimhan, Shri M.D. Dikshit, Principal Director of Research, functioned as the Secretary Incharge.

Appointment

Far-reaching changes have taken place in the country after the enactment of the Indian Police Act, 1861 and the setting up of the Second Police Commission of 1902, particularly during the last thirty years of Independence. Though a number of States have appointed Police Commissions after Independence to study the problems of the Police in their respective States, there has been no comprehensive review at the national level of the police system after independence despite radical changes in the political, social and economic situation in the country. A fresh examination is necessary of the role and performance of the Police — both as a law enforcement agency, and as an institution to protect the rights of the citizens enshrined in the Constitution. The Government of India have, therefore, decided to ap-

---

1. Ministry of Home Affairs, Government of India, New Delhi, 1979, 128 p.

point a National Police Commission. The National Police Commission was appointed under the Government of India, Ministry of Home Affairs Resolution No. VI-24021/36/71-GPA.I, dated November 15, 1977.

Terms of Reference

The following will be the terms of reference of the Commission:

(1) Re-define the role, duties, powers and responsibilities of the police with special reference to prevention and control of crime and maintenance of public order.

(2) Examine the development of the principles underlying the present policing system, including the method of magisterial supervision, evaluate the performance of the system, identify the basic weaknesses of inadequacies, and suggest appropriate changes in the system and the basic laws governing the system.

(3) Examine, if any changes are necessary in the existing method of administration, disciplinary control and accountability.

(4) Inquire into the system of investigation and prosecution, the reasons for delay and failure; the use of improper methods, and the extent of their prevalence; and suggest how the system may be modified or changed, and made efficient; scientific and consistent with human dignity; and how the related laws may be suitably amended.

(5) Examine methods of maintaining crime records and statistics and suggest methods for making them uniform and systematic.

(6) Review policing in rural areas, evaluate any new arrangements that have been made, and recommend changes that are necessary.

(7) Examine the system of policing required in non-rural and urbanised areas including metropolitan areas, and suggest the pattern that would be the most suitable.

(8) Examine the steps taken for modernising law enforcement, evaluate the work of police communications, the computer network, scientific laboratories and agencies for research and development, and examine whether modernisation can be speeded up; examine to what extent, as a result of the modernisation of Police forces, streamlining of its functions and its

re-structuring, it would be possible to economise in the man-power in the various areas of its activities.

(9) Examine the nature and extent of the special responsibilities of the Police towards the weaker sections of the community and suggest steps to ensure prompt action on their complaints for the safeguard of their rights and interests.

(10) Recommend measures and institutional arrangements:

(i) to prevent misuse of powers by the police, and to examine whether police behaviour, out-look, responsiveness and impartiality are maintained at the correct level, and if not the steps such as recruitment and training which should be taken to improve them;

(ii) to prevent misuse of the Police by administrative or executive instructions, political or other pressure, or oral orders of any type, which are contrary to law;

(iii) for the quick and impartial inquiry of public complaints made against the police about any misuse of police powers;

(iv) for the quick redressal of grievances of police personnel and to look after their morale and welfare; and

(v) for a periodic objective evaluation of police performance in a metropolitan area/District/State in a manner which will carry credibility before the public.

(11) Examine the manner and extent to which police can enlist ready and willing cooperation of the public in the discharge of their social defence and law enforcement duties and suggest measures regarding the institutional arrangements to secure such co-operation and measures for the growth of healthy and friendly public-police relationship.

(12) Examine the methods of police training, development, and career-planning of officers and recommend any changes that are required at any time in their service, to modernise the outlook, and to make the leadership of the force effective and morally strong.

(13) Examine the nature of the problems that the police will have to face in the future, and suggest the measures necessary for dealing with them, and for keeping them under continuous study and appraisal.

(14) Consider and make recommendations and suggestions regard-

ing any other matter which the Government may refer to the Commission.

(15) Any other matter of relevance or importance having an impact on the subject.

Contents

Preface; Preamble; The Constabulary; Pay Structure; Housing; Supply of Essential Commodities; Orderly System; Machinery for Redressal of Grievances of Police Personnel; Welfare Measures for Police Families; Recruitment, Training and Career Planning; Modalities for Inquiry into Complaints against Police; Summary of Observations and Recommendations; Financial Implications; Appendices

Recommendations and Financial Implications

Preamble

11.1 Police performance in India today is under close review and critical assessment by a demanding public in far greater measure than at any time in the past. Increasing crime, rising population, growing pressure of living accommodation, particularly in urban areas, violent outbursts in the wake of demonstrations and agitations arising from labour disputes, agrarian unrest, problems and difficulties of students, political activities including the cult of extremists, enforcement of economic and social legislations, etc., have all added new dimensions to police tasks in the country and tended to bring the police in confrontation with the public much more frequently than ever before. (Para 1.1)

11.2 In public estimate the police appear as an agency more to implement and enforce the objectives of the Government in power as distinct from enforcing law as such as an independent and impartial agency. The dividing line between the objectives of Government as such on one side and the interests and expectations of the ruling political party as such on the other side gets blurred in actual practice and the image of police as an impartial law enforcement agency suffers in consequence. (Para 1.1)

11.3 The basic and fundamental problem regarding the police today is how to make them function as an efficient and impartial law enforcement agency fully motivated and guided by the objectives of service to the public at large, upholding the Constitutional rights and liberties of the people. (Para 1.1)

11.4 In the view of the 1902 Commission, the duties of a constable were to be of a mechanical character and he was not to be entrusted with duties requiring the exercise of discretion and judgement. (Para 1.3)

11.5 With the transition from foreign rule to independent, socialist, democratic and welfare State, the style of police handling of public order situations has had to change from an aggressive and mailed first attitude to peaceful and persuasive handling of agitating groups. This change in police methodology has meant the involvement of a much larger number of police personnel to handle a given public order situation as compared to pre-Independance situation. This has, in turn, meant the deployment of a larger number of Constables for interacting with the public and securing their co-operation by persuasion and appeal for maintaining public order. This is a job which the Constabulary visualised by the 1902 Police Commission was not expected to perform in the old days. (Para 1.17)

11.6 The Constable of the present day has moved far from the predominantly mechanical role assigned to him by the 1902 Commission and has now to interact with the public in larger numbers in a variety of situations where he has to apply his mind, exercise his judgement, use his powers of persuasion and appeal and enforce law with public understanding and cooperation. It is the Constabulary who form the cutting edge of police administration and face the public most during their visits to police stations and movement on roads. It is the Constable's behaviour and response which create the first and foremost impact on the public mind. The police image in the country is largely determined by the staff who function at the police station level. The Constabulary constitute a large majority of this staff and form the foundation and base for the entire police structure. Any attempt at a meaningful police reform has necessarily to start at their level only, since no restructuring of the system will be practicable or enduring unless the mass base of the system is rendered healthy and efficient. (Para 1.20)

The Constabulary

11.7 The Constable has been groomed in the existing police system to be an obedient, mechanical functionary, mostly acting in compliance of a specific order from his superior officer and not doing anything positive on his own initiative and judgement. (Para 2.6)

11.8 A sample survey of the actual work currently being done by the Constables in a few police stations in three States and one Union Territory has shown that 49 per cent of their time is spent on duties which require initiative, exercise of discretion and judgement and also interaction with the public, 37 per cent is spent on duties which are of a similar nature but do not involve interaction with public, and only 14 per cent on duties which are mostly mechanical in nature. (Para 2.9)

11.9 The promotional structure within the police system is not conducive to the fulfilment of the legitimate career ambitions of the Constabulary. With the system of direct recruitment at the level of Sub-Inspector and the relatively meagre number of Sub Inspector's posts compared to the vast numbers of the Constabulary, a large majority of the Constables retire as Constables without even one rank promotion in their entire career. No system can remain healthy if such a large chunk of its personnel vegetate and waste out after working for nearly 30 years in the same rank at which they entered the system. (Para 2.14)

11.10 Having regard to the changed needs of policing the country and the importance of making the Constable function as a responsible functionary with due sense of values, discretion and judgement in his interaction with the public, we feel that the existing system should be immediately changed to achieve the following objectives:

(i) The Constabulary should no longer be treated as a cadre meant only for duties of a mechanical character as visualised by the 1902 Commission. They should be so recruited and trained that they could be deployed also on duties involving exercise of discretion and judgement, with due regard to the paramount need for securing public cooperation and understanding in any situation;

(ii) They should be able to assist the Sub-Inspectors in inquiries and investigational work in a positive and purposeful manner;

(iii) They should pick up experience of such work over a period of 5 or 6 years and be in a position to handle investigational work independently and rise to the level of Assistant Sub-Inspector and upwards by promotion; and

(iv) The promotional structure within the police system should be radically revised to permit a smooth and quick promotional flow from the rank of Constable. It should be possible for a Constable to rise by promotion to higher ranks — even the highest-by showing his worth in the performance of police tasks. (Para 2.17)

11.11 In the revised set up a Constable would thus be looked upon as a potential investigating officer who could be entrusted with higher responsibilities in field jobs as he picks up experience and rises further by promotion on the basis of his performance at each level. (Para 2.18)

11.12 The crux of efficient policing, in our view, is the effective and amiable street presence of a well qualified, trained and motivated Constable. (Para 2.18)

11.13 The present position of the Constable is a far cry from the position described above. Long and arduous hours of work without facilities for rest and recreation, continuous employment on jobs under extreme conditions of stress and strain, both mental and physical, prolonged stagnation in the same rank without even one rank promotion throughout their service for a majority of them, constant exposure to criticism and ridicules by a demanding public, a totally inadequate pay structure with no compensation for the handicaps and privations they undergo in their jobs, low status and lack of involvement in planning and executing field jobs with a full understanding of the objectives set by the police organisation, etc., have all had their telling effect on the morale of the Constabulary throughout the country. The increasing educational level of the Constables— a trend noticeable in the recent years — has sharpened the edge of their frustration with their existing lot within the police system. During our visits to several police stations and discussions with the Constabulary, their highly demoralised state was strikingly noticeable. They have nothing to motivate them into meaningful and positive performance of police tasks with a full understanding of the implications and objectives of police action. They function as automations in situations where they are required to exercise their discretion and judgement. They function rigidly in circumstances which require flexibility of approach and understanding of the opposite point of view. We are convinced that more changes in their training schedule will not bring about the necessary improvement in their motivation or performance unless some serious deficiencies in their living and working conditions which have long been neglected are immediately taken up and remedied. (Para 2.19)

Pay Structure

11.14 The Second Central Pay Commission (1959) which went into the question of the pay structure of the police under the Central Government had fixed the pay scale of a Constable at a level equal to that of 'lower semi-skilled' worker. The Third Central Pay Commission (1973) upgraded the status of the Constabulary by taking them out of Class-IV category and fixed their pay scales at a slightly higher level, without specifically expressing an opinion whether or not a Constable should be rated as a skilled worker. (Para 3.3)

11.15 The minimum qualification for recruitment of a constable in many States is now fixed as matriculation. Recruitment is followed by a period of intensive training in specialised skills including a course in law which is very important for a police functionary. The duties on which a constable is even now employed call for considerable initiative and exercise of judgement. In fact, in the revised Police set up we are visualising a role for the Constabulary which will require a lot more initiative and capacity to exercise judgement in dealing with public situations. He will also be required to perform a part of the investigational duties that devolve at the police station level. In many situations even now he has to function by himself, exercising his judgement of the situation and acting according to its needs under the law. A thorough knowledge of law is not required on the part of every constable and will be required in greater measure for satisfactory performance of his duties. All these requirements of the role and duties of a constable clearly make out a case for rating him as an operative somewhere between a highly skilled worker and skilled worker, as defined in a notification issued by the Ministry of Labour in September, 1976. (Para 3.14)

11.16 We feel that full justice has not been done in the past to policeman in regard to his pay structure *vis-a-vis* other services. Despite the relatively low status accorded to him in public services, the policeman has time and again shown commendable loyalty to the call of duty and has always been principally instrumental in maintaining public order even in the most trying situations. In times of crisis brought about by strikes in important and vital sectors of Government as well as Public Undertakings like Railways, civilian employees in Central Government, etc., it is the police that stand by the side of law and maintain order despite severe handicaps and restraints. We strongly feel that the case of the policeman for a rational pay structure should not be deferred any longer but should be resolved in a fair and just manner to sustain police morale which is most important in the context of growing developments in the country. The base of all progress in a country is peaceful existence of law and order and no country can afford to ignore the needs of the machinery and personnel responsible for the maintenance of law and order except at considerable peril of orderly progress. (Para 3.15)

11.17 On a careful consideration of the various factors which attend the working of the Defence Forces and the Police, we feel that there is no rational basis for comparing one with the other in regard to pay and other emoluments. The requirements of each have to be dealt with on its own merits without any comparison as such. (Para 3.16)

11.18 We feel that an armed police Constable as well as a civil police Constable should be rated at the same level with regard to their qualifications for recruitment, professional training and subsequent assessment for further promotion. Having regard to considerations analysed earlier, we recommend that the police Constable, both on the civil side as also the armed side, should be rated as 'skilled worker' for determining his pay structure *vis-a-vis* other public services in the States. (Para 3.17)

11.19 Policemen are obliged to work even on Sundays which are normally off days for all workers. They should be compensated for this extra requirement of duty by having a strict system of giving one day off in a week by rotation among the Constabulary in any working unit. The data underlying this system is to ensure a day of compulsory rest for every Constable once a week. On extraordinary occasions when this is denied to him during one week, this should be given to him in the succeeding week, in addition to that week' rest day. In any case, denial of this off day and compensating him by paying him extra allowance for that day is to be strictly discouraged. (Para 3.19)

11.20 Policemen are also obliged to work on other gazetted holidays which are notified as public holidays and are usually occasions for enjoyment and rest by the community at large. Such occasions invariably call for additional deployment of policemen for law and order duties for containing the exuberance of the holidaying public. Many policemen are unable to avail their normal entitlement of leave every year, being called on to remain on duty to meet the ever increasing demands of manpower for incessant law and order duties. This obligation to work on other gazetted holidays and inability to avail normal entitlement of leave every year should be compensated by entitling a Constable to 15 days' additional leave every year besides what he is normally entitled to in common with other Government servants, and further enabling him to encash the entire leave (including this additional leave) if he is denied leave in 'public interest'. (Para 3.20)

11.21 Policemen work for long and arduous hours on most days of duty, every much in excess of the normal eight hours. A survey has shown that the normal working time put in every day by an average subordinate police officer employed on public order or crime investigational duties is 13 hours. We have carefully examined the question of compensating the policemen for their long and arduous hours of work. The system of overtime allowance provides this compensation to employees in the industrial sector and the civilian staff under the Central Government who come under a prescribed definition of office staff. A policeman has every right to be considered for similar compensatory payment for the enormous load of overtime work he bears in the normal course of discharge of his duties. We feel it would be grossly unfair to him to hold that under the law he is on a 24 hour call of duty and therefore the matter ends there. It would be invidious to deny him the concept of overtime allowance, while large sections of his brother employees in the public sector or under the Government are allowed this facility. We are, however, aware of the practical difficulties that are likely to crop up in working out the overtime allowance system for the police personnel on the same lines as now implemented for the civilian staff. Prior authorisation of overtime work by individual policemen on a day to day basis may not always be practicable because the extent of overtime work is often determined by the developing needs of a growing situation, particularly in the enforcement of public order, as also during investigations of serious crimes which require prolonged pursuit of clues without any let up. We are also aware of the scope for malpractices in the system of maintaining registers and computing overtime allowance on the basis of actual hours of performance of an individual's work from day to day. We are anxious that, as a law enforcement agency, police should be particularly guarded against such malpractices creeping into their system. We, therefore, feel that a different methodology has to be adopted for making this overtime payment to police personnel. (Para 3.21)

11.22 After a careful examination of all aspects of the matter, we feel that payment of overtime allowance for policemen need not be individually determined on the basis of registers and computation of hours of work put in day after day, but may straightway be fixed as 30 per cent of his total emoluments, including DA and CCA. This additional payment, which may be designated as "Overtime Pay", may be stipulated as payable to all police personnel from the rank of Constable up to and inclusive of the rank of Inspector working in police units which deal with public order situations and crime investigations. Having regard to the nature of duties and responsibilities of the different branches of the Police, the State Government may notify from time to time the police branches to which the above system of overtime pay will be admissible. Apart from such notified branches, individual posts in other branches may also be notified for this purpose if the duties attached to the post would entail appreciable overtime work by the subordinate police personnel holding that post. (Para 3.23)

11.23 The facility for encashment of unavailed leave during a year should be extended to the Constabulary in States where the arrangement is not in force now. In most States the facility for encashment of leave on the date of retirement on superannuation already exists for all police personnel in common with the other Government servants subject to a maximum of 180 days. In a few States the maximum is fixed at 120 days. We would recommend that the maximum be increased to 180 days in all States and that this facility be also made available in cases of retirement on any ground, earlier than the date of superannuation. (Para 3.25)

11.24 The conveyance allowance and washing allowance paid to the Constabulary are very low and unrealistic in some States. We would recommend that each of these allowances to the Constabulary be raised to Rs. 10 per month. (Para 3.26)

11.25 The Constabulary should also be provided with financial incentives for acquiring special qualifications as they progress in service which would be useful for bettering their professional performance. We, therefore, recommend that a special qualification pay should be paid to policemen who acquire the following skills or technical/academic knowledge:

(i) proficiency in driving and motor mechanism;
(ii) proficiency in handling wireless equipment for transmitting and receiving messages;
(iii) proficiency in handling computers and electronic data processing machinery;
(iv) acquiring a University degree higher than what he had already secured at the time of entering service in a subject which would be of professional use to him. For example, criminology, forensic sciences, etc.

The quantum of special pay payable to each of these categories may be determined realistically, having regard to the pay and emoluments drawn by similarly qualified personnel working in other services or the private sector in the States. (Para 3.27)

Housing

11.26 Ever since 1861, when the present police system was created, provision of free housing to non-gazetted police personnel has been recognised as the responsibility of the State. (Para 4.1)

11.27 As against the general principle enunciated over 100 years ago regarding provision of 100 per cent accommodation (barrack or family type) of the non-gazetted police personnel, the actual position in the field at present is that more than 50 per cent of the non-gazetted police ranks all over the country have not been provided with Government accommodation of any kind whatsoever. Even among those provided with Government accommodation, a very small percentage alone have family accommodation and the rest are lodged in barracks. For example, in Bihar which has about 49,000 head Constables/Constables, family accommodation has been provided for only 4 per cent among them. Percentage of family accommodation in the rank of sub-inspector/assistant sub-inspector in this State is 27.5 and in the rank of inspector it is 31.1. In Punjab it is only 10.30 per cent of the Constables who have family accommodation. Percentage of family accommodation for the ranks of assistant sub-inspector and sub-inspector and inspector in this State is 17.6, 39.3 and 48.7 respectively. In Uttar Pradesh it is only 14.9 per cent of the Constables that have family accommodation. In Delhi it is only

20.7 per cent of the Constables who have family accommodation. The overall picture that emerges is that the percentage of family accommodation provided to police personnel is very low, and lowest in the rank of Constables. (Para 4.2)

11.28 The deficiency in housing and increasing hardship in paying high rents for private accommodation secured with great difficulty operate as the largest single factor responsible for grievous loss of morale in police ranks, particularly the Constabulary. We, therefore, consider it a matter of great urgency that this condition of service which has remained neglected for many years be taken up for immediate fulfilment. (Para 4.2)

11.29 Among the police personnel yet to be provided with Government accommodation of any kind, as many as 89.1 per cent are in the ranks of Head Constable/Constable. (Para 4.2)

11.30 We recommend that in future, excepting for the requirements of trainees in a training institution or some sections of armed police units, all ranks of non-gazetted police personnel be provided with *family type accommodation*. The existing barrack accommodation may also be replaced by fresh construction of family quarters as and when the barrack accommodation is switched over for the requirements of a training institution or a similar purpose. (Para 4.4)

11.31 We do not find any rationale for the difference in the targets for family accommodation adopted by the States in their police housing programmes for different ranks. The general picture that emerges is that a higher percentage of family accommodation is programmed for the higher ranks among the non-gazetted police personnel as compared to the Constabulary. We recommend that this distinction be immediately given up and the target of 100 per cent family accommodation be uniformly applied to all ranks of non-gazetted police personnel. Having regard to the fact that the existing deficiency of family accommodation is largest in the ranks of Head Constable/Constable we would further recommend that the future police housing programme should be so evolved that the percentage of satisfaction regarding family accommodation for the Constabulary is brought to level with that which obtains for the upper subordinates. (Para 4.5)

11.32 We feel that the indifferent handling of this problem in the past and a persistent tendency to accord low priority to it on account of financial considerations have allowed this problem to assume its present formidable dimensions which now make it appear intractable. We would strongly urge that from the point of view of improving police efficiency and sustaining the sagging morale of the force, the provision of housing to the Constabulary should be given high priority in financial allocations and the pace of investment should be substantially increased so that this problem may be solved within ten years. (Para 4.7)

11.33 We have computed the approximate cost of construction of family accommodation for all the entitled personnel in all the States who are yet to be provided with Government accommodation of any kind. The total expenditure involved in the project to complete the entire housing programme from the position as obtains today is about Rs. 1045 crore. If this programme were to be spread over ten years, the outlay in the first five year period will be Rs. 523 crore. The draft Five Year Plan for 1978-83 provides for Rs. 105 crore for police housing within the Plan scheme. We understand that this is made up of Rs. 60 crore for the State Plans and Rs. 45 crore for the Central Plan. A part of Rs. 45 crore set apart for the Central Plan will be utilised by the Ministry of Home Affairs in the normal course to render financial aid to the States for implementing their police housing programmes under the scheme of Central aid for such programmes. Having regard to the importance of housing for sustaining police morale and efficiency in the increasingly difficult conditions in which police personnel have to perform their tasks, we would strongly recommend that the outlay on police housing under the State Plans in the Five Year Plan (1978-83) be increased to Rs. 523 crore. Of this amount, Rs. 262 crore could be the investment by the States from their own resources and the balance of Rs. 261 crore could be the financial assistance from the Centre. The quantum of Central assistance in this scheme would be inclusive of the amount recommended by the Seventh Finance Commission for allocation to the States for this purpose on the non-Plan side. (The Seventh Finance Commission has recommended capital outlay of Rs. 82.86 crore in the non-Plan budget during the period 1979-84 for police housing in 15 States where the housing deficiency is comparatively large). We would not consider the total outlay of Rs. 523 crore in a Five Year Period as financially unreasonable or impracticable if the importance of this scheme is realised as it should be. In this context, we would like to observe that where the States are determined to make an investment in a scheme they consider important in any context, they are apparently able to find the money without great difficulty, as may be seen from the fact that in 1977-78, nine States, in which Assembly elections were due to be held, had announced several tax concessions and measures to relief to employees which amounted to an additional commitment of Rs. 326 crore from the States' resources in one single financial year, after the State Plans had earlier been finalised — *vide* statement made by the Finance Minister in the Lok Sabha on the 22nd July, 1977. Given the desire to alleviate the hardship of 3.86 lakh police personnel all over the country who have at present no Government accommodation of any kind whatsoever, family or even barrack type, and provide them with suitable accommodation to enable them discharge their heavy duties more efficiently to the satisfaction of the public, the Central Government and the State Governments should be able to find their way to make this investment in the first spell of five years, to be followed by a similar plan in the next five year period which would then see the completion of the entire programme. (Para 4.9)

11.34 We would recommend that the scheme of financial aid from the Centre be limited to housing programmes in States which have not yet reached 80 per cent satisfaction of family accommodation for the different ranks. If a higher level of satisfaction has been reached for any particular rank in a State, further outlay on police housing for that rank should not have the benefit of Central aid. This would also imply that when a State reaches 80 per cent level of satisfaction of housing for all the non-gazetted ranks, the scheme of Central assistance to that State will terminate. (Para 4.10)

11.35 We would recommend the following corrective measures eliminate the gaps in information in the Ministry of Home Affairs and delay in release of funds:

(i) The Ministry of Home Affairs should indicate to the State Government the allocation from the Central Plan outlay for police housing well before the commencement of the financial year, immediately after the Central Plan is finalised. This would enable the State Governments to chalk out their police housing programme well in advance;

(ii) The physical target in the form of specified number of dwelling units to be constructed with the investment of the proposed allocation of Central assistance should also be indicated in advance;

(iii) Achievement of physical targets from time to time should be monitored;

(iv) Funds may be released in instalments commencing with a provisional release at the very beginning of the year, followed by subsequent releases on receipt of progress reports from the States which shall indicate the total provision made in the State budget for police housing, the physical targets reached and the amount spent till then;

(v) During discussions with the Planning Commission regarding their Annual Plan outlays, State Governments should clearly indicate their proposed Plan outlay for police housing. The Plan approval communicated by the Planning Commission should specifically indicate the approved outlay on police housing separately, instead of clubbing it with general housing, as has been done in several letters of approval of the Annual Plan 1978-79 issued in 1978. A copy of the Annual Plan approval letter from the Planning Commission to the State, which is normally issued before the presentation of the State and Central budgets, should be marked to the Ministry of Home Affairs so that they could suitably plan the allocation of Central Assistance well in time for implementation during the year covered by the Plan;

(vi) If persistent failures are noticed in any State in the timely implementation of approved housing programmes, the Ministry of Home Affairs should send an official team to visit the State for identifying the difficulties and deficiencies in the field so that appropriate corrective action could be taken in time; and

(vii) A standard proforma for the periodic submission of all relevant information and data from the States to the Ministry of Home Affairs regarding police housing is indicated in Appendix XI. (Para 4.14)

11.36 We would recommend the constitution of the requisite number special divisions in the PWD of each State for implementing the police housing programmes. These divisions should be earmarked for the Police housing projects only and should not be deployed on other work. While these divisions would be under the administrative and technical control of the Chief Engineer of the PWD, their outturn of work should be subject to a close quarterly review by a Committee consisting of the Inspector General of Police, the Chief Engineer, PWD, and a representative each from the Home and Finance Departments. (Para 4.16)

11.37 Maharashtra, Andhra Pradesh and Bihar have set up Police Housing Corporations to handle construction programmes for police personnel. These corporations get financial aid from HUDCO also to pursue their construction plans. Other States could consider the setting up of similar Police Housing Corporations. (Para 4.17)

11.38 We would recommend the association of State Housing Boards with Police Housing schemes wherever possible. This arrangement could conveniently secure financial assistance from HUDCO. (Para 4.18)

11.39 It is necessary to strengthen the survey and planning organisation in the police and PWD to ensure that at any given time an adequate number of planned building projects with land already acquired and estimates duly approved are kept ready for commencement of work at short notice. Unless all these factors are taken care of at the planning stage, we will continue to have the paradox of paucity of resources on the one side and surrender of funds on the other. Whatever special arrangements are devised, it would be necessary for the police department to maintain close contact with the actual progress in the processing of housing schemes and the execution of sanctioned construction works. For this purpose, it would be advantageous if an officer of the appropriate rank from the PWD is taken on deputation to the Police Departments to function as liaison and monitoring officer. This system has been tried in one State with very useful results. (Para 4.19)

11.40 Nazul land and the excess land that becomes available for disposal by the Government under the provisions of Urban Land (Ceiling and Regulation) Act of 1976 could and should be utilised for police housing schemes wherever feasible. The extent to which this could be implemented in all the urban areas covered by the above mentioned Act, can be gone into by a small working group in each State consisting of representative of the Revenue, Housing and Police Departments. (Para 4.20)

11.41 *Ad hoc* and piecemeal establishment of police stations and outposts resulting from sporadic responses to local demands have aggravated the problem of accommodation for the police personnel who are deputed to man these stations and outposts. It would be a good arrangement if in all future cases of sanction of police stations and outposts the provision of residential accommodation for the police staff concerned is also settled simultaneously and all sanction orders are issued together. (Para 4.21)

11.42 We would recommend that in the future programme for construction of police housing, rural areas and metropolitan cities should be grouped together and given first priority followed by other cities and towns in that order. Availability of family accommodation in rural areas would also act as an incentive for willing acceptance of rural posting by police personnel. We would further recommend that as far as possible police quarters be built in the vicinity of police stations to facilitate group briefing and quick mustering of men as and when required. (Para 4.22)

11.43 We would strongly recommend that police personnel entitled to free accommodation should be fully reimbursed the actual house rent paid on their producing a certificate from their supervisory officer of the rank of D.S.P. that the accommodation occupied by them is not more that what they are entitled to under Government rules or Regulation made in this behalf by the Inspector General of Police. This payment may be subject to a ceiling determined for each rank at the district level by the chief revenue authority in the district in consultation with PWD. These ceilings shall be reviewed every three years. In this arrangement there shall be no need for certificates from the Rent Controller or any other similar authority for deciding individual cases so long as the ceiling limits are observed. (Para 4.23).

11.44 In addition to 100 per cent family accommodation for all non-gazetted ranks in the Civil and in the Armed Police, some barrack accommodation should be available for Constables who come from the moffusil to district headquarters on various duties. Barrack accommodation should also be available for personnel who are called for in-service training. But, in no case should this barrack accommodation be used for residential purposes by personnel posted in the district headquarters. (Para 4.24)

11.45 We recommend that the minimum living accommodation for Constabulary, i.e., Head Constables and Police Constables should consist of two rooms, a kitchen and a bathroom. (Para 4.25)

11.46 Another cause of anxiety and concern for police personnel, particularly the Constabulary, that has been brought to our notice is the problem of their accommodation after retirement. Most of them have no house of their own and view with alarm their accommodation problem which they would face after they retire from service. It would be appropriate in the present context for the Government to aid police personnel in building small houses for themselves. The aid can be in the form of a housing loan repayable in convenient instalments with the condition that the loanee would either live in the house himself or hand it over to the Government in the event of his transfer to some other place, and the Government would pay him monthly rent calculated on the current percentage of return on cash investment of corresponding value. The Government could then utilise the same house for accommodating another policeman posted at that place. We understand that such a scheme is in vogue in Maharashtra and would commend its adoption in all States. (Para 4.26)

11.47 Construction of such houses by the policemen themselves with aid from the Government would be further facilitated by setting up a Cooperative Housing Society in each district for all policemen. This arrangement would help in securing financial assistance from other bodies like the Life Insurance Corporation. Successful management of such Cooperative Housing Societies will need the whole time attention of a senior officer and we, therefore, recommend that an officer of the rank of Superintendent of Police in the welfare wing of the police department be entrusted with the responsibility for promoting these cooperative housing societies in each district. It should be deemed a legitimate charge on the welfare side of police budget to provide expert personnel for running these societies efficiently. (Para 4.27)

Supply of Essential Commodities

11.48 We find an arrangement in West Bengal for the supply of some essential commodities to subordinate police officers at rates which remain fixed irrespective of the rise in prices. In this scheme, which is in force from 1966, all subordinate police officers from the rank of Sub Inspector/Sergeant downwards including Wireless Supervisors, crew of police launches, Subedars and Jamadars of the Eastern Frontier Rifles, etc., are supplied rice, wheat, sugar, dal and mustard/rapeseed oil at fixed concessional rates according to a prescribed scale. The supply covers the family members of each police personnel up to a maximum limit of 4 including the personnel himself. The scheme is operated through supply centres which are opened at convenient places in a district and run by internal arrangement with the existing staff under the Superintendent of Police. The scale of supply at the fixed rates is furnished below:

Item	Quantity per head per week	Rate per kg.
Rice	1 kg.	0.50 p.
Wheat or	(1.50 kg. for policemen.	0.25 p.
Wheat products	1 kg. for family member)	
Sugar	300 grams	0.70 p.
Dal	750 grams	0.60 p.
Mustard Oil/ Rapeseed Oil	250 grams	2.00 p.

We find this scheme has served as an excellent morale booster for the West Bengal Police and is gratefully acknowledged as a great boon by the rank and file of the force. It has sustained their morale while working under severe economic strain and increasing pressure of duties all round. We would recommend the immediate adoption of this scheme for the police in all States. (Para 5.8)

11.49 Apart from the above scheme, we would further recommend that on occasions when police personnel are required to remain on duty for more than 8 hours at a stretch without relief, arrangements should be made for the supply of food packets to them at their places of duty at Government cost. This will be in addition to any daily allowance which they may be entitled to under the normal rules for the duty done that day. (Para 5.9)

Orderly System

11.50 We recommend that the orderly system as it exists at present be abolished. (Para 6.4)

11.51 In lieu of this system, one Constable may be attached to an officer for attending to (i) petitioners, complainants and other visitors who come to see the officer; (ii) attend to telephone calls particularly during the officer's absence and furnish helpful replies to enable the caller to speak to some other appropriate functionary for action; (iii) pass on messages to subordinate officers; and (iv) accompany the officer on his field work and be present with him to afford security and assistance in dealing with any situation. Entitlement to such assistance may be determined, not by the rank of the officer but by the actual need for such assistance with reference to the nature of his duties and responsibilities. (Para 6.5)

11.52 For carrying messages and files from the officer to the local staff stationed nearby, for assisting the officer in keeping his uniform and arms in a neat and smart condition and for maintaining the officer's reception room and office premises in a neat and tidy condition for receiving visitors and transacting official business, we feel that officers hitherto entitled to orderlies for the purpose of this work should continue to have assistance, but by an arrangement of paying the officer a suitable monthly allowance for employing a private person of his choice for performing these duties. The quantum of the monthly allowance may be fixed with reference to the provisions of the Minimum Wages Act, 1948, as applicable to an unskilled worker. The Government's responsibility will be limited to the payment of the monthly allowance to the officer. Employment of the private hand and payment of wages to him will be the officer's responsibility. (Para 6.6)

Machinery for Redressal of Grievances

11.53 There is an urgent need for devising a satisfactory system through which grievances can be effectively voiced and, what is more, some solutions can be found with a proper understanding and assessment of the issues involved. (Para 7.1)

11.54 The Police Forces (Restriction of Rights) Act, 1966 enacted by Parliament implies the recognition of the concept of an association for members of a police force, with due sanction from a prescribed authority. (Para 7.2)

11.55 While the right of police personnel to form associations is already recognised in law, subject to prescribed rules and regulations, we feel it would be useful to set down some general principles which should govern the formation and working of such associations, having regard to the paramount need for guarding against factors that might prejudice the proper discharge of duties by policemen and the maintenance of discipline among them. We recommend that the following guidelines be kept in view by the prescribed authorities while granting recognition to policemen's associations:

(i) Membership shall be restricted to serving policemen only. No outsiders, whether a government servant or not, shall be entitled to membership or function as an office bearer of the Association or be connected with it in any advisory or other capacity;

(ii) Members shall not have the right to strike work or withhold their services or otherwise delay the performance of their duties in any manner;

(iii) The Association shall not resort to any coercive method or agitation for obtaining redressal of grievances;

(iv) The Association shall not do anything which may affect the efficiency of the force or undermine its discipline; and

(v) The Association shall be absolutely non-political in character and shall not be connected directly or indirectly with political activity of any kind.

It would be desirable to have the above stipulations embodied in the Memoranda of Association of these bodies before they are recognised. (Para 7.5)

11.56 We have looked into the existing practice for the election of office bearers of these associations in some States. We appreciate that unless the office bearers come up through some process of election, they will not have the representative character which is important in the entire scheme of ventilation of grievances. We are, however, equally anxious that any electoral process adopted for this purpose among the police personnel should not provide the unintended scope for political forces to operate in a manner prejudicial to the maintenance of discipline and, what is more, the impartial character of the Police as a whole. In our view a process of indirect election of the type we are separately recommending in regard to Police Staff Councils could be adopted for the election of office bearers of police associations. State Governments may also like to consider other alternate methods of indirect election, having regard to local conditions and experience of working of police associations already existing in the State. (Para 7.6)

11.57 We further recommend that policemen's associations may be of the following four categories:

(i) One association may cover Constables and Head Constables and equivalent ranks;

(ii) A second association may cover all Assistant Sub-Inspectors, Sub-Inspectors and Inspectors and equivalent ranks;

(iii) A third association may cover all officers of the State Police Service of and above the rank of Deputy Superintendent of Police; and

(iv) Existing Indian Police Association will cover all I.P.S. officers.

Associations covering the ranks of Constable/Head Constable, Assistant Sub-Inspector/Sub-Inspector/Inspector may be formed on district basis. Representatives of the District Associations may constitute the State level Associations for these ranks. The Association of State Police Service Officers of an above the rank of Deputy Superintendent of Police may be organised on State basis. (Para 7.6)

11.58 Police Associations may only facilitate collective articulation of grievances but that by itself would not help in evolving practicable solutions. The existing system does not provide an adequate sense of participation for all members of the police force particularly at the lower levels, in the evolution of professional norms and techniques for handling police problems and for removal of grievances which stand in the way of efficient performance of duties. We have, therefore, to devise a forum at which representatives of Policemen's Associations can sit together in a kind of federal body and discuss the problems of evolving concrete and practicable solutions. (Para 7.7)

11.59 We recommend the immediate formation of a Joint Consultative Machinery in the shape of Staff Councils for the police personnel at the district level and the State level to provide such a forum and also a scheme for compulsory arbitration. (Para 7.10)

11.60 The District Police Staff Council – hereinafter referred to as DPSC – shall be made up of the following:

Superintendent of Police	1	(ex-officio Chairman)
Dy. Superintendent of Police	1	(Member Secretary)
Inspector of Police	1	(Member)
Sub-Inspector and Assistant Sub-Inspector	2	(Member)
Head Constable and Constable	4	(Member)
Total	9	

Note: Representatives from the rank of Head Constable/

Constable shall include at least 2 Constables. Representatives in the rank of Sub-Inspector/Assistant Sub-Inspector shall include at least one Assistant Sub-Inspector.

Members from the rank of Constable up to Deputy Superintendent of Police shall be nominated by the respective Service Associations. But, where no such associations exist, these members shall be elected through a process of indirect election covering all the personnel in the district. (Para 7.11)

11.61 At the State Police Headquarters, there shall be a State Police Staff Council – hereinafter referred to as SPSC — composed of the following:

Inspector General of Police	1 (ex-officio Chairman)
Deputy Inspector General of Police incharge of Welfare Wing	1 (ex-officio Member)
Assistant Inspector General of Police in charge of Administration	1 (ex-officio Member Secretary)
Superintendent of Police/Asstt. Superintendent of Police	2 (Member)
Deputy Superintendent of Police	2 (Member)
Inspector	2 (Member)
Sub-Inspector and Assistant Sub-Inspector	4 (Member)
Head Constable and Constable	8 (Member)
Total	21

Note: Representatives from the rank of Head Constable/ Constable shall include at least 4 Constables. Representatives in the rank of Sub-Inspector/Assistant Sub-Inspector shall include at least 2 Assistant Sub-Inspectors.

All Members of the SPSC, excepting the ex-officio functionaries, shall either be nominated by the State level Service Associations covering the respective ranks or shall be elected through a process of indirect election. (Para 7.14)

11.62 A candidate has to satisfy the following conditions to be eligible for membership of these Councils either through election or nomination as described above:

(i) He shall have put in at least five years of service in the police force on the first day of January of the year in which the election is held; and

(ii) He shall not have received any major punishment in the previous three years.

Note: Major punishment for this purpose shall mean reduction in rank or to a lower stage in the time scale and suspension from service, if imposed as a specific punishment. (Para 7.15)

11.63 Elected members of the DPSCs and SPSC shall hold office for a term of two years at a time. On expiry of one term, a member shall be eligible for re-appointment in either of these Councils if he comes up again through the same process of election as detailed above, but no such member shall hold office for more than two consecutive terms. A term of office held in either of these councils shall count for membership of the other council under this rule. Vacancies caused by death, retirement or transfer shall be filled for the unexpired term. (Para 7.16)

11.64 DPSC shall meet once in three months and the SPSC shall meet once in six months and discuss all matters pertaining to morale, welfare and other allied establishment problems which fall within the administrative purview of the State Government. They shall, however, be precluded from discussing individual cases of disciplinary proceedings or postings or transfers or similar establishment matters. The DPSC shall dispose of all matters regarding which remedial measures are feasible at the district level. Matters requiring further consideration and decision at higher levels shall be remitted to the SPSC. Service conditions of officers of the Indian Police Service or any other related matter which will require decision at the Central Government's level, shall be beyond the purview of the DPSCs and SPSCs. (Para 7.17)

11.65 There shall be a Joint Consultative Council (JCC) at the State Headquarters to deal with matters which require consideration and decision at the government level. This Council shall consist of an official side and a staff side. The official side shall be appointed by the Government and may consist of up to 7 members including the

Chief Secretary, Secretary in charge of police, Finance Secretary and Personnel Secretary in the State Government. The entire body of the SPSC, as described earlier, shall constitute the staff side of the Joint Consultative Council. The Minister in charge of Police shall be the Chairman of the Joint Consultative Council. It shall meet as often as necessary to deal with matters that arise from the deliberations of the SPSC or otherwise. (Para 7.18)

11.66 The scope of the JCC shall include all matters relating to conditions of service and work, welfare of the police personnel and improvement of efficiency and standards of work, provided, however, that: (i) in regard to recruitment, promotion and discipline, consultation will be limited to matters of general principles, and (ii) individual case shall not be considered. (Para 7.20)

11.67 The official side shall conclude matters at meetings of the council and shall not reserve them for later decision by the Government. (Para 7.21)

11.68 If there is no agreement between the two sides, the matter may be transmitted to a committee of the JCC for further examination and report. But, if a final disagreement is recorded, and the matter is one for which compulsory arbitration is provided, it shall be referred to arbitration, if so desired by either side. In other cases, the Government will take action according to its own judgement. (Para 7.24)

11.69 Arbitration shall be limited to:

(i) pay and allowances;
(ii) leave; and
(iii) any other matter that the SPSC and the State Government mutually agree to refer to arbitration. (Para 7.27)

11.70 Cases of individuals shall not be subject to arbitration. (Para 7.28)

11.71 A dispute shall not be referred to arbitration unless it has been considered by the JCC and final disagreement between the two sides has been recorded. (Para 7.29)

11.72 On a final disagreement being recorded as mentioned above, the State Government shall appoint a Board of Arbitration as soon as possible, in any case not later than one month from the date of recorded disagreement. The Board shall consist of three members, one drawn from a panel of 5 names submitted by the officials side, one from a similar panel submitted by the staff side of the JCC and a Chairman who shall be an independent person, preferably a retired or serving Judge of the High Court or senior administrator. The members and the Chairman shall be selected by the Minister in charge of Police. (Para 7.30)

11.73 Subject to the overriding authority of the State Legislative Assembly, recommendations of the Board of Arbitration shall be binding on both sides. (Para 7.33)

11.74 If, for reasons to be recorded in writing, the State Government is of opinion that all or any of the recommendations of the Board of Arbitration should on grounds affecting national economy or social justice be modified, the State Government shall, as soon as may be, lay before the state Legislative Assembly the report of the Board containing such recommendations together with the modification proposed and the reasons therefore, and thereupon the Legislative Assembly may make such modifications in the recommendations as it may deem fit. (Para 7.34)

11.75 Orders made by the State Government in pursuance of the recommendations of the Board of Arbitration shall, unless otherwise specified in these recommendations of modified by mutual agreement, remain in operation for a period of three years. (Para 7.35)

11.76 In making these recommendations, we have taken into account the currently growing trend of attitudes and feelings among the rank and file of the police force and the urgent need for the officer cadres and the leadership of the force to start a joint endeavour with the rank and file for a meaningful and collective discussion of service problems and evolve solutions in a manner which would satisfy the rank and file and foster in them feelings of professional pride, dignity and sense of participation in the decision-making processes in the system. We are fully convinced that unless the steps as envisaged above are taken in hand quickly, the rank and file will soon be enveloped by growing demoralisation and the entire system would get dangerously weakened. (Para 7.36)

11.77 We would recommend that the Staff Councils and the Joint Consultative Council as detailed above may be brought into being in the first instance through administrative orders. After gaining practical experience in working the scheme for some time, they may be given a statutory cover by appropriate modifications and additions to the Police Forces (Restriction of Rights) Act, 1966 and the rules framed thereunder. (Para 7.37)

11.78 We would further recommend that this Act be appropriately amended straightway to:

(i) enable the Central Government or the prescribed authority impose such conditions as may be deemed fit to ensure the proper discharge of police duties and the maintenance of discipline among policemen before granting sanction to any proposed association;
(ii) include the guidelines for the working of the associations as detailed in para 7.5;
(iii) enable the formation of associations to cover more than one rank, on the lines indicated in para 7.6; and
(iv) impose the same obligations on members of the families of policemen as applicable to policemen themselves in regard to their membership or other links with such associations. (Para 7.40)

11.79 Individual grievances have to be looked into by the departmental authorities at the supervisory levels. A rigid insistence on rituals in the name of discipline, before a subordinate police officer could approach the senior ranks for redressal of his grievances should be avoided. Any officer with a grievance should feel free to articulate it before his own superiors. Any attempt to stifle such articulation would only result in the affected personnel airing their grievances outside the system and that would lead to undesirable results. Supervisory officers should take the initiative and avail every opportunity to identify individual grievances in the normal course of their tours and inspections and take effective remedial measures. One of the points for assessing the supervisory capacity of an officer should be the measure of success achieved by him in identifying and redressing the grievances of his subordinates. Expeditious sanction and payment of increments and such other allowances as fall due from time to time, prompt settlement of leave, pension, provident fund, gratuity, etc., are matters that require close and constant attention from the supervisory officers to avoid build up of individual grievances on that account. (Para 7.41)

Recruitment, Training and Career Planning

11.80 We consider the educational qualification of Matric/SSLC as the very minimum for a Constable recruit to get trained properly and fit into the police system and in due course assume higher positions of responsibilities as envisaged by us. (Para 9.1)

Modalities for inquiry into Complaints against Police

11.81 One of the fundamental requisites of good government in a democracy is an institutionalised arrangement for effectively guarding against excesses or omissions by the executive in the exercise of their powers or discharge of their mandatory duties which cause injury, harm, annoyance or undue hardship to any individual citizen. This is specially necessary in the police who have vast scope for exercise of powers by a large number of personnel affecting the rights and liberty of individual citizens in daily life. (Para 10.1)

11.82 Statistics regarding complaints against police in many States reveal that:

(a) a sizeable percentage of complaints of police misconduct are preferred before police authorities higher than the Superintendent of Police;
(b) the percentage of substantiated complaints is low both in regard to the inquiries held by the District Magistrates and their officers and the inquiries held by the Superintendent of Police;
(c) percentage of substantiated complaints of police torture is highest in Judicial inquiries, lower in magisterial inquiries and lowest in inquiries conducted by other agencies; and
(d) a very large number of private criminal complaints filed against police officers in courts have failed. (Para 10.6)

11.83 There is imperative need to ensure that the complaints that are made, irrespective of their number, are handled in a manner that affords maximum satisfaction and carries credibility to the complainant in particular and the public in general. (Para 10.7)

11.84 Any arrangement for inquiry into complaints against police should be acceptable both to the police and to the public as fair and just, not favouring one at the expense of the other and not damaging the morale of the police and reducing their effectiveness in maintaining law and order. (Para 10.11)

11.85 A large number of complaints against police can

legitimately and rightly be looked into and disposed of by the supervisoy ranks in the police hierarchy itself. (Para 10.11)

11.86 Inquiries into any complaint of police misconduct shall be conducted by an officer of the rank of Inspector of Police or above only, on the following pattern:

Complaints against	*To be inquired into by*
Head Constables/Constables	An officer not below the rank of Inspector of Police.
Sub-Inspectors/Assistant Sub-Inspectors	An officer not below the rank of Deputy Superintendent of Police.
Inspectors of Police/Deputy Superintendents of Police/Assistant Superintendents of Police	An officer not below the rank of Superintendent of Police
Superintendents of Police and above	Complaint Cells directly supervised by the Deputy Inspector General or Inspector General, as the case may be. (Para 10.13)

11.87 While the above categorisation would apply to inquiries conducted by the authorities in the hierarchy in the normal course, there shall be a special complaint cell headed by a Deputy Superintendent of Police in each district working under the Superintendent of Police to handle inquiries into allegations of police misconduct in which the normal hierarchical levels are likely to take a biased view for any local reason. The discretion to entrust special inquiries to this cell shall be exercised by the Superintendent of Police having regard to the circumstances of each case. (Para 10.14)

11.88 There shall be a similar cell working directly under each Range DIG for handling inquiries which may involve scrutiny of the part played by the Superintendent of Police himself in any particular situation. At the State headquarters, there shall be a special cell under a Superintendent of Police with supporting staff of Deputy Superintendents of Police and Inspectors working directly under the Inspector General of Police to handle such inquiries which require attention at the State level. (Para 10.15)

11.89 Regarding the actual manner of conducting inquiries, the following points have to be kept in mind by Inquiry Officers:

(i) The complainant should be heard in detail and every effort must be made by the Inquiry Officer himself to ascertain the truth by examining such other witnesses as he may deem necessary, without insisting on the complainant himself to secure the presence of witnesses;
(ii) Important witnesses shall as far as possible be examined in the presence of the complainant so that he has the satisfaction of hearing what they depose;
(iii) Throughout the conduct of inquiry, the Inquiry Officer shall scrupulously avoid doing anything which might create a doubt in the complainant's mind about the objectivity and impartiality of the inquiry;
(iv) The inquiry shall, as far as practicable, be conducted in an appropriate public building or place, in or near, the complainant's resident village; and
(v) If the Inquiry Officer reports that the complainant himself does not want to press his complaint in any particular case, the facts and circumstances of that case shall again be verified by either the next superior officer or the district complaint cell. (Para 10.17)

11.90 In regard to the following categories of complaints against police, a judicial inquiry shall be mandatory and be held immediately according to a set procedure described in the Report:

(i) alleged rape of a woman in police custody;
(ii) death or grievous hurt caused while in police custody; and
(iii) death of two or more persons arising from police firing in the dispersal of an unlawful assembly as defined in Section 141 of the Indian Penal Code. (Para 10.19)

11.91 A judicial inquiry in the above cases shall be held by an Additional Sessions Judge nominated for this purpose in every district by the State Government in consultation with the High Court. He will be designated as the District Inquiry Authority—hereinafter referred to as 'DIA'. (Para 10.20)

11.92 In conducting the inquiry the DIA shall be assisted by an Assessor who shall be an Additional Superintendent of Police or senior Deputy Superintendent of Police nominated for this purpose in each district or group of districts as required by the Inspector General of Police. (Para 10.20)

11.93 The inquiry by the DIA shall be in the nature of a fact finding inquiry and shall, as far as possible and consistent with the provisions of the scheme described in the Report, conform to the procedure prescribed in the Commissions of Inquiry Act, 1952. (Para 10.23)

11.94 The inquiry shall also cover the circumstances leading to the alleged incident and any other matter which the DIA may consider relevant for the inquiry. (Para 10.23)

11.95 Proceedings before the DIA shall normally be open to the public. They may, however, be held in camera at the discretion of the DIA on the application made by the complainant or the Superintendent of Police, furnishing reasons therefor. (Para 10.23)

11.96 The DIA may take the assistance of an Additional Public Prosecutor or an Assistant Public Prosecutor in the district for examining witnesses, but no one shall be entitled to be represented by a legal practitioner in any proceedings before the DIA. (Para 10.23)

11.97 An inquiry taken up by the DIA under this scheme shall be given priority in his work and shall be proceeded with expeditiously through day-to-day hearings and completed within four months from the date on which the DIA receives the report or complaint on which the inquiry is started. If in any exceptional case the inquiry is held up beyond the specified period of four months, the DIA shall immediately inform the Government of the reasons for the delay and the probable time for the completion of inquiry.

11.98 On completion of inquiry, the DIA shall send his report with his findings to the State Government, simultaneously marking a copy to the Inspector General of Police. Thereupon the State Government shall in consultation with the Inspector General of Police, decide the course of further action, whether to prosecute the accused persons in court or deal with them in departmental disciplinary proceedings or dispose of the case in any other appropriate manner. It shall be mandatory on the part of the State Government to publish the report of the DIA and the State Government's decision thereon, within two months of receipt of DIA's report by the Government. If the DIA's inquiry had commenced on a complaint, a copy of the DIA's report and the State Government's decision thereon shall be furnished to the complainant simultaneous with the aforesaid publication of the report. (Para 10.26)

11.99 The DIA shall also serve as an independent authority to oversee the ultimate disposal of complaints dealt with by the administrative officers themselves in the normal course. Any complainant aggrieved by the disposal given on the conclusion of an inquiry, by the administrative authorities into his complaint of police misconduct, shall have the right of appeal to the DIA. The DIA shall be authorised to call for the connected records from the department and deal with the appeal. (Para 10.30)

11.100 A Police Complaints Board set up at the State level will generally oversee the satisfactory implementation of the new scheme throughout the State. (Para 10.31)

11.101 Complaints against police which are linked with their conduct in a specific case under active investigation, are best looked into by the supervisory ranks at some appropriate level so that the investigation of the main case is not prejudiced. Even in such instances if the complaint refers to a serious misconduct of the type which would automatically attract the jurisdiction of the DIA for inquiry, it shall be inquired into by the DIA only. (Para 10.34)

11.102 Complaints against police which predominantly involve a corruption angle are best looked into by the State Anti-Corruption Department who have the experience and expertise to deal with such complaints. Modalities for conducting inquiries into such complaints when they arise in the course of active investigation of a specific case should be settled by discussion between the police and Vigilance Branch at the level of DIG/IG. (Para 10.35)

Financial Implications

12.1 The likely financial implications of the recommendations made in the different chapters of the report are briefly indicated in the following paragraphs:

Preamble and the Constabulary (Chapters I and II)

12.2 No cost is involved because these chapters contain some fundamental and basic observations only, relating to the police structure in general and the Constabulary in particular.

Pay Structure (Chapter III)

12.3 (i) An important recommendation having a cost factor is that a Constable should be rated as a "skilled" worker for determining his pay structure *vis-a-vis* other public services in the State, in view of his revised role in the new set up as visualised by us, where he will be employed on inquiry and investigational work and other duties requiring frequent interaction with the public with due exercise of discretion and judgement. We are not making any recommendations for any particular pay scale as such. The cost of implementing this recommendation will vary from State to State, depending on the existing degree of difference between the skilled worker's pay and the pay of a Constable in the State. In one State, the Constable's pay has already been revised to this level and, therefore, it will not mean any cost as far as that State is concerned. All that we are projecting in this recommendation is a recognition of a fundamental principle so that the policemen's pay structure will have a particular status in the overall pay structure of the services in the State.

(ii) In view of the fact that several policemen are required to work even on gazetted holidays which are normally occasions for rest and holidaying by the general public and several other services, a recommendation has been made that, besides his normal entitlement to leave, a Constable/Head Constable should be entitled to additional leave for 15 days every year with facility to encash that leave if it is denied to him in public interest. The extent to which this additional leave is denied to the Constables will be a variable factor and, therefore, the cost involved in payment of equivalent cash cannot be precisely estimated.

(iii) In view of the prolonged and arduous hours of work put in by policemen in certain branches of the police on every working day, we are recommending overtime pay at the rate of 30 per cent of total emoluments including DA and CCA for all police personnel from the rank of Constable upto and inclusive of the rank of Inspector working in police units which deal with public order situations and crime investigations. It is for the State Governments to notify from time to time the police branches to which the above system of overtime pay will be admissible and, therefore, it will not be possible to estimate the actual cost right now.

(iv) It is recommended that the conveyance allowance and washing allowance paid to the Constabulary which are low and unrealistic in some States should each be raised to Rs. 10 p.m. The cost involved in this recommendation will vary from State to State. In Delhi, it will amount to about Rs. 8.6 lakh per year.

(v) It is recommended that a special qualification pay be paid to policemen, who acquire the following skills or technical/academic knowledge:

(a) proficiency in driving and motor mechanism;
(b) proficiency in handling wireless equipment for transmitting and receiving messages;
(c) proficiency in handling computers and electronic data processing machinery; and
(d) acquiring a University degree higher than what he had already secured at the time of entering service in a subject which would be of professional use to him. For example, criminology, forensic sciences, etc.

We are not recommending any particular quantum of special pay but are leaving it to the State Governments to fix it realistically, having regard to the pay and emoluments drawn by similarly qualified personnel working in other services or the private sector in the States.

Housing (Chapter IV)

12.4 (i) The approximate cost of construction of family accommodation for all the entitled personnel in the States who are yet to be provided with Government accommodation of any kind is Rs. 1045 crore. If this programme is spread over 10 years, the total outlay in the first 5 year period will be Rs. 523 crores, of which we are recommending Rs. 262 crore to be met by the States from their own resources and the balance of Rs. 261 crore to be the financial aid from the Centre.

(ii) For speeding up the construction programme we have recommended constitution of the requisite number of special divisions in the PWD of each State for looking after these programmes exclusively. The actual number of divisions will have to be determined in each State depending on the existing working workload of their PWD set up. Cost on this account cannot possibly be calculated at this stage.

Supply of Essential Commodities (Chapter V)

12.5 We have recommended a scheme similar to the one that obtains in West Bengal for supply of certain essential commodities like rice, dhal, etc., at fixed rates, which are to be maintained independent of the inflationary price rise in the market. In West Bengal the cost of this scheme is of the order of Rs. 6.5 crore per year.

Orderly System (Chapter VI)

12.6 The existing system is proposed to be abolished and replaced by a system in which some officers will get a regular Constable for their assistance in the performance of certain duties and some others will get a monthly allowance to engage a civilian servant for purposes of certain other types of duties currently being done by a uniformed orderly. The number of officers to whom this monthly allowance may be paid is to be determined by the State authorities. The exact cost cannot, therefore, be calculated, but since this arrangement is in lieu of an existing orderly who get paid more as a Constable, it is likely to result in some saving to Government.

Machinery for Redressal of Grievances of Police Personnel (Chapter VII)

12.7 No cost is involved in the proposed formation of Staff Councils as such, but some small additional cost may arise on account of movement of the Members of the Councils to the District headquarters and State headquarters from time to time in connection with the Council elections and other connected work. If a Board of Arbitration is set up, some minimal secretariat assistance has to be provided for the Board.

Welfare Measures for Police Families (Chapter VIII)
Recruitment, Training and Career Planning (Chapter IX)

12.8 Our detailed recommendations are yet to be made and no cost is involved in the preliminary observations we have made in this report.

Modalities for Inquiry into Complaints against Police (Chapter X)

12.9 Cost is involved in:

(a) setting up Complaint Cells at the district level/range level and State level; and
(b) setting up of the District Inquiry Authority.

As regards the Complaint Cells we are recommending that an existing functionary may be asked to look after this work and an exclusive post for this purpose may be created in major districts only. In regard to the DIA set up also, we have left it to the State authorities to nominate an existing functionary in the district judiciary as the DIA and create an exclusive post for this purpose only where the workload is heavy. The cost cannot, therefore, be precisely estimated at this stage. It will depend on the arrangements actually made on the needs of the situation.

NATIONAL POLICE COMMISSION, 1977 — SECOND REPORT[1]

Chairman Shri Dharma Vira, retired Governor

Members Shri N.K. Reddy; Shri K.F. Rustamji; Shri N.S. Saksena; Prof. M.S. Gore

M. Secy. Shri C.V. Narasimhan

Alterations Shri C.V. Narasimhan, former Director of Central Bureau of Investigation, functioned as Member Secretary of the Commission from its inception till 19th April, 1980 when he left to take a posting in his parent cadre in Tamil Nadu on replacement of his services from the Central Government to the State Government. After the departure of Shri Narasimhan, Shri M.D. Dikshit, Principal Director of Research, functioned as the Secretary Incharge.

Appointment

Far-reaching changes have taken place in the country after the enactment of the Indian Police Act, 1861 and the setting up of the Second Police Commission of 1902 particularly during the last thirty years of Independence. Though a number of States have appointed Police Commissions after Independence to study the problems of the Police in their respective States, there has been no comprehensive review at the national level of the police system after Independence despite radical changes in the political, social and economic situation in the country. A fresh examination is necessary of the role and performance of the Police—both as a law enforcement agency, and as an institution to protect the rights of the citizens enshrined in the Con-

---

1. Controller of Publications, Delhi, 1979, 103 p.

stitution. The Government of India have, therefore, decided to appoint a National Police Commission. The National Police Commission was appointed under the Government of India, Ministry of Home Affairs Resolution No. VI-24021/36/77-GPA.I, dated November 15, 1977.

Terms of Reference

The following will be the terms of reference of the Commission

(1) Re-define the role, duties, powers and responsibilities of the police with special reference to prevention and control of crime and maintenance of public order.
(2) Examine the development of the principles underlying the present policing system, including the method of magisterial supervision, evaluate the performance of the system, identify the basic weakneses of inadequacies, and suggest appropriate changes in the system and the basic laws governing the system.
(3) Examine, if any changes are necessary in the existing method of administration, disciplinary control and accountability.
(4) Inquire into the system of investigation and prosecution, the reasons for delay and failure, the use of improper methods, and the extent of their prevalence; and suggest how the system may be modified or changed, and made efficient, scientific and consistent with human dignity; and how the related laws may be suitably amended.
(5) Examine methods of maintaining crime records and statistics and suggest methods for making them uniform and systematic.
(6) Review policing in rural areas evaluate any new arrangements that have been made, and recommend changes that are necessary.
(7) Examine the system of policing required in non-rural and urbanised areas including metropolitan areas, and suggest the pattern that would be the most suitable.
(8) Examine the steps taken for modernising law enforcement, evaluate the work of police communications, the computer network, scientific laboratories and agencies for research and development, and examine whether modernisation can be speeded up; examine to what extent, as a result of the moder-

nisation of Police forces, streamlining of its functions and its re-structuring, it would be possible to economise in the man-power in the various areas of its activities.

(9) Examine the nature and extent of the special responsibilities of the Police towards the weaker sections of the community and suggest steps to ensure prompt action on their complaints for the safeguard of their rights and interests.

(10) Recommend measures and institutional arrangements:

(i) to prevent misuse of powers by the police, and to examine whether police behaviour, out-look, responsiveness and impartiality are maintained at the correct level, and if not the steps such as recruitment and training which should be taken to improve them;

(ii) to prevent misuse of the police by administrative or executive instructions, political or other pressure, or oral order of any type, which are contrary to law;

(iii) for the quick and impartial inquiry of public complaints made against the police about any misuse of police powers;

(iv) for the quick redressal of grievances of police personnel and to look after their morale and welfare; and

(v) for a periodic objective evaluation of police performance in a metropolitan area/District/State in a manner which will carry credibility before the public.

(11) Examine the manner and extent to which police can enlist ready and willing co-operation of the public in the discharge of their social defence and law enforcement duties and suggest measures regarding the institutional arrangements to secure such co-operation and measures for the growth of healthy and friendly public-police relationship.

(12) Examine the methods of police training, development, and career-planning of officers and recommend any changes that are required at any time in their service, to modernise the out-look, and to make the leadership of the force effective and morally strong.

(13) Examine the nature of the problems that the police will have to face in the future, and suggest the measures necessary for dealing with them, and for keeping them under continuous

study and appraisal.

(14) Consider and make recommendations and suggestions regarding any other matter which the Government may refer to the Commission; and

(15) Any other matter of relevance or importance having an impact on the subject

Contents

Welfare measures for police families; Police role, duties, powers and responsibilities; Interference with and misuse of police by illegal or improper orders or pressure from political executive or other extraneous sources: Remedial measures; Gram Nyayalayas; Maintenance of crime records and statistics; Summary of observations and recommendations; Appendices.

Recommendations

Welfare Measures for Police Families

18.1 Among the many deficiencies that got exposed in the situation following the recent agitation by policemen in some States, one relates to the inadequacy of welfare measures for police families. (Para 13.1)

18.2 Governments have tended to accord low priority to the funding of police welfare measures. Police leadership does not appear to have realised its responsibility to take the initiative and organise such measures with a total and complete involvement of the personnel in maintaining them. The rank and file themselves have tended to view these measures as a responsibility of the Government and have been disinclined to perform their own contributory role in full measure. (Para 13.2)

18.3 The Ashwini Kumar Committee has given a report recommending several welfare measures to cover housing, education, medical care, recreational facilities, financial aid and special retirement benefits in distress situations arising from death or physical disability caused by service conditions, etc. Extracts from Ashwini Kumar Committee's Report are furnished in Appendix II. We broadly agree with these recommendations and would advise their adoption in planning police welfare measures in the States. (Para 13.4)

18.4 One category of welfare measures would cover such items like pension/family pension/gratuity, medical facilities, housing, etc., which should be deemed as a part of conditions of service of police personnel and, therefore, should be funded fully and adequately by the Government. Another category would cover such measures like welfare centres to provide work for police families and help in augmenting their income, financial aid and encouragement for pursuing higher studies by police children who show special merit, financial relief in distress situations not provided for under regular rules, etc. For organising welfare measures of the second category, an adequate welfare fund should be built up initially by contributions from the police personnel themselves, supplemented by *ad hoc* grants from the Government and sustained by recurring contributions and grants. In organising such measures and building up the necessary fund, a lot will depend on the initiative and interest taken by the personnel themselves and the continuous lead, guidance and support given by supervisory officers. The officer cadre of the force should realise their special responsibility in this regard and act accordingly. (Para 13.5)

18.5 The work done by an officer in organising welfare measures for the personnel under his command should be specifically commented on in his annual confidential report. (Para 13.5)

18.6 Wives of officers can play a significant role in bringing together the families of police personnel and encouraging their collective involvement in welfare work of different kinds. (Para 13.5)

18.7 A brief assessment of the existing welfare measures for the police personnel in different States is furnished in Appendix III. It indicates under different headings the most advantageous and beneficial arrangement that a few States have found it possible to introduce in regard to their own police personnel. The remaining States may immediately examine the feasibility of introducing similar arrangements for their policemen also. (Para 13.6)

18.8 Government should take special care of the family of a policemen who happens to die or get disabled in circumstances arising from the risks of his office. In the case of a policeman who dies in such circumstances we would recommend financial aid to the family on the following lines:

(i) *Gratuity* equivalent to 8 months' pay last drawn by the deceased;

(ii) *Monthly pension* to the family equal to the last pay drawn by the deceased till the date on which the deceased would have normally reached the age of superannuation, and thereafter a monthly pension equal to the amount of pension to which the deceased would have been entitled if he had continued in service till the date of his superannuation; and

(iii) *Ex-gratia grant* of Rs. 10,000 as immediate financial assistance. (Para 13.7)

18.9 Arrangements for line visits by a Government doctor should be made by authorising a small monthly allowance to the doctor from Government funds, if need be, depending on the frequency of calls and the distances involved. (Para 13.8)

18.10 Medical treatment in all police hospitals should also be extended to retired police personnel and their families. (Para 13.9)

18.11 We endorse the following important recommendations of various State Police Commissions in regard to the educational facilities for policemen's children:

(1) There should be free education up to high school standard;
(2) The children of policemen should get a grant of Rs. 50 p.a. per child in lump sum for purchase of books;
(3) There should be no fees charged in Government or Government aided schools;
(4) Scholarships should be provided for vocational education;
(5) There should be hostel accommodation for the children of policemen at every divisional headquarters; and
(6) Special scholarships should be given on grounds of exceptional merit for university education. (Para 13.11)

18.12 The first requisite of any arrangement for this purpose would be the creation of a separate police education fund in each State, made up of contributions from the police personnel themselves and supplemented and assisted by *ad hoc*/recurring grants from the State Government. The fund should be built up with the ultimate object of establishing at least one police school in each district headquarters which could take in police children for education up to the 12th standard. Hostel accommodation for children of police personnel located outside the district headquarters should also be planned. Admission to such schools should be governed by suitable tests to recognise merit and facilitate the development of bright young police children. In the curriculum of these schools, there should be special emphasis on discipline and a healthy combination of rigorous outdoor exercises with intensive academic pursuits. Management of all such police schools in a State may be supervised by the Head of the training wing of the Police Department and overseen by a Police School Board whose chairman could be the Head of the Department of Education in the State and the Member Secretary could be the Head of the training wing in the police. A couple of eminent educationists could also be nominated to the Board. The pay and allowances of the police personnel on the staff in the school could be borne by the Police Department. The deputation allowance and other incentives provided to the other teaching staff drawn on deputation from the other Government schools may also be borne by the Police Department. The rest of the expenditure may be borne by the Education Department. Police children who do exceptionally well in these schools may be encouraged with scholarship from 'police welfare fund' to pursue higher collegiate studies. (Para 13.13)

18.13 Every effort should be made to finalise pension papers in good time so that every policemen receives his full pension order along with the gratuity amount and other dues on the very day of retirement itself. We were told in one metropolitan city about the initiative shown by the Commissioner of Police in arranging for farewell parades for all policemen who retired every month and seeing them off in a solemn ceremony with the full payment of their dues and pension order. We commend this initiative to all police units. (Para 13.14)

18.14 Inadequate leave reserve is one of the reasons behind the organisation's inability to sanction and rotate leave promptly among the operating personnel. This deficiency in the strength of police personnel should be looked into and made good. (Para 13.15)

18.15 Different types of 'group insurance schemes' are now available for all categories of employees in Government. Details of two special schemes which appear to be specially attractive and have been adopted in two State are furnished in the note in Appendix III. We recommend their adoption in other States as well. (Para 13.16)

18.16 Regarding the sources and mechanisms for the initial building up of police welfare fund and its sustained maintenance, the Ashwini Kumar Committee has made specific recommendations with which we agree. The broad principle which may guide the working arrangements in this matter should be that 60 per cent of he requirements of the fund comes from contributions from the police personnel themselves, 20 per cent is made up from Government grants and they balance 20 per cent is covered by the interest generated by the interest generated by the initial lump sum grants which may be kept in fixed deposits or invested otherwise. (Para 13.17)

18.17 Management of the welfare fund should be by a committee constituted by the police staff council. (Para 13.18)

18.18 The audit of the welfare fund at the battalion/district level should be made the responsibility of a sub-committee of the battalion/district staff council which would be representative in character and adequately reflect the interests of the rank and file. It will be open to this sub-committee to take the assistance of a qualified professional accountant or auditor to get this job done. (Para 13.19)

18.19 Wages for work done by police families at welfare centres in stitching police uniform or for other similar occupation should be determined by a local committee in which the Government secretariat and the police management could both be involved to take a realistic view of all the relevant factors. (Para 13.20)

18.20 Retired police personnel and educated girls in police families may be given first preference for employment to manage and run police canteens and stores. (Para 13.21)

18.21 A recurring deposit scheme as organised in the Border Security Force for augmenting the pension/gratuity assistance for the police personnel at the time of their retirement may be adopted by all police units. (Para 13.22)

18.22 Every State police must have a whole-time police welfarc officer at the State Headquarters who, by his initiative and interest, should organise welfare measures on a sound basis in every district/battalion and, what is more, ensure satisfactory delivery of welfare services on the ground. We leave it to the State Governments to decide the rank of this officer at State Headquarters, while observing that it is not the mere rank but the initiative and genuine interest shown by the officer and the example set by him that would count more in this matter. (Para 13.24)

18.23 Resettlement of ex-policemen who retire in the normal course will need assistance and advice to keep themselves occupied and settled in reasonable comfort. There is considerable scope for rendering assistance in the matter of securing allotment of land for cultivation, or facilities for productive self-employment from various developmental agencies under the Government or otherwise. The State Police Welfare Officer should deem it a part of his responsibility to render this help on a systematic basis for retired police personnel. (Para 13.25)

Police Role, Duties, Powers and Responsibilities

18.24 Police, prosecutors, advocates, judges, functionaries in the correctional services and jails form the different distinct organised wings of the criminal justice system. The role, duties, powers and responsibilities of the police with special reference to prevention and control of the crime cannot be defined in isolation in absolute terms, but has to be fitted into the overall requirements for the success of the criminal justice system as a whole. (Para 14.1)

18.25 The classification of offences and limitations of police response to complaints thereof, as spelt out in the existing laws, do not conform to the understanding and expectation of the common people who, when they become victims of a crime or are otherwise subjected to a distress situation, naturally turn to the police for help. Police become a much misunderstood force when their action gets limited by law contrary to the natural expectations of the people. There is, therefore, immediate need to examine the procedural laws and allied regulations for modifying them to enable police response to confirm to public expectations, consistent with the resources potential of the police. (Para 14.2)

18.26 The rules which govern the present accusatorial system of criminal trials make various demands from and place various restrictions on the prosecution so that the defendant gets all the help he can to defend himself. At the end of the trial the prosecution must prove their case beyond reasonable doubt, but the accused may, however, only raise a doubt and get its benefit to secure his acquittal. The severe limitations placed on the admissibility of evidence from the prosecution side and the norms for determining the value of the admitted evidence make it difficulty for the police as the investigating agency to carry forward all the material uncovered during their investigation to the final point of success in getting the offender convicted under the law. (Para 14.5)

18.27 We are convinced of the need for effective interaction between the police and the prosecuting agency at the stage of court trial for proper marshalling and presentation of all the evidence uncovered during investigation. Facilities for such interaction should be provided without in any manner affecting the professional independence of the prosecuting agency. The need for such interaction should also be suitably recognised in law instead of being left as a mere administrative arrangement. (Para 14.6)

18.28 The rituals of court trials under the existing law and the general attitude shown by the legal counsel tend to delay the proceedings in court. Apart from the delays at the stage of investigation which are attributable to deficiencies in police, the further delay at the stage of trial results in considerable harassment to the victims of a crime while at the same time the effect of deterrence of quick conclusion of proceedings in court is lost on the offender himself. Pendency of criminal cases undertrial in courts has gone up enormously in the recent years and the system itself will soon get clogged up beyond repair if the existing law is allowed to operate without any modification. (Para 14.7)

18.29 There is urgent need for a comprehensive reform in the procedural laws relating to investigation and trial in our system. (Para 14.9)

18.30 Though well-conceived and based on progressive concepts, the institutions and services contemplated under the Probation of Offenders Act, the Children Act, the Suppression of Immoral Traffic Act and similar enactments in the category of social legislation suffer in practice because of a totally inadequate infrastructure. (Para 14.9)

18.31 Our jails are terribly overcrowded. The population of undertrial prisoners in relation to convicts has rapidly increased. The huddling together of a large number of undertrials with convicted prisoners and the mixing together of old and hardened criminals with young first offenders tend to promote in the minds of all inmates feelings of criminality instead of remorse and regret for their previous conduct and a desire to reform. (Para 14.13)

18.32 Apart from the over-crowding in jails, the general manner in which the rituals of the daily life inside the jails are rigidly administered and enforced tends to dehumanise the prisoner who is cowed down by the oppressive atmosphere around with all its brutalities, stench, degradation and insult. Instead of functioning as a reformatory house to rehabilitate the criminal to reform him and make him see the error of his ways and return a better and nobler man, the ethos inside our jails to-day is tragically set in the opposite direction, making it practically difficult for any reformatory process to operate meaningfully. (Para 14.13)

18.33 The deficiency in the functioning of their correctional services has meant the weakening of their corrective influence on the behaviour and conduct of all the delinquents who pass through the system. Police, who appear in the first part of the system to investigate crimes and identify the offenders involved, have gain to contend with the likely continued criminal behaviour of the same offenders, without the expected aid and assistance from the other agencies of the system to contain their criminality. We are, therefore, of the opinion that in whatever way we may define the role, duties and responsibilities of the police, they cannot achieve ultimate success in their role performance unless all the wings of the criminal justice system operate with simultaneous efficiency. This would require our having some kind of body which will have the necessary authority and facilities to maintain a constant and comprehensive look at the entire system, monitor its performance and apply the necessary correctives from time to time, having in view the overall objective of the system. In view of the primacy of law in the entire system, our first thoughts in this matter go to the Law Commission. We feel it would be advantageous to enlarge the concept of the Law Commission and make it function as a Criminal Justice Commission on a statutory basis to perform this overseeing role on a continuing basis. For this purpose it would be desirable for appropriate functionaries from the police and correctional services to be actively associated with the deliberations of the new Commission. This arrangement at the Centre should be supported by a similar arrangement at the State level in which a high powered body under the Chairmanship of the Chief Justice of the High Court, either serving or retired, and with members drawn from the police, bar and the correctional services, would perform this monitoring role and evaluate annually the performance of the system as a whole. (Para 14.14)

18.34 Police role in maintaining public order has even greater limitations specially in a democracy. Maintenance of order implies a certain measure of peace and avoidance of violence of any kind. Public order is deemed to have been upset, in public estimate, if violence breaks out in public in a noticeable form. The characteristic features of the existing social structure in India are (i) inter-group conflicts on account of religion, language, caste, etc; (ii) increasing pressure of poverty; (iii) increasing unemployment; and (iv) rapid urban growth rate with a concentration of organised protest groups in urban areas like Government employees, industrial workers, political groups students, etc. All these factors, combined with the general belief among the havenots that the only way to evoke response from administration is to launch an agitation or a strike or any form of protest activity involving violence of some kind or other, induce an atmosphere of continuing pressure and proneness to break into situations of public disorder. (Para 14.16)

18.35 Public urge for reform and relief from pressure situations of the above kind are often articulated by political parties, particularly those in opposition to the ruling party. Protest activity, therefore, gets mixed up with political dissent. Police methodology in dealing with such situations has necessarily to conform to democratic traditions and cannot have the trappings of the technique of an authoritarian regime to sustain itself in power. In such circumstances, the police have the most difficult role to perform to maintain order. Any step taken by them for this purpose is immediately viewed by the agitating public as partisan conduct to maintain the *status quo* and oppose the changes for which the agitators clamour. Police invariably get dubbed as being on the side of the conservative and the no changer. Police action in such situations is severely handicapped on this account. Police cannot be expected to handle such situations, all by themselves but they should have accommodation, co-operation, assistance, sympathy and understanding from organised section of the public themselves. (Para 14.17)

18.36 The basic role of the police is to function as a law enforcement agency and render impartial service to law, in complete independence of mere wishes, indications of desires, expressed by the Government as a matter of policy which either come in conflict with or do not conform to the provisions in our Constitution or laws duly enacted thereunder. We recommend that this basic role of the police may be specifically spelt out in categorical terms in the Police Act. (Para 14.28)

18.37 A Code of Conduct for the police in India was adopted at the Conference of Inspectors General of Police in 1960 and circulated to all the State Governments. We recommend that clause (12) of the above Code may be modified to read as under:

(12) The police should recognise that their full utility to the people of the country is best ensured only by maintaining a high stan-

dard of discipline, faithful performance of duties in accordance with law and implicit obedience to the directions of commanding ranks and absolute loyalty to the force and by keeping themselves in a state of constant training and preparedness. (Para 14.29)

18.38 Having regard to the objectives mentioned in the Preamble to our Constitution, we would hold that law enforcement by police should cover the following two basic functions:

(i) Upholding the dignity of the individual by safeguarding his constitutional and legal rights. Police secure this objective by enforcing laws relating to the protection of life, liberty and property of the people; and
(ii) Safeguarding the fabric of society and the unity and integrity of the nation. Police secure this objective by enforcing laws relatable to maintenance of public order. (Para 14.31)

18.39 We are of the view that police have a direct and more or less exclusive responsibility in the task of investigating crimes but have a limited role in regard to the prevention of crime for the reason that the various contributory factors leading to crime do not totally and exclusively fall within the domain of police for control and regulation. A co-ordinated understanding and appreciation of these factors not only by the police but also by several other agencies connected with social defence and welfare would be necessary for effective prevention of crime. Police responsibility for the prevention of crime has thus to be shared to some extent with other agencies. We feel that this distinction in police responsibility for investigation of crime on the one hand and prevention of crime on the other should be clearly understood and indicated in the Police Act itself, which would also thereby institutionalise and facilitate appropriate associative action by other social welfare agencies for preventing crime. (Para 14.32)

18.40 We recommend a system of licensing with appropriate statutory backing to control the working of private detective agencies which have come up in the country in the recent years. (Para 14.35)

18.41 Police responsibility for investigation of crimes may be spelt out in general terms in the basic law, namely, the Police Act, but in actual procedural practice there should be graded situations specifying different degrees of police responsibility in regard to different types of crimes. (Para 14.36)

18.42 Certain types of crimes will require police intervention on their own initiative and on their own intelligence, without waiting for a complaint as such from any aggrieved person. Certain other types of crimes may justify police intervention only on a specific complaint from a member of the public. A third category of crime can be visualised where police may intervene only on a complaint from an aggrieved party and not by any member of the public. (Para 14.36)

18.43 With regard to police role in the enforcement of social legislation, we are of the view that as the primary law enforcement agency available to the State, police cannot escape involvement in the enforcement of social and economic laws also in some form or the other. Police have a duty to enforce these laws but the manner of enforcement can certainly be regulated and controlled to avoid some possible evils that may arise from this involvement. (Para 14.40)

18.44 Police responsibility for prevention and investigation of ordinary crimes may ultimately lead them on to involvement in containing law and order situations, public order situations and threats to internal security, in that order. When the country's internal security is threatened, the Central Government has a direct responsibility for taking appropriate counter measures. It has been the practice for the Central Government to come to the aid of State Governments by deputing armed forced of the Centre like CRP and BSF to aid the State police in dealing with serious public order situations. Police is at present a State subject in the 7th Schedule of the Constitutions. It is for consideration of the Central Government and the State Governments whether the Central Government should be constitutionally facilitated to coordinate and direct police operations in situations which threatened internal security. In our view, the addition of Entry 2A in the Union List of the 7th Schedule following the Constitution (Forty Second) Amendment Act, 1976 recognises this need to some extent. We understand that no law has yet been enacted and no rules or regulations have yet been laid down governing the jurisdiction, privileges and liabilities of the members of the armed forces of the Union when they are deployed in a State in accordance with Entry 2A of the Union List. We recommend that appropriate law/rules/regulations for this purpose be enacted soon. (Para 14.42)

18.45 Under the existing law—Section 23 of the Police Act,

1861— the police are responsible for collecting intelligence affecting public peace only. We recommend that police powers for collection of intelligence should cover not only matters affecting public peace but also matters relatable to crimes in general including social and economic offences, national integrity and security. The legal provisions in this regard should be in the nature of enabling provisions which can be availed by the police to collect intelligence as and when required. Law should not place the exclusive responsibility on the police only for collection of all intelligence on these matters because we are aware that a variety of intelligence relevant to these matters may fall within the jurisdiction of some other developmental or regulatory agencies as well. We further recommend that a police agency should not have the power or facilities for collection of any intelligence other than what is specified in law, as proposed. (Para 14.44)

18.46 There is considerable scope for exercise of discretion at various stages in the discharge of police functions, particularly in regard to preventive policing measures before a crime occurs, as distinct from investigation which starts after the occurrence of crime. We are of the view that exercise of discretion in all such situations should be based on the assessment and judgement of the police functionaries concerned only. To prevent freakish or whimsical decision in such matters some broad guidelines should be laid down to cover all such conceivable situations. Police Manuals which do not contain such guidelines at present should be appropriately amplified. These guidelines should be set out in clear terms and also made known to the public. *Ad hoc* views or policies declared on the spur of the moment and conveyed orally or otherwise from the executive hierarchy above should not be deemed equivalent to guidelines for such purposes. In the absence of a guideline, the matter should be left to the sole discretion of the police officer directly involved in the situation and should not be subject to directions from above, except where it falls within the legitimate supervisory responsibility of a higher functionary under the law. (Para 14.45)

18.47 Counselling and warning should be deemed as legitimate police activities towards prevention of crime and recognised as such in law. (Para 14.46)

18.48 The police should have a duly recognised service-oriented role to play in providing relief to persons in distress situations like those arising out of natural calamities like cyclones, floods, etc. The police should be trained and equipped properly to perform these service-oriented functions. (Para 14.50)

18.49 We recommend that the New Police Act may spell out the duties and responsibilities of the police to —

(i) promote and preserve public order;
(ii) investigate crimes, and where appropriate, to apprehend the offenders and participate in subsequent legal proceedings connected therewith;
(iii) identify problems and situations that are likely to result in commission of crimes;
(iv) reduce the opportunities for the commission of crimes through preventive patrol and other appropriate police measures;
(v) aid and co-operate with other relevant agencies in implementing other appropriate measures for prevention of crimes;
(vi) aid individuals who are in danger of physical harm;
(vii) create and maintain a feeling of security in the community;
(viii) facilitate orderly movement of people and vehicles;
(ix) counsel and resolve conflicts and promote amity;
(x) provide other appropriate services and afford relief to people in distress situations;
(xi) collect intelligence relating to matters affecting public peace and crimes in general including social and economic offences, national integrity and security; and
(xii) perform such other duties as may be enjoined on them by law for the time being in force.

Item (ii) above will give legal scope for police to be associated with the process of prosecution and have effective interaction with the prosecuting agency. Items (iii) and (v) will afford scope for police to be associated in a recognised manner with the other wings of the criminal justice system for preventing crime and reforming criminals. Items (ix) and (x) will facilitate the performance of service-oriented functions and will also recognise a counselling and mediating role for the police in appropriate situations. (Para 14.51)

Interference with and Misuse of Police by Illegal or Improper Orders or Pressure from Political Executive or Other Extraneous Sources—Remedial Measures

18.50 While steering the country towards the promised objectives of the socialist welfare State for its hundreds of millions of people, the Government have had to control and regulate in an increasing degree the conduct and business of different sections of people through progressive legislation and other related measures. This has meant increasing exercise of power by the Government through its widely spread apparatus of the executive in several matters affecting the daily life of the people. National leaders, who were at the helm in different parts of the country in the first decade after Independence, conducted the affairs of the Government with great vision and wise statesmanship and set down patterns of conduct and inter-relationship between the political leadership in Government on the one side and the civil services on the other. Though not precisely defined, their respective roles were mutually understood fairly well and followed in practice. While the civil services had the benefit of lead and guidance in policy from the political leadership having in view the expectations and aspirations of the public, the political masters had the benefit of professional advice from the civil services regarding the different dimensions of the problems they had to solve. Great leaders and statesmen like Jawaharlal Nehru, Sardar Patel, Abul Kalam Azad, Rajagopalachari, Govind Ballabh Pant, Rafi Ahmed Kidwai, K. Kamaraj, B.C. Roy and Sri Krishna Sinha provided an atmosphere of dignity and sense of direction for the civil services to function honestly and efficiently, with public interests constantly held in view. Passing years saw the entry of a large variety of people into the field of politics and increasing contact between politicians and the executive at various levels in a variety of situations, including those caused by decreasing majorities in legislatures. Scope for exercise of power through the political leadership in Government induced political functionaries outside the Government to take undue interest in the conduct of Government affairs, and gradually the spectre of 'political interference' appeared on the scene. Police, as a part of the civil services, came within the ambit of this interference. In fact the police became specially vulnerable to interference from politicians because of the immense political advantage that could be readily reaped by misuse of police powers. The quality of police performance was and continues to be adversely affected by such interference. (Para 15.2)

18.51 After long years of tradition of law enforcement subject to executive will under the British rule, the police entered their new role in independent India in 1947. The foreign power was replaced by a political party that came up through the democratic process as laid down in our Constitution. For a time things went well without any notice of any change, because of the corrective influences that were brought to bear on the administrative structure by the enlightened political leadership. However, as years passed by there was a qualitative change in the style of politics. The fervour of the freedom struggle and the concept of sacrifice that it implied faded out quickly, yielding place to new styles and norms of behaviour by politicians to whom politics became a career by itself. Prolonged one-party rule at the Centre and in the States for over 30 years coupled with the natural desire of ruling partymen to remain in positions of power resulted in the development of symbiotic relationship between politicians on one hand and the civil services on the other. Vested interests grew on both sides. What started as a normal interaction between the politicians and the services for the avowed objective of better administration with better awareness of public feelings and expectations, soon degenerated into different forms of intercession, interventions and interference with *mala fide* objectives unconnected with public interest. (Paras 15.4)

18.52 Consequent on the agitationist posture taken up by some political parties in opposition, protest demonstrations, public meetings, processions, politically motivated strikes in the industrial sector, *dharnas, gheraos,* etc. have become a recurrent feature of political activity in the country. Police have been increasingly drawn into the resultant law and order situations and are expected by the ruling party to deal with all such situations with a political eye. Putting down political dissent has become a tacitly accepted objective of the police system. (Para 15.6)

18.53 Some typical situations or matters in which pressure is brought to bear on the police by the political, executive or other extraneous sources are listed below:

(i) Arrest or non-arrest of a person against whom a case is taken up for investigation by the police;
(ii) Deliberate handcuffing of a person in police custody merely to humiliate him;
(iii) Release or non-release on bail after arrest;
(iv) Suppression of material evidence that becomes available during searches by police;
(v) Inclusion or non-inclusion in the chargesheet placed in court

on conclusion of investigation;

(vi) Posting or non-posting of police force in an area of apprehended trouble to create an effect to the advantage of one party or the other;

(vii) Taking persons into preventive custody to immobilise them from legitimate political activity in opposition to the party in power;

(viii) Foisting false criminal cases against political functionaries for achieving political ends;

(ix) Discretionary enforcement of law while dealing with public order situations, with emphasis on severity and ruthlessness in regard to persons opposed to the ruling party;

(x) Manoeuvring police intervention by exaggerating a non-cognizable of offence or engineering a false complaint to gain advantage over another party in a situation which will lie outside the domain of police action in the normal course; and

(xi) Preparation of malicious and tendentious intelligence reports to facilitate action against an opponent. (Para 15.13)

18.54 Pressure on the police takes a variety of forms, ranging from a promise of career advancement and preferential treatment in service matters if the demand is yielded to, and a threat of drastic penal action and disfavoured treatment in service matters if the pressure is resisted. While it is not possible to punish a police officer with a statutory punishment under the Discipline and Appeal Rules without adequate grounds and following a prescribed procedure, it is very easy to subject him to administrative action by way of transfer or suspension on the basis of an alleged complaint taken up for inquiry. While suspension acts as a great humiliating factor, a transfer acts as a severe economic blow and disruption of the police officers' family, children's education, etc. The threat of transfer/suspension is the most potent weapon in the hands of the politician to bend down the police to his will. (Para 15.14)

18.55 During our tours in the States several officers brought to our notice this phenomenon of frequent and indiscriminate transfers ordered on political considerations. We analysed the frequency of transfers in different ranks in the States in the five year period 1973–77 and found the following position in many states:

Rank	Average period of stay in the same post/ same station	
I.G.	1 year and 8 months	(In one State 6 IsG were changed, in three States 5 IsG were changed in this period).
S.P.	1 year and 7 months	(In one State it is as low as 11 months and in three others it was 10 months).
Sub Inspector	1 year and 2 months	(In one State it is as low as 7 months and in three others it was 10 months).

In computing the above period, we have excluded the transfers arising from normal administrative reasons like promotion to a higher post, deputation to training or to a post under the Central Government, retirement, removal/dismissal from service, etc. The frequent changes of officers, particularly at the operational level of Sub Inspectors in Police Stations and Superintendents of Police in districts coupled with frequent changes at the apex, namely, Inspector General of Police, have no doubt largely contributed to the sharp decline in the quality of police service down the line. Inspectors General in some States have been changed as often as the Chief Minister or the Home Minister changed! The interests of real professional service to the public have been sacrificed at the altar of political expediency. (Para 15.15)

18.56 We are also aware that the unhealthy influences and pressures that are brought to bear on the police do not always originate from political sources alone. Capitalists, industrialists, businessmen, landlords and such others who form the richer and more influential sections of society have immense capacity to generate such pressures to operate at different levels in the police, either directly or indirectly through political sources, and influence the course of police action. (Para 15.17)

18.57 Interference with the police system by extraneous sources, especially the politicians, encourages the police personnel to believe that their career advancement does not at all depend on the merits of their professional performance, but can be secured by currying favour with politicians who count. Deliberate and sustained cultivation of a few individuals on the political plane takes up all the time of a number of police personnel to the detriment of the performance of their normal professional jobs to the satisfaction of the general public at large. This process sets the system on the downward slope to decay and total ineffectiveness. (Para 15.18)

18.58 Interference at the operational level in police stations, police circles, etc. results in the total by-passing of the supervisory officers in the hierarchy. The frequent by-passing of the normal chain of command results in the atrophy of the supervisory structure. It, therefore, fails to operate effectively even in matters which do not attract any such extraneous interference. This was strikingly seen in the situation arising from the policemen's stir in certain States in May-June 1979. (Para 15.19)

18.59 In their anxiety to ensure police performance in accordance with the appreciation of the situation by the political party in power, some State Governments are known to have issued executive instructions restricting the scope for police action even in situations where a specific line of action by police is enjoined on them by law itself. (Para 15.20)

18.60 A police force which does not remain outside politics but is constantly subjected to influences and pressures emanating within the system from the politicised police personnel themselves will in turn seriously disturb the stability of the duly elected political leadership in the State itself and thereby cause serious damage to the fabric of our democracy. This danger has to be realised with equal seriousness and concern by the politician as well as by the police. (Para 15.25)

18.61 The experience of several other democracies has also shown the need for evolving healthy norms in the interaction between the political leadership in Government and the executive services, to ensure that each section performs its duly recognised role and benefits by the corrective influence from the other in constantly serving the cause of public interest. (Para 15.31)

18.62 We have already observed how in the early years after independence the political leadership provided by well-motivated administrators and statesmen had in fact enabled the services including the police to function effectively in the best interests of the public at large. We feel confident that the existing situation can certainly be corrected and we can evolve practicable remedial measures to bring about a healthy functioning of the police with helpful and wise guidance from the elected representatives of the people. (Para 15.32)

18.63 We feel that it would be appropriate to lay down that the power of superintendence of the State Government over the police should be limited for the purpose of ensuring that police performance is in strict accordance with law. (Para 15.38)

18.64 Police tasks may be broadly divided into three categories for the purpose of analysing the relevance of supervision by Government. They are (i) investigative; (ii) preventive and (iii) service-oriented. Investigative tasks will include all action taken by police in the course of investigating a case under Chapter XII of the Code of Criminal Procedure. Preventive tasks will cover such actions like preventive arrests under Section 151 Cr.P.C., initiation of security proceedings, arrangement of beats and patrols, collection of intelligence and maintenance of crime records to plan and execute appropriate preventive action, deployment of police force as a preventive measure when breach of peace is threatened, handling of unlawful assemblies and their dispersal, etc. Service-oriented functions will include rendering service of a general nature during fairs and festivals, rescuing children lost in crowds, providing relief in distress situations arising from natural calamities, etc. (Para 15.39)

18.65 As far as investigative tasks are concerned we have a clear ruling from the Supreme Court that the nature of action to be taken on conclusion of investigation is a matter to be decided by the police only and by no other authority—*vide* para 18 of the Supreme Court judgement in criminal appeal No. 218 of 1966 reported in AIR 1968 Supreme Court 117 (V 55 C 32). It may, therefore, be safely projected as a fundamental principle governing police work that the investigative tasks of the police are beyond any kind of intervention by the executive or non-executive. Any arrangement in which the investigative tasks of the police are sought to be brought under executive control and direction would go against this fundamental principle spelt out by the Supreme Court and hence should be deemed illegal. We would, therefore, recommend in the first place that all the executive instructions issued by the government having a bearing on investigative tasks of the police may be scrutinised and either cancelled or modified to conform to the above principle. (Para 15.40)

18.66 In the performance of preventive tasks and service-oriented functions, the police will need to interact with other governmental agencies and service organisations. For example, in planning preventive measures in a near-strike situation in an educational institution or an industrial unit, police will have to keep in touch with the educational authorities or the labour departmental authorities to have a proper perception of the developing situation. In the performance of such preventive tasks there is considerable scope for exercise of discretion, having in view the overall public interests involved in any particular situation. Every police officer should normally be left free to exercise this discretion on his own judgement but there may be situations the disposal of which may have repercussions beyond the jurisdiction of one police officer and it will become necessary in such cases for the supervisory ranks to step in and exercise discretion at their level. Extending this analogy one can visualise a State-wide situation in which the exercise of discretion in regard to preventive tasks may have to take into account several factors of Statewide significance and it would be appropriate in public interest that the exercise of discretion in such situations conforms to some policy approach that may be evolved at the highest political level in the government which has the ultimate responsibility for proper governance of the State. We, therefore, recommend that in the performance of preventive tasks and service-oriented functions police should be subject to the overall guidance from the government which should lay down broad policies for adoption in different situations from time to time. There should, however, be no instructions in regard to actual operations in the field. The discretion of the police officer to deal with the situation, within the four corners of the overall guidance and broad policies, should be unfettered. An erring officer can always be made accountable for his action. Such policy directions should be openly given and made known to the State Legislatures also as and when occasion demands. (Para 15.42)

18.67 We have already referred to the weakening of the normal chain of command resulting from unauthorised interference with police work by political and other extraneous sources. To restore the capacity of the police as an organisation to resist such pressures and illegal or irregular orders, we consider it would be extremely useful if the Chief of Police in a State is assured of a statutory tenure of office. Such a tenure will strengthen his position and enable him to stand up effectively against unhealthy pressures on the system. The tenure may be fixed as a period of four years or a period extending up to the date of his retirement or promotion in the normal course, whichever is shorter. This tenure should be put on a statutory basis by being included in a specific provision in the Police Act itself. It shall also be provided that the removal of the Chief of Police from his post before the expiry of the tenure period shall require approval from the State

Security Commission whose set up is being recommended separately. (Para 15.43)

18.68 We recommend that the posting of the Chief of Police in a State should be from a panel of IPS officers of that State cadre prepared by a Committee of which the Chairman of the Union Public Service Commission will be the Chairman and the Union Home Secretary, the senior most among the Heads of Central Police Organisations, the Chief Secretary of the State and the existing Chief of Police in the State will be members. The panel should not have more than three names at any time. Posting from the panel should be according to seniority: We visualise that in the future police set up at the Centre and in the States, the Chiefs of State Police and the Heads of Central Police Organisations will be of comparable status and it should be possible for the Central and State Governments to arrange for periodic interchange of officers at this level without involving any loss of rank or status as experienced now. The association of the Central Government and the State Government in jointly preparing this panel would ensure its acceptability to both and facilitate smooth interchange of officers at the highest level in the normal course. (Para 15.45)

18.69 There is immediate need to devise a new mechanism of control and supervision which would help the State Government to discharge their superintending responsibility in an open manner under the framework of law, with due regard to healthy norms and conventions that may develop in due course. For this purpose we recommend the constitution of a statutory Commission in each State which may be called the State Security Commission which shall have the State Minister incharge of police as the ex-officio Chairman and six others as Members. Two members shall be chosen from the State Legislature, one from the ruling party and another from the opposition parties. They shall be appointed to this Commission on the advice of the Speaker of the State Legislature. The remaining four members of the Commission shall be appointed by the Chief Minister, subject to approval by the State Legislature, from retired judges of the High Court, retired Government servants who had functioned in senior positions in the Government while in service, social scientists or academicians of public standing and eminence. The Chief of Police will ex-officio function as Secretary of this Commission which shall have its own Secretariat for the transaction of its business. Arrangement of funds for the functioning of this Commission will be made on the same lines as for the State Public Service Commission. (Para 15.46)

18.70 The term of the Members of the Commission (other than the Chairman) shall be three years. If any among the four non-political Members were to join a political party after being appointed to the Commission, he shall immediately cease to be a Member of the Commission and the vacancy shall be filled by fresh appointment from the non-political category. (Para 15.47)

18.71 The functions of the State Security Commission shall include:

(i) laying down broad policy guidelines and directions for the performance of preventive tasks and service-oriented functions by the police;
(ii) evaluation of the performance of the State Police every year and presenting a report to the State Legislature;
(iii) functioning as a forum of appeal for disposing of representations from any police officer of the rank of Superintendent of Police and above regarding his being subjected to illegal or irregular orders in the performance of his duties;
(iv) functioning as a forum of appeal for disposing of representations from police officers regarding promotion to the rank of Superintendent of Police and above; and
(v) functioning as a forum of appeal for disposal of the police in the State. (Para 15.48)

18.72 The Commission shall devise its own procedures for transaction of business. It shall be open to the Chairman and Members of the Commission and also the Chief of Police to bring up for consideration by the Commission, any subject falling within its jurisdiction. (Para 15.49)

18.73 The Commission shall meet at least once every month and may meet more often, if required by the Chairman or Members of the Commission or the Chief of Police for considering any particular subject proposed by them. (Para 15.50)

18.74 As the Chairman of the Commission, the Minister-in-charge of police will be able to project the government point of view during the Commission's deliberations. Any policy direction or guidelines which the government desire to issue shall have to be agreed to by the Commission before they are passed on to the police for implementation. However, in an emergency the Government may directly issue a policy direction or guidelines in regard to a specific situation, but such direction or guidelines shall as soon as possible be brought before the Commission for ratification and be subject to such modifications as the Commission might decide. (Para 15.51)

18.75 The Constitution of such a Commission will, in our opinion, help considerably in making police performance politically neutral. While retaining governmental responsibility for overseeing the police, this Commission will ensure that this responsibility is discharged in an open manner with publicly known policy directions and guidelines. The arrangement of an annual evaluation report from the same Commission and constant review of the functioning of the police by it would also further ensure that police performance in any given period has conformed to the prescribed policy directions and guidelines and has served public interests in the best possible manner. We recommend that the limits of supervisory responsibility of the State Government in regard to police performance as earlier observed by us, and the Constitution of a State Security Commission as proposed above to help the State Government in discharging this responsibility may be spelt out in a new provision in the Police Act in replacement of the existing Section 3 of the Act. (Para 15.54)

18.76 A sensitive area of police functions with considerable scope for misuse of police relates to collection of intelligence. Under the garb of having to collect intelligence regarding matters which have a bearing on the law and order situation, the intelligence wing of the State Police frequently collects a variety of information regarding activities of political parties and individual politicians. (Para 15.55)

18.77 The Shah Commission of Inquiry has referred to some aspects of the functioning of the Intelligence Bureau and the Central Bureau of Investigation at the Centre and pointed out the need for appropriate safeguards to be evolved to ensure that these organisations are not put to misuse by the Government or some one in the Government. We would like to point out that the tendency to misuse these organisations would get accentuated by political instability in Government and, viewed from this angle, the functionaries in these organisations would need protection from improper and unhealthy pulls and pressures that might operate in such situations. We understand from the Ministry of Home Affairs that they have recently received the report of the high-level Committee headed by Shri L.P. Singh, a former Home Secretary and presently Governor of Assam,

Meghalaya, Nagaland, Manipur and Tripura, which was appointed in pursuance of the observations of the Shah Commission of Inquiry regarding the Intelligence Bureau and the Central Bureau of Investigation. The points that may emerge from the analysis of L.P. Singh Committee Report would, in our opinion, be applicable in a substantial measure to the working of the intelligence wing in the State Police as also the State Anti-Corruption agencies. We recommend that the Central Government may communicate to the State Governments the essential observations and recommendations emanating from the L.P. Singh Committee Report for their information and further action in regard to their own agencies, not only for overseeing their performance but also for protecting them from unhealthy influences. (Para 15.55)

18.78 Conduct Rules prohibit all Government servants including the police personnel from being members of or otherwise being associated with any political party, or any organisation which takes part in politics. However, in practice this important provision in the Conduct Rules does not appear to have been enforced with the required strictness and severity. (Para 15.56)

18.79 We would recommend that the administration should take a severe view of any infringement of the above mentioned Conduct Rule and deal with erring officers in a deterrent manner. In appropriate cases resort may also be had to Article 311(2)(b) or (c) to weed out such personnel from the system. In cases where this constitutional provision is invoked, all the available material against the police personnel concerned should be scrutinised by a small Committee under the Chairmanship of the Chief of Police. Members of this Committee may be drawn from senior ranks in the prosecuting agency set up of the State and police officers of the rank of Deputy Inspector General of Police (other than the one who may have been concerned either directly or in a supervisory capacity with the situations or instances that figure in the material for consideration by the Committee). (Para 15.56)

18.80 While we do not hold any brief for or against any political party to say that the membership thereof or association therewith should not or should act as a bar for recruitment to the police at any level, we would state emphatically that the continued involvement in political activity of any kind either directly or indirectly by any personnel after joining the police at any level should not be tolerated in any circumstances. The weeding out of such persons should receive special attention of the Chief of Police from time to time. Here again, recourse may be had to the provisions of article 311(2)(b) or (c) of the Constitution, if need be in appropriate cases. (Para 15.57)

18.81 We feel that police officers should be effectively protected from whimsical and *mala fide* transfer/suspension orders. One step for securing this protection could be to incorporate a provision in the Police Act itself specifying the authorities competent to issue transfer/suspension orders regarding different ranks. Such a statutory provision would render null and void any transfer/suspension order passed by any authority other than those specified in the Act. (Para 15.58)

18.82 Another step could be to lay down as a rule that every transfer/suspension order should also contain a brief paragraph indicating the reasons for the issue of the order, and making it a further rule that any transfer/suspension order which does not contain this explanatory paragraph shall not be valid order. The advantage in this arrangement would be that the recipient of the transfer/suspension order will have some material with him which he can agitate before the authorised available forums if he feels that the reasons are *mala fide* or otherwise not sustainable. (Para 15.59)

18.83 In regard to the issue of oral orders, our recommendations are that oral orders should be avoided as far as possible and may be resorted to only in situations which call for immediate executive action and cannot wait for the issue of written orders in confirmation of the oral order; a record of every oral order be kept both by the issuing officer and the recipient officer in the relevant files; and a subordinate officer receiving oral orders from a higher ranking officer shall be entitled to ask for and get confirmatory orders in writing from the higher functionary, for record. (Para 15.60)

18.84 We feel that if it is laid down as a code of conduct that elected representatives will interact with the police at the level of the Deputy Superintendent of Police or above only, it would avoid situations in which the executives at the operational level in police stations and circles may be overawed by the stature of the political functionary and may be inclined to accept and act upon whatever information he passes on to them without making the necessary check and verification which they might make normally. (Para 15.61)

18.85 We would recommend that the Conduct Rules applicable to Police personnel of all ranks in the States may embody provisions similar to those in Rule 3(3) of the All India Services (Conduct)

Rules which emphasise the responsibility of a member of the Service to act according to his own best judgement and not evade this responsibility by seeking instructions or approval from a higher authority, where such instruction or approval is not necessary according to normal working procedures. (Para 15.62)

18.86 In the Government of India, Department of Personnel and Administrative Reforms letter No. 25/19/64-Ests(A) dated 29th April, 1975, addressed to the Chief Secretaries of all the State Governments, it was indicated that a Code of Conduct for Legislators was being separately processed by the Ministry of Home Affairs. Our enquiries reveal that this Code of Conduct for Legislators has not yet taken any shape. We recommend that the Ministry of Home Affairs complete their exercise expeditiously and have the Code issued very soon so that the elected representatives as also the general public at large may know and appreciate the requirements of ethics and propriety in this important and sensitive matter. (Para 15.63)

18.87 We also trust that the contemplated exercise on the political plane as decided at the Chief Minister's Conference of 6th June, 1979 will be taken up in right earnest and completed soon. (Para 15.63)

18.88 To bring home the primacy of the rule of law in a democracy and the paramount duty of every police officer to recognise this primacy and stoutly resist any interference with the course of his duties as enjoined by law and in accordance with the Constitution, we feel it would be appropriate if every member of the police is made to swear or solemnly affirm a declaration embodying this fundamental principle, at the time of his joining the police, whatever be the rank of entry. (Para 15.64)

18.89 Apart from the initial declaration at the time of joining the police, it would further serve the purpose and embed the principle firmly in the minds of all the police officers if this declaration is remembered and repeated by them in groups and assemblies of police personnel drawn on an annual ceremonial occasion like the 'Police Commemoration Day' which is observed on 21st October, every year. (Para 15.64)

18.90 The structuring of the initial training courses and the later in-service training courses for all police personnel should be suitably designed to facilitate the growth of proper attitudes and sense of values on the part of every police officer, viewing himself throughout as a servant of law to uphold and protect the dignity and rights of every individual fellow citizen of the country. (Para 15.65)

Gram Nyayalayas

18.91 The mounting pendency of cases in court in the present system of trials with emphasis on procedures and rituals rigidly spelt out in law, cannot be brought down within manageable limits except by devising a totally new system with simpler procedures to deal with ordinary crimes involving simple and straight evidence. Such a new system would not only ensure inexpensive and speedy justice but, what is more, would also help in preserving the harmonious relationships in the community which usually get affected if criminal matters are subjected to prolonged trials which might ultimately involve prison sentences also. This is particularly relevant in the rural areas where community opinion and village harmony have been and continue to be perceptible factors of life. (Para 16.2)

18.92 During our tours in the States and discussions with a wide cross section of the public as also the services, we got the impression that the working of Nyaya Panchayats, though well conceived in principle, suffered in practice, mainly because of the lay members of the Panchayat being subjected to local influences and pressures which defeated the purpose of an objective and fair disposal of cases handled by the Panchayats. It was also pointed out that a Nyaya Panchayat solely made up of lay members was unable to handle the judicial work with requisite attention to the minimum requirements of a judicial process. It was further mentioned that Nyaya Panchayats would function far more effectively if they were manned by trained persons with a certain minimum knowledge of law, rules and procedure. (Para 16.10)

18.93 We appreciate that if the Nyaya Panchayats are made up of knowledgeable and academically competent persons alone, they would lose their lay character and, therefore, would merely appear as an extension of the existing sophisticated court system which, for a variety of reasons, does not command the confidence of the rural folk. On the other hand, if the Nyaya Panchayats are made up only of lay men who come up through a process of election, direct or indirect, they would become susceptible to unhealthy influences and pressures which may conflict with the interests of justice. We have, therefore, to adopt a *via media* which would preserve the lay character of the Nyaya Panchayat and at the same time ensure the disposal of cases with due regard to certain minimum judicial requirements. (Para 16.11)

18.94 The observations of Justice Bhagwati Committee on the advantages of the Nyaya Panchayat system and its recommendations regarding the composition of Nyaya Panchayat and procedures for transaction of its business are set out in paragraphs 6.11 to 6.31 of the Committee's report which are furnished in Appendix VIII. (Para 16.13)

18.95 We have carefully gone through Justice Bhagwati Committee's report and we find ourselves in whole-hearted agreement with it. We fully endorse the recommendations therein, subject to the modifications and refinements as spelt out in the following paragraphs, which we consider desirable in the present context. (Para 16.14)

18.96 The new courts proposed at the grass roots level may be called "Gram Nyayalayas", avoiding any reference to Panchayat as such so that they may not be viewed as an adjunct or extension of the Panchayats which are totally executive bodies with which political functionaries are associated. (Para 16.15)

18.97 A Gram Nyayalaya shall be made up of three members. One shall be the Presiding Judge who will be appointed by the District Judge from retired judicial officers or other retired Government servants who, from their experience while in service, would have acquired the requisite knowledge of law and minimum requirements of judicial processes. (Para 16.16)

18.98 Two other members of the Gram Nyayalaya shall be lay members appointed by the District Judge from a panel of names prepared by the local elected body that goes by the name of Panchayat Samiti/Panchayat Union/Block Committee or its equivalent, in the manner described below. (Para 16.17)

18.99 One Gram Nyayalaya shall cover about 25 to 30 villages coming under 8 to 10 Panchayats. This would mean about 5 or 6 Gram Nyayalayas in the jurisdiction of one Panchayat Union/ Panchayat Samiti. The headquarters of each Gram Nyayalaya shall be fixed at some suitable place within the group of villages in its jurisdiction. (Para 16.18)

18.100 The Presiding Judge for all the Gram Nyayalayas within the jurisdiction of a Panchayat Samiti shall be the same person appointed by the District Judge in the manner prescribed earlier. The lay members of each Gram Nyayalaya will, however, be separate for each Nyayalaya. The Panchayat Pradhans relevant to the jurisdiction of each Gram Nyayalaya will be associated in proposing the names of lay members for that Gram Nyayalaya. The Presiding Judge shall hold proceedings of each Gram Nyayalaya in the Panchayat Samiti by visiting the respective headquarters once a month by turn, or more often if required by the volume of work to be handled, and associate the two local lay members with the proceedings in each place. (Para 16.19)

18.101 The Presiding Judge and the two lay members shall normally hold office for a term of 3 years from the date of appointment. They shall be deemed to be public servants as defined in the Indian Penal Code while they hold office. (Para (16.20)

18.102 Gram Nyayalayas shall have exclusive criminal jurisdiction over the offences that are assigned to them in the relevant law. (Para 16.21)

18.103 Gram Nyayalayas shall not be bound by procedural codes or laws of evidence. Their proceedings shall be in the nature of an inquisitorial inquiry which would mean that the Gram Nyayalaya would itself take a positive role in the inquiry to ascertain the facts regarding the involvement or otherwise of the person concerned instead of merely functioning as an adjudicating body to give its view on two versions put before it, one by the prosecution and the other by the defence. (Para 16.25)

18.104 Parties to the proceedings before the Gram Nyayalayas shall not be allowed to be represented by lawyers. Exceptions may arise when a person happens to be arrested or otherwise detained in custody in connection with an offence related to the proceedings before the Gram Nyayalaya, in which case the provisions of Article 22(1) of the Constitution may get attracted. The observations of the Supreme Court in the case of State of Madhya Pradesh versus Shobharam and others (AIR 1966 SC 1910) would be relevant in this connection. (Para 16.26)

18.105 The findings of the Gram Nyayalaya shall be based on the majority view of the component members including the Presiding Judge, subject to the provision that in any case where the two lay members agree on a finding with which the Presiding Judge does not agree, and the Presiding Judge is clearly of the opinion that it is necessary for the ends of justice to submit the case to a higher court, he shall record the ground of his opinion and submit the case for adjudication by the Chief Judicial Magistrate. We are recommending this procedure specially to guard against local unhealthy influences and pressures operating on the system. (Para 16.29)

18.106 Punishment awardable by a Gram Nyayalaya shall be limited to fines not exceeding to Rs. 500. Fines shall be recoverable by processes applicable to arrears of revenue. A Gram Nyayalaya shall not be competent to award any sentence of imprisonment, even in default of payment of fine. (Para 16.30)

18.107 If in any particular case, having regard to the circumstances thereof, the Gram Nyayalaya feels that the person found guilty by it merits a more serious punishment than is awardable by the Gram Nyayalaya, it shall remit the case to the Chief Judicial Magistrate of the district for further action on the lines indicated in Section 325 Cr.P.C. (Para 16.31)

Maintenance of Crime Records and Statistics

18.108 Maintenance of crime records at the police station level and submission of periodic reports and returns from there to the district level and the State level should be so designed as to fit into a scheme of computerised maintenance of data/information at the State level/National level. (Para 17.5)

18.109 Changes in the existing crime record system in different States should be minimal for the limited purpose of achieving the objective mentioned above. (Para 17.5)

18.110 Detailed recommendations made by a Committee of DIGs set up in 1962 regarding the type of records to be maintained at police stations may be kept as model and worked upon further in states. (Para 17.5)

18.111 A District Crime Record Bureau, State Crime Record Bureau and the National Crime Record Bureau should be set up with legal backing and adequate staff. (Para 17.5)

18.112 The Central Finger Print Bureau which is now located in Calcutta should merge with the National Crime Record Bureau which may be located either in Delhi or Hyderabad. Hyderabad location will facilitate useful interaction with the SVP National Police Academy. (Para 17.5)

18.113 Collection and maintenance of data for national and Interpol purposes, at present handled by the Bureau of Police Research and Development and the Central Bureau of Investigation, may be integrated with the proposed National Crime Record Bureau. (Para 17.5)

18.114 Computerisation of Finger Prints at the State level and National level should be taken up on hand and completed within a reasonable time frame, say five years. (Para 17.5)

18.115 Communication channels in the shape of VHF telephones and teleprinters between police stations, and district headquarters, between district headquarters and State headquarters and the final link up with the headquarters of the National Crime Record Bureau should be built up to facilitate prompt exchange of data/information. This will be very necessary to aid investigational work and reduce infructuous arrests and prolonged detention of persons on mere suspicion without adequate grounds. (Para 17.5)

18.116 One or more educated constables must be specifically designated in every police station as Collators who will be responsible for maintenance of crime records at the police station, preparation of the input forms originating from the police station in respect of all police computer applications, placing all computer outputs received in the police station before the Station House Officer for their effective utilisation, handling the P&T telephone and other technical equipment, if any, in the police station, and generally assisting the Station House Officer in all correspondence with the District Crime Records Bureau and the State Crime Records Bureau. (Para 17.5)

18.117 The existing "Identification of Prisoners Act, 1920" should be replaced by a new comprehensive law which may be called "The Crime and Offender Records Act" which would facilitate the collection of wide ranging data and information regarding crimes and criminals which would be of use not only to the police in the performance of their investigative jobs but also to the functionaries in probation services and correctional institutions besides criminologists and social scientists, in their respective fields of correctional work and analytical studies. A draft for the proposed new Act is enclosed to the report as Appendix XII. (Para 17.7)

18.118 Government of India should continue financial aid in increasing measure to the States for installing computers in the police communication and record systems and complete a time bound computerisation plan. (Para 17.8)

NATIONAL POLICE COMMISSION, 1977 – THIRD REPORT[1]

Chairman Shri Dharma Vira, retired Governor

Member Shri N.K. Reddy; Shri K.F. Rustamji; Shri N.S. Saksena; Prof. M.S. Gore

Secretary Shri. C.V. Narasimhan, presently Director, CBI, full-time Member-Secretary of the Commission (on relief from his present post

Alterations Shri C.V. Narasimhan, former Director of Central Bureau of Investigation, functioned as Member Secretary of the Commission from its inception till 19th April, 1980 when the left to take a posting in his parent cadre in Tamil Nadu on replacement of his services from the Central Government to the State Government. After the departure of Shri Narasimhan, Shri M.D. Dikshit, Principal Director of Research, functioned as the Secretary Incharge.

Appointment

Far-reaching changes have taken place in the country after the enactment of the Indian Police Act, 1861 and the setting up of the second Police Commission of 1902 particularly during the last thirty years of Independence. Though a number of States have appointed Police Commissions after Independence to study the problems of the Police in their respective States, there has been no comprehensive review at the national level of the police system after Independence despite radical changes in the political, social and economic situation in the country. A fresh examination is necessary of the role and performance of the Police—both as a law enforcement agency, and as an institution to protect the rights of the citizens enshrined in the Con-

---

1. Controller of Publications, Delhi, 1980, 95 p.

stitution. The Government of India have, therefore, decided to appoint a National Police Commission. The National Police Commission was appointed under the Government of India, Ministry of Home Affairs Resolution No. VI-24021/36/77-GPA.I, dated November 15, 1977.

Terms of Reference

The following will be the terms of reference of the Commission :

(1) Re-define the role, duties, powers and responsibilities of the police with special reference to prevention and control of crime and maintenance of public order.

(2) Examine the development of the principles underlying the present policing system, including the method of magisterial supervision, evaluate the performance of the system, identify the basic weaknesses of inadequacies, and suggest appropriate changes in the system and the basic laws governing the system.

(3) Examine, if any changes are necessary in the existing method of administration, disciplinary control and accountability.

(4) Inquire into the system of investigation and prosecution, the reasons for delay and failure, the use of improper methods, and the extent of their prevalence; and suggest how the system may be modified or changed, and made efficient, scientific and consistent with human dignity; and how the related laws may be suitably amended.

(5) Examine methods of maintaining crime records and statistics and suggest methods for making them uniform and systematic.

(6) Review policing in rural areas evaluate any new arrangements that have been made, and recommend changes that are necessary.

(7) Examine the system of policing required in non-rural and urbanised areas including metropolitan areas, and suggest the pattern that would be the most suitable.

(8) Examine the steps taken for modernising law enforcement, evaluate the work of police communications, the computer net-work, scientific laboratories and agencies for research and development, and examine whether modernisation can be speeded up; examine to what extent, as a result of the modernisation of Police forces, streamlining of its functions and its

restructuring, it would be possible to economise in the manpower in the various areas of its activities.

(9) Examine the nature and extent of the special responsibilities of the Police towards the weaker sections of the community and suggest steps to ensure prompt action on their complaints for the safeguard of their rights and interests.

(10) Recommend measures and institutional arrangements:

(i) to prevent misuse of powers by the police, and to examine whether police behaviour, out-look, responsiveness and impartiality are maintained at the correct level, and if not the steps such as recruitment and training which should be taken to improve them;

(ii) to prevent misuse of the Police by administrative or executive instructions, political or other pressure, or oral order of any type, which are contrary to law;

(iii) for the quick and impartial inquiry of public complaints made against the police about any misuse of police powers;

(iv) for the quick redressal of grievances of police personnel and to look after their morale and welfare; and

(v) for a periodic objective evaluation of police performance in metropolitan area/District/State in a manner which will carry credibility before the public.

(11) Examine the manner and extent to which police can enlist ready and willing co-operation of the public in the discharge of their social defence and law enforcement duties and suggest measures regarding the institutional arrangements to secure such co-operation and measures for the growth of healthy and friendly public-police relationship.

(12) Examine the methods of police training, development, and career-planning of officers and recommend any changes that are required at any time in their service, to modernise the outlook, and to make the leadership of the force effective and morally strong.

(13) Examine the nature of the problems that the police will have to face in the future, and suggest the measures necessary for dealing with them, and for keeping them under continuous study and appraisal.

(14) Consider and make recommendations and suggestions regard-

ing any other matter which the Government may refer to the Commission; and

(15) Any other matter of relevance or importance having an impact on the subject.

Contents

Police and the Weaker Sections of Society; Village Police; Special law for dealing with serious and widespread breaches of public peace or disturbance of public order; Corruption in Police; Economic offences; Modernisation of law enforcement; Scriptory work in police; Summary of observations and recommendations; Appendices I to XIV.

Recommendations

Police and the Weaker Sections of Society

26.1 For determining the special role and responsibility of the police towards weaker sections of the society, it would be possible to evolve precise parameters for identifying and labelling any particular section of the society as weak in absolute terms. It is the relative state of helplessness or defencelessness of a person or class of persons in securing the legal rights to which they are entitled under the law of the land in regard to their life, property and other matters that should determine his or their 'weakness' for this purpose. Those who are subjected to social injustice and different forms of exploitation on account of poverty or ignorance besides age old traditions, customs, beliefs and the interplay of vested interests that have grown around them, would constitute the weaker sections as viewed from this angle. We would, therefore, adopt this parameter for the police to identify the weaker section in any given context and determine police response to their situation in accordance with our observations and recommendations in this Chapter. (Para 19.1)

26.2 State Governments may set up Special Courts under section 15A(2)(iii) of the Protection of Civil Rights Act to bring down the large pendency of cases in court. (Para 19.6)

26.3 Government may consider further amending the Act to specify that no appeal or applications for writ or an order passed by the State Government for imposing a collective fine under Section 10A shall be entertained by any court until the fine amount is deposited with a specified authority. (Para 19.7)

26.4 In the recording and reporting of crime statistics regarding atrocities on Scheduled Caste, no uniform criteria appear to have been adopted in the States. The Ministry of Home Affairs may issue comprehensive guidelines for classifying crimes as 'atrocities' to ensure proper recording and analysis of all such offences over a period of time on a country wide basis. (Para 19.9)

26.5 An undue emphasis on mere statistical reviews is likely to induce suppression of crime by non-registration of cases. Complaints from individual members of Scheduled Castes regarding isolated instances of victimisation may get ignored by the police unless they are backed by a collective demand from a group for appropriate police action under the law. State Government also tend to rely on statistics of recorded crimes to claim improved performance in the maintenance of law and order. It is important for all concerned to see the danger of a false statistical picture deluding them into a belief that all is well while in fact atrocities might be continuing without any notice by the police. Police inaction would in turn encourage further atrocities and the situation would thus deteriorate in the field, contrary to statistical claims in Legislature debates. (Para 19.10)

26.6 Special Cells may be set up in the police department in each State to:

(i) monitor the progress of investigation of cases under the PCR Act or other atrocities against Scheduled Castes/Tribes registered in district police stations;

(ii) make inquiries or investigations into complaints from Schedule Castes/Tribes or other weaker sections of the people that may be received directly in the cell;

(iii) discuss with the prosecuting staff the progress of cases pending trial to ensure satisfactory marshalling and presentation of evidence in court;

(iv) collect statistical and other relevant data for reviewing the state of implementation of the PCR Act from time to time; and

(v) collect intelligence regarding the actual ground situation and identify areas which require special attention for protecting the Scheduled Castes/Tribes and other weaker sections of the people from exploitation and injustice. (Para 19.12)

26.7 Besides the above-mentioned cell which would function as a part of the police set up in the State, a composite cell may be constituted at the district level to look into a wide variety of complaints that might emanate from the Scheduled Castes/Tribes, not necessarily linked with criminal offences as such but relatable to lapses in administrative measures meant for their relief. Since the work of this cell will be mostly in the nature of making an inquiry after scrutiny of departmental documents and ascertaining the factual position in the field by examining affected persons, it would be desirable to staff this composite cell with senior and experienced officers from the Revenue, Police, Social Welfare, Education, Cooperation and Development departments within the district. It would be further helpful to this cell if an auditor or accounts officer from the local fund audit set up in the State or any other similar agency is also associated with the cell in the inquiry work wherever necessary. (Para 19.14)

26.8 The head of this composite cell at the district level should be an officer of the rank of Sub-Divisional Officer and its work may be overseen and periodically reviewed by a District Committee of which the District Collector could be the Chairman and the District Superintendent of Police could be the Vice-Chairman, with the District Social Welfare Officer and District Educational Officer as its members along with some representatives from the public, known for their interest and involvement in social work. (Para 19.14)

26.9 A suitably constituted State level Committee under the chairmanship of the Minister in charge of Social Welfare can periodically review the working of the composite cells in districts. (Para 19.14)

26.10 The Special cell envisaged as part of the police set up for handling inquiries and investigational work connected with the PCR Act and atrocities on Scheduled Castes/Tribes may be referred to as "Special Investigating Cell". The composite cell at the district level which will have a wider charter of duties and responsibilities to look into a variety of complaints relating to the interests of Scheduled Castes/Tribes may be called the District Civil Rights Cell (DCRC). The State level Committee to oversee the working of DCRCs may be called the State Civil Rights Committee (SCRC). The SCRC and the DCRCs may be declared as committees set up under Section 15A(2)(iv) of the PCR Act and clothed with necessary authority and powers under the relevant rules. (Para 19.14)

26.11 An important cause for the dissatisfaction of the Scheduled Castes and other weaker sections of society about lack of police response to their plight in certain situations is that the police do not take cognizance of their complaints of ill-treatment at the hands of the upper castes, pleading the excuse that the complaints are non-cognizable under the law. Such complaints usually relate to non-cognizable offences like hurt under Section 323 I.P.C., assault under Sections 352 or 355 I.P.C. and insult or criminal intimidation under Sections 504 or 506 I.P.C. Police response to a non-cognizable complaint should be suitably specified in law to facilitate effective response on either of two grounds; namely, (i) to protect a member of the weaker section from exploitation or injustice or (ii) to prevent a possible breach of public peace and might result from absence of effective action on the complaint of a non-cognizable offence which has the potential for generating public reaction with consequent repercussion on public order. Section 155 of the Code of Criminal Procedure may be amended on the lines indicated in the report to facilitate this response by police. (Paras 19.15 and 19.17)

26.12 A sample survey has disclosed several deficiencies in the scheme of allotment of land to the landless poor who include a large number of Scheduled Castes. The following remedial measures are suggested:

(i) There is clear need for a separate comprehensive legislation setting out the procedure for the allotment of land (house site as well as agricultural land) to landless poor, particularly Scheduled Castes and Scheduled Tribes. This legislation should also spell out an effective procedure for eviction of unauthorised occupants after the allotment has been duly made under the law. The State itself should assume responsibility to initiate eviction proceedings on the basis of information or intelligence that may be available to it, instead of leaving it to the aggrieved allotted to make a complaint as such;

(ii) Section 441 IPC relating to criminal trespass may be amended on the lines adopted in Uttar Pradesh;

(iii) Police officers from the local police station should also be associated with the act of formally handing over vacant possession of land to the landless as and when it is done by the Revenue or other authorities directly concerned with it. A brief record should be made in the police station records' also about the fact of such handing over and the identity of the parties concerned;

(iv) It should then be deemed a part of police duties to collect intelligence about violations of such allotment orders and make a report thereof to the Revenue authorities concerned for immediate corrective action under the law. Police should also simultaneously take action for investigating the connected offence of criminal trespass. While police responsibility will be confined to the investigation and prosecution of the offender, his actual eviction from the land will be done by the Revenue or other authorities concerned under the provisions of the existing law or the separate law as proposed earlier; and

(v) While framing a separate legislation to govern the allotment of land to the landless poor, State Governments might keep in view some of the provisions of Public Premises (Eviction of Unauthorised Occupants) Act, 1971, which appear to be very effective for purposes of eviction of unauthorised occupants. (Para 19.22)

26.13 Police headquarters in each State should periodically compile and circulate among the field officers a detailed note indicating the scope and responsibility of the police for the investigation of specified offences under several Central and State Acts meant for the economic and social uplift of the weaker sections of the society like the Bonded Labour System (Abolition) Act of 1976, Minimum Wages Act of 1948, Assam Moneylenders Act of 1934, Rajasthan Scheduled Debtors (Liquidation of Indebtedness) Act of 1976, etc. (Para 19.23)

26.14 One of the situations resulting in considerable distress and hardship of the weaker sections of the community relates to motor vehicle accidents resulting in death or serious injury to persons on the road. A system has been institutionalised in Tamil Nadu in which the police are required to furnish relevant information and data in a prescribed form to the Motor Vehicle Accident Claims Tribunal as soon as investigation is taken up in any accident case. Copies of these statements are also simultaneously furnished to the district committee of the State Legal Aid and Advice Board which immediately gets into action for initiating the prescribed processes for getting the compensation amount to the victim. The Tamil Nadu State Legal Aid and Advice Board has reported that the total amount of compensation awarded during the period from 1st January, 1979 to 31st October, 1979 in respect of motor accident cases has totalled to Rs. 2,76,250 which is a vast improvement over the position as it obtained before the scheme came into operation. This scheme is commended for adoption in all States and Union Territories. (Para 19.25)

26.15 There is also another scheme in Tamil Nadu for immediate payment of cash relief to the victim or his family in motor vehicle accident cases on the assessment and recommendations of the investigating police officer. This payment is sanctioned through a simple procedure at the district level itself and, therefore, the cash relief is promptly secured for the victim, on the initiative of the police. This monetary relief may go upto Rs. 1,000 depending on the circumstances of the case, and is without prejudice to any further payment that may be ordered later as compensation by the Motor Vehicle Accident Claims Tribunal. This scheme is also commended for adoption in all States and Union Territories. (Para 19.26)

26.16 Motor Vehicle Accident Claims Tribunals may be conferred with the powers of a criminal court for enforcing attendance of witnesses. (Para 19.27)

26.17 Section 110E of the Motor Vehicles Act may be amended to provide for the execution of the compensation award as a decree of the court so that the amount can be recovered through court earlier than by the present procedure of recovery of arrears of land revenue. (Para 19.28)

26.18 In the Second Report of the Commission the setting up of a State Security Commission has been recommended to oversee the working of the police in certain aspects. The overall quality of police response to complaints from weaker sections in different situations would be assessed and taken note of by the State Security Commission in the normal course. It might facilitate a better appreciation of police performance in this regard if it could be so arranged that one of the non-official members of the State Security Commission is from the Scheduled Castes/Scheduled Tribes. (Para 19.29)

26.19 Beyond observing that the composition of the staff in the police system as a whole should reflect the general mix of communities as exist in society and thereby command the confidence of the different sections of society that the system would function impartially without any slant in favour of any community as such, we would not advise the fixation of any rigid percentages for staffing the police system on the basis of caste or community. (Para 19.30)

26.20 Police personnel at different stages of training may be motivated and oriented to deal with the problems of weaker sections with due understanding and sympathy. (Para 19.31)

Village Police

26.21 Though the village *chowkidar* has become practically useless as far as regular police work is concerned, a total abolition of this system without an alternate scheme, equally simple and inexpensive, for aiding police work in the villages would create difficulties for the regular police who now have in the village chowkidar at least one contact point, however, inefficient it may be, to attempt collection of information in any specific situation. Since collection of information is a fundamental requisite of all field work in the police, the police will be greatly handicapped if they do not have at the village level at least one functionary who will have his ears to the ground and be in a position to help them with useful information whenever needed. (Para 20.4)

26.22 The village chowkidari system should not, therefore, be given up altogether but should be made to function effectively by eliminating the existing deficiencies and, what is more important, linking it effectively with the functioning of a group also at the village level. While the services of an individual functionary like the chowkidar would be required on a continuing basis to keep a general vigil in the village from the police angle, the services of a group as such may be required only at intervals in specified situations. For example, arranging crime prevention and relief work in a cyclone or flood affected area, organising preventive measures against movements of dacoit gangs that might be suspected at any particular time, arranging preventive patrols against sabotage of communication lines or other vital installations that might lie in the rural area when there is a threat of such sabotage, etc., are tasks for the performance of which a village level defence group would be more effective than a lone village chowkidar. (Para 20.16)

26.23 The existing chowkidari system may be retained and strengthened with the following provisions built into the system:

(i) Minimum age limit of 20 years for appointment and maximum age limit of 60 years for remaining in service may be adopted;

(ii) Ability to read and write the regional language should be insisted upon;

(iii) He should be a resident of the village. Preference should be given to a persons having some avocation in the village which would give him the means of reasonable livelihood without total dependence on the remuneration he might get from

Government;

(iv) He may be assigned some village common land for cultivation and enjoyment of its produce, subject to his continued functioning as chowkidar satisfactorily;

(v) He should be under the administrative control of the Police Department and should be paid through them on a regular monthly basis;

(vi) His pay should be fixed at a reasonable level which would appear attractive by the standards of village economy;

(vii) He should not be involved in the performance of tasks concerning other Government departments. If the other departments require the services of a similar village level functionary for their purposes, they should be separately appointed and administered by them; and

(viii) His duties will include—

(a) general maintenance of vigil in the village from the point of view of crime prevention; and

(b) being alert and sensitive to any intelligence regarding village affairs which are likely to lead to a law and order situation and pass on such intelligence promptly to the regular police.

(ix) He should also have powers to arrest and detain persons who may be either caught red handed while committing certain specified offences in the village or may be found in possession of property in circumstances which create the suspicion of the commission of any of the specified offences. The chowkidar will land over to the regular police without delay any person so arrested along with the property seized from him, if any. (Para 20.19)

26.24 Besides the village chowkidar there should be village defence parties organised in such a manner that they can be get together whenever an occasion needs their services for collective action to deal with any specific situation in the village. They may be organised for one village or a group of villages as may be found operationally convenient. One of the members of the village defence party should be designed as the dalapati who will function as their leader. The village chowkidar shall, *ex officio,* be a member of the village defence party. The organisation and set up of the village defence party and the dalapati including the procedure for their appointment and administrative control and their duties and responsibilities may be broadly on the lines of the Karnataka pattern as detailed in paragraphs 206 to 20.11 of the report. (Para 20.21)

26.25 While the administrative control over the village defence parties and dalapatis will remain with the police, it would be desirable to associate a functionary at the Panchayat Union or Block level in the Panchayat administration in exercising supervision over the work of dalapatis. (Para 20.24)

26.26 It would greatly facilitate prompt exchange of information relvant to their tasks if a residential telephone is provided for the dalapati in each village defence party wherever technically feasible. In fact this telephone can function in the manner of a Public Call Office which would also facilitate its use by the other members of the village community in an emergency. Such facility would greatly enhance the status of the dalapati and his utility to the village community. Government may consider the grant of an advance to help purchase of cycles by the members of the village defence parties including the chowkidar. The grant of a small allowance to the chowkidar for the maintenance of his cycle may be also considered. (Paras 20.26 and 20.27)

26.27 The scheme of village policing as detailed in this report envisages a comprehensive set up including the village chowkidar, village defence parties and the dalapati with appropriate administrative and supervisory control measures to secure the ultimate objective of the system, namely, effective involvement of the village community in self-defence, besides co-operating with the regular police in the performance of police tasks. Village chowkidars are at present functioning in some States under a separate Act enacted a long time ago. Village defence parties have been set up in a few States under some recent legislation. We recommend the legislation of a separate comprehensive Act by the State Governments to set up the village police system including both as proposed. (Para 20.28)

Special Law for dealing with serious and widespread breaches of public peace or disturbance of public order

26.28 It is clear from a close assessment of the present crime trends that the administration has to be fully geared to handle situations in which violent crimes are most likely to increase, intensity of physical harm and damage done to persons and property will be more, and there will be widespread disturbances to public order. The present style of police functioning in the event of communal outbursts or other serious breaches or public peace has been more in the nature of a fire fighting operation focused on the immediate objective of restoring order on the spot. Police operations have not been successful in effective follow-up action through the processes of investigations and court trials to bring home to the law-breakers the penal consequences of their action. Investigations get seriously hampered by the reluctance of witnesses to speak in evidence against the accused persons who even if arrested by the police, get easily enlarged on bail under the existing law and wield threatening influence on the witnesses. Further, the evidence normally available in such situations does not always establish a direct nexus between the offences and the real instigators to the extent required under the existing law and procedure to attract penal notice. Criminal liability of individuals when they participate in group violence is difficult to establish under the existing law which is essentially designed to deal with acts based on individual knowledge and intention. The consequent ineffectiveness of the existing processes of law is an important cause for the continued prevalences of criminal attitudes and behaviour of the law breakers. The legislative armoury should be specially designed and strengthened to facilitate effective police action in such situations. (Para 21.18)

26.29 In the context of the law and order situations of the country as it has developed now, we would need some special provisions in law, which would lie between the provisions in normal law applicable to ordinary crime situation on one side and the stringent provisions of an Emergency on the other. These special provisions should be made available in a comprehensive Central legislation which could be invoked and applied to any specified area as and when necessary. An area may be deemed to be a disturbed area and proclaimed as such for this purpose by a State Government if it is satisfied that there is extensive disturbance of the public peace and tranquillity in that area by reason of—

(i) differences, or disputes between members of different religious, racial, languages or regional groups or castes or communities, or
(ii) occurrence of acts of sabotage or other crimes involving force or violence, or
(iii) a reasonable apprehension of the likelihood of occurrence of

sabotage of other crimes as aforesaid. (Para 21.19)

26.30 Section 151 Cr.P.C. may be amended to enable the police get the arrested person remanded to custody for a period not exceeding 15 days in any case, as a preventive measure. (Para 21.22)

26.31 A special law to deal with widespread disorder and breaches of public peace should provide for—

(i) notification of any specific area disturbed by widespread disorder and breach of peace as a 'proclaimed areas' to which certain provisions of the Act will apply;
(ii) suitable definitions of 'riotous mob' 'instigator', 'public property' and 'sabotage' to identify crimes connected with them;
(iii) control over movements of persons in the proclaimed area;
(iv) tighter control over possession and use of arms and explosives;
(v) externment of bad characters from a specified area;
(vi) preventive detention for a period not exceeding three months;
(vii) attachment of criminal liability to instigators for unlawful acts committed by riotous mobs on their instigation;
(viii) Special Courts to deal with offences under the Act as also other specified offences;
(ix) presumption regarding culpable mental state unless rebutted by the accused;
(x) presumption regarding some aspects of evidence arising from documents;
(xi) tightening the provisions regarding 'bail'; and
(xii) fixing time limits for the completion of investigations and commencement of proceedings in court.

A draft for the proposed special law which may be called "The Disturbed Areas (Criminal Law Amendment) Act" is furnished in Appendix IX of the report. (Para 21.35)

Corruption in Police

26.32 Several administrative and legal measures for plugging the loopholes and securing better supervision over police performance for the avoidance of corruption and allied malpractices have been recommended to the States following the Conference of Inspectors General of Police and the Heads of State Anti-Corruption Bureaux.

Most of these malpractices can be substantially reduced by a system of surprise checks and inspections and effective supervision by honest and well motivated officers at different levels of command within the hierarchy itself. However, the reward and punishment mechanism of the system has become totally ineffective because of increasing political interference and, therefore, the senior officers, however, determined and committed they might be to the cause of anti-corruption work, find themselves unable to deal with some corrupt officers who have political contacts and are able to draw political intervention on their behalf whenever anything is attempted to be done to discipline them. The patent inability of a superior officer to deal with a known corrupt subordinate immediately lowers his prestige in the department and induces other subordinates also to seek and develop political contracts as a protective cover to escape punishment for their malpractices. We earnestly believe and trust that the implementation of the measures suggested in chapter XV of our Second Report to insulate the police system from political interference would go a large way in promoting an appropriate climate for effectively dealing with the problem of corruption in police. (Para 22.7)

26.33 The basic responsibility for maintaining the honesty of the force and weeding out the corrupt elements should rest on the supervisory levels in the force and they should be enabled to discharge this responsibility effectively. In this context, their capacity to punish the dishonest personnel should not be diluted in any manner, and likewise their capacity to place honest officers in important and sensitive posts should not also be interfered with. (Para 22.8)

26.34 To secure honesty and integrity for the system as a whole it is important that the postings of officers in charge of police stations should be the exclusive responsibility of the district Superintendent of Police and likewise the Chief of Police should have the exclusive responsibility for selecting and posting Superintendents of Police in charge of districts. (Para 22.9)

26.35 The provisions in the service rules for compulsory retirement after completion of 20 years of service should be resorted to without hesitation to weed out officers with corrupt reputation. Evidence regarding this reputation should be assessed by a suitably constituted high level committee in the police headquarters whose satisfaction on the adequacy of material for this purpose should be held final and acted upon. A senior representative from the State Judiciary or the Law Department of the State may be associated with this high level committee to ensure an objective assessment of the available material. This Committee should function as a Standing Committee and go through this exercise every year without full. In the case of compulsory retirement ordered on an assessment report from the Committee an appeal may lie to the Government except in cases where the compulsory retirement has been ordered by the Government itself when the appeal shall lie to the State Security Commission envisaged in our Second Report. There shall be only one appeal and the matter shall be deemed closed after the disposal of that appeal. It would be desirable to lay down a time limit of three months for the disposal of such appeals. (Para 22.10)

26.36 In extreme cases where the stipulated minimum number of years of service may not have been crossed, action for weeding out corrupt officers should be taken by availing the provisions of Article 311(2)(e) of the Constitution. To avoid any doubt regarding the legal propriety of such action under this Article, we would recommend that sub-clause (c) of the proviso to this Article may be amended to read as under:

"(c) Where the President or the Governor, as the case may be, is satisfied that in the interest of the security of the State or the maintenance of integrity in public services in the State it is not expedient to hold such an inquiry." (Para 22.11)

26.37 There should be constant interaction and exchange of intelligence between the Chief of Police and the Head of the State Anti-Corruption Bureau to identify officers of doubtful integrity and plan conjoint action for collection of intelligence to expose their corruption. For this purpose the Chief of Police should freely use his powers under the Conduct Rules to demand from a suspect officer a complete statement to his assets, movable and immovable either owned in his name or in the name of any member of his family, either acquired from his own resources or from the resources of his family members. (Para 22.12)

26.38 The Conduct Rules applicable to the State police personnel in different ranks may be suitably amended to incorporate a provision on the lines of Rules 16(5) of the All India Services (Conduct) Rules, where it does not exist. (Para 22.12)

26.39 It is most important that the highest standards of rectitude and straightforward dealings are maintained at the stage of recruitment and training. Personnel for manning these branches in the police should be specially selected with reference to their record honesty, integrity and commitment to genuine police work, and enabled and encouraged to function without interference. (Para 22.13)

26.40 Procedures for recruitment to any level in the police (other than the Indian Police Service, regarding which our recommendations will be made separately) should be evolved within the police system itself without involving non-officials or functionaries outside the police department. (Para 22.13)

26.41 While assessing the qualities of supervisory officers at various levels, the positive action taken by the officer to detect the corrupt elements under his charge and deal with them effectively should be specifically commented upon. A new column with an appropriate heading should be included for this purpose in the Annual Confidential Report. (Para 22.14)

26.42 The present arrangement of recording the integrity certificate in the Annual Confidential Report may be revised to give the reporting officer three options; one will be to record a positive certificate of integrity if he is convinced that the reported officer enjoys a good reputation and has performed his work with honesty and rectitude, the second will be to say that he has no material to express a precise opinion on the reported officer's integrity at that stage, and the third will be say specifically that the reported officer lacks integrity, if the reporting officer becomes aware of any material to suspect the former's integrity. (Para 22.15)

26.43 If annual entries regarding an officer's integrity are recorded in the manner suggested above, there will be no need to obtain a special certificate of integrity at the time of an officer's promotion if he has a consistently good record with positive entries of integrity to this credit. But in cases where the entries do not disclose a precise assessment of integrity, a special certificate of integrity should be called for from the officer who is designated as reviewing officer for the purpose of his annual confidential report, and in the case of officers of the rank of Inspector of Police and above an additional certificate of integrity should be obtained from the Head of the State Anti-Corruption Bureau. (Para 22.16)

26.44 In line with the procedure we have earlier recommended for the appointment of the Chief of Police in a State we suggest that the posting of the Head of the State Anti-Corruption Bureau should be from a panel of I.P.S. officers of that State cadre prepared by a committee of which the Central Vigilance Commissioner will be the Chairman and the Secretary in the Department of Personnel and

Administrative Reforms at the Centre, the Head of the Central Bureau of Investigation, the State Vigilance Commissioner (or in his absence the Chief Secretary of the State) and the existing Head of the State Anti-Corruption Bureau will be members. Posting of the other staff for the Bureau should be left to the Head of the Bureau. (Para 22.17)

26.45 The tempo of anti-corruption work within the department will largely depend on the initiative and seriousness of purpose shown by the senior officers. If their conduct in day-to-day administration and the manner in which they treat and move with known corrupting elements in society do not inspire confidence among the subordinates from the angle of integrity, it will be very difficult to sustain effective anti-corruption work in their charge. Senior officers whose time is mostly taken up in the management of their own private business in the shape of farms or other property to the prejudice of their regular official duties can hardly inspire and enthuse the subordinate officers to remain straight and honest in all their dealings. We would, therefore, like to underline the special responsibility of the senior cadres in police to function effectively as champions of integrity and cleanliness in all that they do. (Para 22.18)

26.46 Several policemen are under an erroneous impression that an arrest is mandatory under the law while investigating a cognizable case. A sample study has disclosed that a major portion of arrests made by the police is really not justified from the point of view of crime prevention. There is a clear case for reducing the number of arrests in police work. This will also reduce the scope for allied corruption. (Paras 22.33 and 22.25)

26.47 Sections 2(c) and 2(1) Cr.P.C. should be amended to remove the emphasis in arrest in the definition of cognizable and non-cognizable offences. (Para 22.25)

26.48 Section 170 Cr.P.C. may be amended to remove the impression that it is mandatory to make an arrest in non-bailable cases. In the amended form as recommended in the report, the section would also provide for taking security from an accused for appearance before the investigating officer or the court, without a formal arrest as such. (Para 22.26)

26.49 Guidelines may be laid down for making arrest as indicated in the report. Departmental instructions may insist that a police officer making an arrest should also record in the case diary the reasons for making the arrest, thereby, clarifying his conformity to the specified guidelines. (Para 22.28)

26.50 We endorse the recommendations in the 78th Report of the Law Commission regarding release on bail. (Para 22.29)

26.51 While on one hand the suggested amendments in law would secure release on bail for a larger number of persons than at present, we are anxious that it should not on the other hand enable hardened criminals to escape restraint on their movements which may be very necessary in the context of certain situations. We are aware of many instances in several States in which hardened professional criminals after getting released on bail in a case under investigation or trial had committed further offences while on bail, and again got released on bail after the second arrest! To provide for such cases we recommend that the following proviso be added under sub-section (3) of Section 437 Cr. P.C.–

"Provided that before ordering the release on bail of such person, the Court shall have due regard to–

(a) the likely effect on public order and public peace by the release of such person, and
(b) his conduct after release on bail in a previous occasion, if any, as may be brought to the notice of the Court by the police officer investigating the case in connection with which the aforesaid person was taken into custody." (Para 22.30)

26.52 Guidelines may be issued for the use of handcuffs on arrested persons, on the lines indicated in the report. (Para 22.31)

26.53 Police stations may be provided with adequate imprest amount to meet a variety of contingent expenditure in day to day work. It is very important to remove this deficiency in police stations since it compels even honest officers to wink at certain malpractices by their subordinate officers which in turn breed downright corruption for personal gain. (Para 22.32)

Economic Offences

26.54 Tax evasion, manipulation of stocks and share, frauds in licences and permits, profiteering, black-marketing, hoarding, adulteration of drugs, food stuff, and other essential commodities are examples of economic offences. But their very nature these crimes have no overt aggressive physical aspect as the traditional crimes like murder, dacoity or theft have, but are committed in a highly organised manner involving a lot of background activities and sophisticated methods under a facade of law abiding life to escape detection. These crimes involve high economic stakes and the offenders gain at the enormous expense of the government and the community as a whole. (Para 23.1)

26.55 Failure in dealing with economic crimes generates cynicism among the ordinary people who tend to exclaim that the rich and influential can get away with non-payment of taxes, dishonest trade practices, etc., which help them make more and more money, while the processes of criminal law are severe with the ordinary people who happen to commit ordinary crimes in situations of economic distress. To restore the confidence of the ordinary man in the efficacy of the rule of law it is most important to ensure that these economic offences are effectively handled by the police and accused persons concerned are demonstrably brought to book. (Para 23.3)

26.56 A separate economic offences wing may be set up in the State police on the pattern adopted in Assam where they have a Bureau of Investigation (Economic Offences) headed by an officer of the rank of Additional Inspector General of Police and staffed by offices drawn from the Police, Sales-Tax, Transport, Forest, Excise, Agriculture, Supply and Audit departments. It is the composite nature of the inquiry staff in this organisation that increases its effectiveness in the investigation of economic offences requiring a deep probe into several matters affecting more than one department. (Para 23.8)

26.57 Financial considerations should not deter the State Governments in setting up these wings since it has been amply demonstrated in the case of CBI and a few States that the cost of the additional staff is more than off set by the gain to the State exchequer by way of recovery of concealed income, besides heavy fines realised through courts. (Para 23.8)

26.58 It would be advantageous from the point of view of building up expertise and optimising the utilisation of the investigating staff if the Economic Offences Wing functions under the overall charge of the Special Inspector General of Police or Additional Inspector General of Police who is incharge of the State CID. (Para 23.9)

26.59 A small training course may be developed in the Police training institution in each State which can be conveniently attended by the investigating staff of the State Economic Offences Wing. Lectures on appropriate subjects can be arranged at this course from senior officers of the different departments in the State dealing with the various subjects like sales-tax, entertainment tax, agricultural loans, subsides, etc. (Para 23.11)

26.60 A concerted drive in all the States to expose the embezzlement in Co-operative Societies, recover large amounts of embezzled money from the accused concerned and get the powerful and influential accused duly convicted in court, would put down this crime considerably and enable the financial benefit of cooperative movement to reach the sections for whom it is really intended. (Para 23.12)

26.61 In their Forty-seventh Report (1972) the Law Commission had recommended that the minimum fine for an economic offence should not be less than the amount of the ill-gotten gains of the offender arising from the offence committed by him. We, however, notice that no amendment has been made in individual economic enactments like the Essential Commodities Act or Drugs and Cosmetics Act or the Prevention of Food Adulteration Act, etc., to give effect to this recommendation. This omission may be made good now with appropriate amendments in the different laws concerned. (Para 23.13)

26.62 The scope of the Smugglers and Foreign Exchange Manipulators (Forfeiture of Property) Act, 1976 (SAFEMFOPA) may be enlarged to cover economic offenders also by—

(i) appropriately amending the heading and preamble of the Act, to include economic offenders;
(ii) including a person convicted under certain specified economic offences like Essential Commodities Act, Prevention of Food Adulteration Act, and Drugs and Cosmetics Act in the category described in Section 2(a) of the Act;
(iii) including under Section 2(b) of the Act any person in respect of whom an order of detention has been made under the provisions of the Prevention of Blackmarketing and Maintenance of Supplies Essential Commodities Ordinance, 1979 or any similar law for the preventive detention of hoarders and blackmarketeers; and
(iv) including in the definition of "illegally acquired property" in Section 3(1)(c) of the Act any property in the possession of the person which is disproportionate to his known sources of income and for which he cannot satisfactorily account. (Para 23.14)

26.63 The State Security Commission envisaged in our Second Report should specially oversee the working of the Economic Offences Wing, assess the results achieved every year and make an annual report in his regard to be laid before the State Legislature. (Para 23.15)

Modernisation of Law Enforcement

26.64 From 1969-70 to 1977-78 all the State Governments put together had spent only Rs. 21.76 crore as compared to the Central Government aid amounting to Rs. 43.841 crore in the same period for modernising their police forces. There is need of a greater involvement of the resources of the State Governments in this matter. (Para 24.4)

26.65 Priority may be given for acquisition of scientific equipment in preference to construction of buildings from the Central grant given to States. (Para 24.5)

26.66 A Central team may be constituted with representatives from the Ministry of Home Affairs, Bureau of Police Research and Development and Institute of Criminology and Forensic Science to visit the States once in two years and assess the actual ground position in regard to modernisation of the State police. The quantum of Central assistance to the States may be decided with due regard to the assessment reports of this team. (Para 24.6)

26.67 The Central assistance scheme which operated up to 1978-79 should be continued for another ten years with substantial increase in allotment. (Para 24.7)

26.68 In the interests of national security as well as police efficiency, the police wireless network should develop its own independent multi-channels for communication through UHF and micro-wave and they may be immediately allotted the necessary frequencies in this range for providing links between with State headquarters and any point in the districts. (Para 24.14)

26.69 Teleprinter links should be made to cover all the districts and cryptographic machine should be introduced for transmission of classified information. (Para 24.17)

26.70 Portable pocket sets should be provided to police officers on patrol duty. (Para 24.18)

26.71 The Bharat Electronics Limited which is now the sole supplier of wireless equipment for the police has not been able to meet their requirements fully from 1974 because of priority accorded to the needs of the Ministry of Defence. Ministry of Home Affair may quickly examine the following three alternatives and arrange for a satisfactory source of supply of equipment for the police—

(a) a separate captive factory; or
(b) dedicating an adequate part of the available capacity of BEL, preferably a complete self-contained unit of the organisation, to police needs; or
(c) farming out standard designs to selected Electronics Corporations set up by various State Governments, or selected industrial units in the private sector having collaboration with leading manufacturers abroad. (Para 24.19)

26.72 Control rooms with attendant patrol vans should be introduced in all cities with a population exceeding one lakh. (Para 24.20)

26.73 Proposals for the expansion of the Central Police Radio Training Institute and the enlargement of the Directorate of Coordination (Police Wireless) to include a Forward Planning Branch which are now pending consideration of the Ministry of Home Affairs may be quickly decided to implement the expansion plans. (Para 24.22)

26.74 A fully equipped Radio Workshop may be set up in the headquarters of each State and supplemented by regional workshops wherever called for. (Para 24.23)

26.75 Investigating Officer's Kit Boxes which are lying in disuse in police stations should be brought up to date in their contents by localised arrangements and put to effective use. (Para 24.24)

26.76 Scene of Crime Vehicles may be developed and made available in all district headquarters and other important towns. (Para 24.25)

26.77 Two more Central Forensic Science Laboratories may be established, one in the western region and another in the north-eastern region. (Para 24.26)

26.78 Some allied Units like the Chemical Examiner's Laboratory, State Handwriting Bureau, Fire Arms Examination Section, etc., which are functioning separately in certain States should all be brought under the fold of the State Forensic Science Laboratory. (Para 24.27)

26.79 Regional laboratories may be established to handle certain types of tests which frequently arise in the normal crime work of the State. These regional units may have staff and equipment to deal with chemicals (including alcohol), toxicology, documents and photography. (Para 24.28)

26.80 The ultimate results achieved by the research studies under the Research Fellowship Scheme of the Ministry of Home Affairs should be properly followed up and documented in the Institute of Criminology and Forensic Science. (Para 24.30)

26.81 The annual grant given to the Indian Academy of Forensic Sciences by the Ministry of Home Affairs may be increased substantially to meet its financial needs and enable its journal to be issued quarterly instead of half yearly. (Para 24.31)

26.82 Single Digit Finger Print Bureaux should be developed in all district headquarters. The Single Digit Bureaux and the State level Finger Print Bureau should all function under the fold of the State Forensic Science Laboratory set up which in turn should be under the administrative control of the Inspector General of Police. (Para 24.32)

26.83 A 'Central Forensic Science Service' may be set up with a cadre structure suitably designed to provide the personnel for the science wing in the staff of the Bureau of Police Research and Development, Institute of Criminology and Forensic Science, National Police Academy, Central Detective Training Schools, Units of the Government Examiner of Questioned Documents, Central Finger Print Bureau and all Central Forensic Science Laboratories. Modalities for constituting this service and determining its structure and spelling out different methods of recruitment and other service conditions may be gone into by a special committee which may be set up by the Ministry of Home Affairs. (Para 24.34)

26.84 The existing scheme of Central financial aid to the States for a phased programme of installing computers for police use may be continued to cover all the States very early and meet the requirements of the State Crime Record Bureau and National Crime Record Bureau as recommended in our Second Report. (Para 24.35)

26.85 The provision of transport for the police at the different levels from the police station upwards may be on the following lines: –

(i) A jeep should be supplied to each police station. Where the officer in charge of a police station is an Inspector of Police, the Sub-Inspector in charge of traffic and law and order work may additionally be provided with motor-cycle;

(ii) Jeeps should be supplied to Inspectors in charge of circle;

(iii) Sub-Divisional police officers should be provided with a pick-up van;
(iv) Superintendents of Police and higher officers should be provided with cars or jeeps, whichever would be more suitable for the type of their field duties and responsibilities. A jeep would be more useful to an officer mostly engaged in law and order work;
(v) Armed police units in the district should be supplied with vehicles at the rate of one for 25 men; and
(vi) Vehicular needs of specialised agencies like Forensic Science Laboratory, Finger Print Bureau, etc., should be determined separately on the merits of each case. (Para 24.36)

26.86 Police personnel should be encouraged with grants or loans on easy terms for equipping themselves with some kind of transport and also paid a suitable monthly allowance for their maintenance. (Para 24.37)

26.87 A survey of the ground position of vehicles in the different States shows that about 10 to 15 per cent of vehicles in most States are lying off the road undergoing repairs. It takes about three months on an average for the repairs of a vehicle to be attended to 7 per cent of the vehicles are lying condemned and no replacement has been made. Fifteen per cent of the vehicles are awaiting condemnation. This is a very sorry state of affairs and needs rectification. We recommended the setting up of separate police motor workshops at least at the range level for expeditious handling of all repair work for police vehicles in each range. (Para 24.38)

Scriptory Work in Police

26.88 The Station General Diary which was introduced by the Police Act of 1861 has now come to be regarded as a kind of general purpose register in the police station to record a large variety of information and notes to provide corroboration for the police version of any matter. Enormous scriptory work developed on this account may be avoided by revising the instructions in the Police Manual and limiting the entries in the Station General Diary to the purpose spelt out in the Police Act. (Para 25.3)

26.89 Several other provisions in the Police Manuals which prescribe a number of other registers and returns relating to the day to day work in police stations may be scrutinised and suitable revised to limit scriptory work to what is really relevant and important in the present context of police work and realities in the field. (Para 25.4)

26.90 A Standing Committee may be formed in every State Police Headquarters which should include, among others, a couple of officers from the police station level and Circle Inspector level, for examining if the periodicity of some of the returns could be altered or some of the returns could be lumped together or even discontinued. The Committee could also devise suitable proformae to standardise the collection of data and reduce the load of repetitive scriptory work. (Para 25.6)

26.91 We would like to draw attention to the existing instructions in the Central Government that no action is to be taken on anonymous or pseudonymous complaints. We commend the adoption of this police in all States in regard to anonymous and pseudonymous complaints. (Para 25.7)

26.92 A small statistical cell may be constituted at the State Police Headquarters to compile information from the material already available in police headquarters whenever required for answering Parliament or State Legislature questions, without making unnecessary references to the subordinate units in the field. (Para 25.8)

26.93 Repeated inspections of police stations by several officers in the hierarchy generate a lot of scriptory work. It would be adequate if a detailed inspection of the police station is periodically conducted by officers at the sub-divisional level. The administrative cadres at the higher levels may confine themselves to an overall assessment of the quality of police performance at the circle level and above. Their visits to police stations should be more to acquaint themselves with the actual field conditions and difficulties of the operating staff rather than to do a fault finding exercise in the name of inspection. (Para 25.10)

26.94 Adequate staff should be sanctioned for the police to handle the scriptory work arising from having to furnish copies of prosecution documents to the accused under Section 173(7) Cr. P.C. (Para 25.11)

26.95 The supervisory ranks in the police hierarchy, particularly at the level of Inspectors and Sub-divisional officers who do not have a full-fledged office to give them ministerial assistance, should be provide with adequate stenographic assistance for expeditious handling of their scriptory work. (Para 25.12)

26.96 Provision of mechanical aids like typewriters and taperecorders at the police station level would be very helpful in reducing the load of scriptory work presently borne by the investigating staff. They may also be encouraged to buy such aids wherever possible by giving them loans or grants for the initial purchase and paying them a monthly allowance for their maintenance. A system of payment of typewriting allowance to the investigating staff is an vogue in the Central Bureau of Investigation in the recent years and we commend it to the State police agencies as well. (Para 25.13)

26.97 Adequate supply of the standardised forms and registers for police use should be ensured by developing a separate press for the police department, if the Government press a found unable to cope with the requirements. (Para 25.14)